My
Mad
Fat
Diary

My
Mad
Fat
Diary

RAE EARL

St. Martin's Griffin ⋘ New York

www.stmartins.com

Library of Congress Cataloging-in-Publication Data

Names: Earl, Rae, author.
Title: My mad fat diary / Rae Earl.
Other titles: My fat, mad teenage diary
Description: First U.S. edition. | New York : St. Martin's Griffin, 2016. | Originally published as: My fat, mad teenage diary. London : Hodder, 2007.
Identifiers: LCCN 2016006332| ISBN 9781250116499 (trade paperback) | ISBN 9781250116505 (e-book)
Subjects: LCSH: Earl, Rae—Diaries. | Teenage girls—Great Britain—Diaries. | BISAC: BIOGRAPHY & AUTOBIOGRAPHY / Women.
Classification: LCC HQ799.G72 E17 2016 | DDC 305.235/20941—dc23
LC record available at http://lccn.loc.gov/2016006332

Our books may be purchased in bulk for promotional, educational, or business use. Please contact your local bookseller or the Macmillan Corporate and Premium Sales Department at 1-800-221-7945, extension 5442, or by e-mail at MacmillanSpecialMarkets@macmillan.com.

First published in Great Britain under the title *My Fat, Mad Teenage Diary* by Hodder & Stoughton, a division of Hodder Headline

First U.S. Edition: April 2016

10 9 8 7 6 5 4 3 2 1

For

My husband – for not letting me burn these diaries when I wanted to . . .

Kevin Earl – for three decades of comedy genius but especially for the card game 'Wolf'

But most of all

For my mum – for not letting me watch *Threads* and for saying the immortal words 'You can print what you like if I can have a new cooker'

A FEW THINGS YOU MIGHT NEED TO KNOW
IF YOU DON'T LIVE IN LINCOLNSHIRE

A Levels and the British Education System
It's very easy to explain the British education system
– chaos. Every few years, different governments blame
the last government for making a mess of everything,
and ruining a generation of young minds. Then that
government changes everything again. For example:
In the 1970s, children were told that expression
was more important than punctuation. This means
that, even though my job is technically a writer,
I'm honestly still unsure of the actual purpose of a
semicolon.

I'm telling you this because even since my diaries
were written, the British education system has changed
at least seventeen times. I wish I was joking.

In the days covered by the diaries, we did GCSEs –
General Certificate of Secondary Education. These were
taken by all school students between 14 and 16 years
of age. These exams were graded from A to G, with
A being the best grade, and G being the 'thanks for
turning up and writing your name' mark. Most people,
depending on their academic ability, took between
five and ten GCSEs. These would normally include
compulsory subjects like English Language (my grade
A), English Literature (A), French (C), Biology (E), and
Maths (yes, we use the plural – and I don't want to talk
about the grade).

After receiving these results, you could leave school to find a job. Unlikely though, as Mrs Thatcher was in power. Do Google her. Alternatively, you could go to a college and do a vocational course – like mechanical engineering or catering. Or you could join what was commonly known as a sixth-form college and do your Advanced Levels – a.k.a. 'A' Levels.

Still with me? Good. This should be easier, shouldn't it?

There were some specialty sixth-form colleges but many were just an extension of the school you were already in – like mine. You picked between 2 and 4 'A' Level subjects. You studied these courses between the ages of 16 and 18. These were the grades that could get you into universities and polytechnics. The weird thing was, you applied to the higher education establishments BEFORE you took your exams, so you had to fill in forms: the UCCA form for universities, and PCAS for polytechnics. Teachers would predict your grades, and you'd go for an interview at the universities and/or polytechnics you wanted to attend.

You also had to write a personal statement about all the extracurriculum activities that made you a fully rounded character. This, in mine and many other cases, was a well-constructed exaggeration of hobbies and things that you'd like to do, if only you could get out of your bedroom or the pub.

From ALL of that information, the higher education establishments concerned would reject you, give you a conditional offer (you MUST get certain grades in certain subjects), or an unconditional offer (VERY rare – this meant they either REALLY loved you, or your mum worked there).

There was also the option of having a year off and applying when you had your grades, but only the really sensible mavericks did this. They went travelling and came back with amazing stories of gorillas in Rwanda, wild moped rides, parties in Thailand, and camels in the Australian outback. Sometimes it really pays to ignore teachers.

For the elite universities, Oxford and Cambridge, the system was slightly different. But I had no interest in that. I had just come out of a psychiatric ward. Besides, possibly, maybe my academic aptitude was lacking a bit . . .

It's all changed now. An A* is the best grade at GCSE. Polytechnics don't exist – they are now called new universities. People apparently have to tell the truth on their personal statement, and everyone goes travelling. Sometimes I feel very last century.

Bogs
British slang for toilets. I want to tell you that it originates from when the Ancient Celts would leave their house to go and wee in the actual muddy bog that was by their mud hut, but the truth is I have no idea. Let's pretend that's the truth, and change it on Wikipedia.

Budgies
Budgies are budgerigars – small parrots. They are either green or blue, and people in Britain love to have them in cages. There they sit, eating seed and cuttlefish carcasses, while talking to specially made tiny hanging mirrors. I'm not making this up. Sometimes they are allowed to fly around lounge rooms. People also have aviaries in the back garden to house lots of them.

Either way, they really should be flying free in their native Australia. Can you imagine having wings and not being able to use them properly? It still makes me feel cross. Yes, I do feel guilty about Nelson Mandela the budgie – he will stay with me forever. But was it better for him to have a moment of freedom, than a lifetime of imprisonment in the feathery equivalent of Robben Island? I don't know. I do know that I STILL hate caged birds.

Chunder

To chunder is to vomit. Otherwise known as the 'Rainbow Yawn.' Again, I have no idea where this comes from. All I know is that when the cartoon *Thundercats* was on TV, it was fun to sing 'Chunder-Chunder-Chunder CATS!' to anyone that felt sick. This was usually alcohol related.

Cow

Interesting one, this . . . 'Cow' can be used in many different ways. It's a very British thing to be both offensive AND affectionate at the same time. It's all in the intonation. For example: I might say to my friend Dobber "You daft cow!" when she does something silly that makes me laugh.

However, it can also be used to describe a woman that says something mean, or is consistently nasty. The sort of woman that criticises your looks or flirts with your boyfriend.

It's all ridiculous, really, as cows (the mammal) are lovely in my experience, and are a main contributing factor to Brie cheese. They therefore should be praised.

Dates

North America. Can we chat?

In Britain we write dates as DAY/MONTH/YEAR. Now, forgive me, but that does make more sense, as we go from smallest amount of time to the biggest. You, however, do MONTH/DAY/YEAR. The thing is we could easily, in online dating, make some terrible astrological errors. For example: A handsome American chap says he's born on 11/5 and we think BINGO! Nice reliable Taurean. In reality we are getting a Scorpio, and we ALL know what Scorpio men can be like.

I think we've got to sort this date thing out and at the highest level. It's causing problems. Please lobby your president on this issue.

Fag

This simply means a cigarette. It has nothing to do with being gay. Though homosexual men and women can smoke in Britain, and they can get married too. A fact that makes me very proud.

Jibbing

In simple terms, 'jibbing' means to deliberately opt out of something. However, the word carries a sense of shame and/or weakness with it. To 'jib on the beers' or to 'jib on a party' is to act in a pathetic way. Jibbing, then, usually refers specifically to missing out on something good. One would never jib on root canal work, or a school test. Jibbing is the deliberate act of not having enough stamina to enjoy all the good times. And when you're 17 – that's ludicrous.

Knackered

Either very, very tired, or broken beyond repair. It comes from 'Knacker's Yard' – slang for a slaughterhouse. After the age of 40, it is used more in the latter rather than the former sense.

Pillock

Pillock is a magnificent word that means a STUPID person. I'd like to see it used globally. Again, much like cow, it can be used both offensively and affectionately. For example: Someone who did something stupid but didn't cause any harm (reversed their car into yours but only caused a scratch) could be called a 'total bloody pillock.' However, when I had a small altercation with my son's Minion beanbag and spilt stuffing all over the carpet, my mother, through laughter, called me a 'useless pillock.' Again – it's all in the way it's said.

Piss

Piss is glorious. Its versatility is ENDLESS.

To 'take the piss' is to mock someone – their personality, their habits, their clothes. ANYTHING. However, as we have seen with other words, affection in Britain is often displayed via aggression and what could be perceived in other cultures as negative comments. So gently 'taking the piss' out of someone may be a sweet thing to do. You may love them and/or fancy them.

'Pissed' also means very drunk. We also use the phrase 'pissed as a newt.' A newt is a small amphibian. I have never seen one with a gin, and have no idea where that phrase comes from. Like many things in Britain, someone thought it was a good phrase in 1653 and no one has bothered to change it.

Alternatively, to 'take a piss' is to urinate, but to be 'pissed off' is to be very annoyed indeed. We would never say 'I'm pissed' in the North American sense to indicate that we were angry. If you said that in Britain, you would be handed a strong black coffee to help you sober up.

Posh

Ah! The wonderful British class system. It's so complicated. For the sake of sanity, let's keep it REALLY simple.

A 'posh' person is usually someone who has breeding – like racehorses. They only reproduce from certain sectors of society. Put it this way – Prince William was never going to marry a cashier from Walmart. The poshest person in Britain is clearly the Queen or King. However, posh can also mean someone who is rich (although not all rich people are posh), or something or someone that is of superior quality.

Posh can be used in either a positive or negative way. You could walk into a fantastic, swanky hotel and say, 'Ohhh! This is posh.' Alternatively, you could be treated badly by someone who clearly thinks she is better than you, and mutter 'posh cow' under your breath.

You will often hear me in my diaries refer to my posh school. This is because I won an academic scholarship when I was 11. The sort of school I attended is called a private or independent school, and parents pay a fee for their children to go there. Most people who attend will therefore be rich, and many will be 'posh.'

The government paid all of my fees. It was an attempt implemented in the 1950s to make sure that poor but clever people, who were not posh, had access to the best education possible. Universities were also free, and I got a grant for living expenses. I KNOW! How lucky was I? Don't get me started on social mobility. This should be the standard in ALL countries. In YOUR country too.

Anyway, I am still not posh, but I loved school and I loved, and love, loads of the girls I went to school with. To quote my mother: 'You're no better or worse than anybody else.'

Sixth Form
Where you do your 'A' Levels. Named after the fact that it's your sixth year of secondary school. For further information, see 'A Levels and the British Education System.'

Slag
A woman who is sexually promiscuous. A girl who has dared to sleep with one man, more than one man, or 'snogged' (see below) lots of men. Please note in 1989 and, at the time of writing, this derogatory term does not seem to apply to men. Which in my opinion is bollocks and unfair.

You can also 'slag' somebody off. This means to criticise them – not necessarily about their sexual technique. About anything.

Snogging

Snogging is French kissing. All the tongues wrapping round all the tongues. In the American sitcom *Happy Days* they called it 'making out' at 'Make Out Point.' I should point out here 'Happy Days!' is a great British phrase we use when things are going well. We also put our thumbs up like the Fonz.

If you don't know who the Fonz is, please Google. The Fonz means cool.

Stone

You weigh in pounds. We weigh in stones and pounds. I think we are the only country that still does it to my knowledge. Europe, Asia, and Australasia all use kilograms. This is because we refuse to change – even if it makes more sense to change. We are British. Secretly we believe everyone else is wrong and we are right. We are just too polite to say.

There are 14 pounds in a stone. So I weighed 203 pounds when I wrote the diary. I am 5 foot 4 inches, and 164 centimeters tall, or 1.7 yards. I'm covering all bases.

Swizzing

Cheating. When you are swizzed, you have been conned out of something. A swizz is something that has been deliberately designed to get more out of you than you wanted to give, or an unwinnable game. Swizz. It's a lovely word to say for an essentially lousy thing. Perhaps we should swap swizzing with snogging. Snogging has always sounded too much like snot for my liking. There are good and bad bodily fluids.

Tossers

Unlike many British insults, acting like a tosser
is never really a good thing. A tosser is someone
behaving like a really nasty piece of work. A tosser
will disregard any sensitive feelings you may have,
and make remarks about you just to get a laugh even
if they can see you are CRUSHED by them. At that
moment a tosser doesn't care about anything except
their own gratification. The word comes from 'tossing
off,' which relates to male masturbation. Although
masturbation – for both genders – is a great thing, so
let's not get confused. Tossing is good. But TOSSERS
ARE ALWAYS BAD.

The most difficult thing is when someone you love
acts like a tosser. Being a tosser may not be a terminal
condition, but being with a tosser can be really, really
testing to your soul and your friendship.

And yes, I am thinking of someone in particular from
my diaries. Even though I still love them. Emotions, like
tossers, are complicated.

Vs

North Americans do one finger. We do two. The Vs is a
standard insult, and is used daily. To tell someone you
disapprove of their behaviour, simply position the two
fingers nearest your thumb in a V shape, raise them
purposefully with your palm facing towards you, and
flick those Vs. You MUST ensure you do the Vs with your
palm facing towards you because otherwise you will be
doing Winston Churchill's 'V for Victory' gesture. You do
NOT want to be wishing any success to the person who
is, in fact, pissing you off.

If you want to show added levels of frustration, anger, or annoyance, use both hands and raise the Vs up and down repeatedly. This is particularly effective behind someone's back. Whole games have been created in schools to see how long you can get away with flicking the Vs to a teacher without them noticing. My record – 12 seconds.

My
Mad
Fat
Diary

Preface

THIS IS *MY FAT, MAD TEENAGE DIARY*, Volume 1 – 1989.

It's pretty self-explanatory, but for things to make sense, you need a bit of background. And I need to warn you – some of it is odd. As in a juicy-episode-of-*Trisha* odd.

When I tell people about my life, some of it does sound like a load of bullshit. I mean, most 35-year-olds don't have a 64-year-old mother who is married to a Moroccan champion bodybuilder 20 years her junior. Most people don't have a mum who has a photo of the aforementioned bodybuilder tattooed on her backside. I do. So it's that sort of detail you are just going to have to accept.

At the time of writing these diaries I was a 17-year-old public schoolgirl who had recently been released from a psychiatric ward. The public school was courtesy of the 11-plus scholarship scheme. (Lincolnshire has always been 50 years behind the rest of Britain – education policy no different.)

The psychiatric ward? Courtesy of a complete nervous breakdown.

The funny thing was, in the late 1980s healthcare professionals seemed to think it was a good idea to put you in a mental hospital with adults, overlooking fields and fields of root crops – when it's common sense that anybody would go over the edge if they were forced to look at Brussels sprouts and sugar beet *in the Fens* all day.

So I was still a bit loopy, though I managed to finish essays on Henry VIII's foreign policy, while my mum's second adolescence was about to crash headlong into mine. The main bone of contention was that Mum was getting man action – and I was getting none.

In 1989 my mum was still married to her second husband. He turned out to be homosexual. (Lousy bloke, but what a record collection! Nobody had 1970s coloured vinyl European disco imports like we did.) He lived abroad teaching English in Morocco. Like many mothers and teenage daughters then and now, we lived together in an atmosphere of almost constant intense mutual antipathy. She had very high hopes for me. She wanted me to get away from the lack of opportunities in our small Lincolnshire town, and to avoid the thing that she thought was the cause of most of her problems – men.

She was right to be worried. Frankly, to use late 1980s terminology, I was gagging for it. Like most teenagers, I was desperate to lose my virginity. However, I already had a lover that made me look pregnant but actually ensured that I would never, ever become a teenage pregnancy statistic: Food.

I can't remember when I fell hook, line and sinker. I think it was a packet of Happy Shopper violet creams in 1981. I took one. Then another. Then another. From that point on, Food and I cavorted with each other for most of the waking day. At home, it was chocolate multi-packs and blocks of cheese sliced daintily but consumed in bulk. Once at school, the problem was compounded by dinner ladies – they've always loved me. I think they see a fat kid as a chance to make one of their own.

4

I've always had the 'feed me more' look – even when I was spilling out of my clothes. Mrs Cook at St George's Primary School first deemed me 'Cheeky Face' (really meaning 'fat cheeks') and that woman was impossible to melt – but by class three I was getting extra milkshake and pink custard and 'tarmac' (technical late 1970s term for chocolate goo on Rice Krispies). Secondary school was even more food-intensive – my school was so posh we could have cheese and biscuits for dessert, so an average day meant a full cooked breakfast, then a three-course school dinner, then tea at home (something shoved in the slow cooker – but even stews are fattening when you're eating a whole chicken a night). All this was in addition to endless chewing the cud of whatever thing in a shiny wrapper came my way.

So at 17, and at five foot stumpy four, I was pushing 14 and a half stone. And once you are that fat, the 'fuck-it factor' comes into play. The fuck-it factor means that you know (even with the most basic grasp of nutrition) it will take ages to lose your excess weight, so you might as well get an easy lay by sticking half a packet of Hula Hoops into a tub of cheese spread.

Fat girls were quite an unusual sight in 1989. These days you see chubby children everywhere, but then we were a rare breed. We had more enforced PE tortures, less human rights, more fresh air, more calories expended and consequently less flabby flesh. You really had to be going some to be young and fat in the 1980s. But fat girls were there. We didn't just turn up with supersizing in the drive-thru. You may just not have spotted us. Funnily enough, it's pretty easy to cling to a wall when you're five stone overweight, downing Cadbury's Mini Rolls and chanting the Fat Girl's Prayer:

Please let it be true that men secretly fancy Alison Moyet and Dawn French . . .
Please make my big personality count more than a little waist squeezed into something small and revealing . . .
Please let my inner beauty REALLY matter like Oprah Winfrey says it does, and let me grow up to look like Kylie Minogue . . .
So some man can free my inner minx that's squashed underneath these pounds of flesh . . .
And please . . .
Oh, please . . .
Make Walkers prawn-cocktail crisps fat-free.
Amen.

PS Even Dannii Minogue will do.

So this little fat girl was fed up, lonely and stuck in a small town in the 1980s surrounded by a sea of thin. Every day I boiled over with a stew of hormones, sexual frustration, jealousy and lust, and so, as all these things were banned in Lincolnshire until the late 1990s, I threw down everything I felt into three top-secret exercise books I'd nicked from school.

That's where the diary started.

So that was me, my mum and Food. It's January 1989 in Stamford, and we are living with a deaf white cat in a council house with a mint-green bathroom suite and a larder full of naughty things. It's a small town – famed ironically for being the burial place of Britain's fattest man, Daniel Lambert. There are no mobile phones, we are scared of the Russians, Charles and Di are still married, the Berlin Wall is still up, Kylie Minogue isn't expected to last another year in the charts, and I am about to start a diary that will take me all the way through sixth form and beyond.

Everything I've written is true. I've changed people's names, but they all existed. (One person is actually a mixture of three people: Bethany – she's three girls rolled into one. There is never just one bitch in a fat, mad girl's life.) I've taken some liberties with time, but everything happened. Every word. I'm sharing it because these days it makes me laugh – and because I still see fat girls everywhere labelled as 'bubbly with a nice personality'. And I suppose I want to tell them (and everyone else) that in the end it's all OK. You can be fat and nuts and a virgin when you are –17 – and things can still turn out OK.

Volume 1 starts on Tuesday, 24 January 1989.

Tuesday 24.1.89

I'VE GOT THIS REALLY MAD urge to start a diary up again. I don't know what it is but I think things are on the 'up and up' as it were. My last entry in the other diary was nearly two years ago. God, that was the biggest load of bullshit ever – it was CRAP! (in its rawest form). Actually, I think I am going to burn it. It is no longer entertaining or useful, so I'm reading it and then I'm binning it. So what's happened? Urmm . . .

- Record collection's pretty impressive. Over 1,000 singles because of the record sale every three months where the bloke sells off ex-jukebox records for 10p. Half of them are scratched – my copy of 'China in Your Hand' by T'Pau lasts less than a minute – but who cares?
- Had 'diffy' illness. OK, I lost the plot. Ended up in psychiatric ward 4 of Edith Cavell Hospital for the weekend – jigsaws, mashed potato and group exercises. I had to get out so I lied to them that I felt better. I know some of the stuff I think and some of the stuff I do is wrong as hell but I will never make the mistake of telling anyone what's really in my head ever again. I don't want to be locked up in a brown room with a personal stereo that's run out of batteries and 58 copies of *Reader's Digest* – it was as bad as it gets.

8

- I've still got 'women's problems' but they keep fobbing me off by saying it's my age. They say the same thing to my mum and she's going through the menopause. So I've only got another 30 years of this. Great.
- Doing 4 A levels. English. Politics. History. And theatre arts.
- Chloe is pregnant! Can you believe it? She has had to leave school and everything. She told me in the sixth-form toilets as she was sitting on a windowsill downing a Twix, like it was the most normal thing in the world.
- I'm fat – really fat. I'm fatter than Chloe and she is up the duff.
- The bloke out of Soft Cell has made a record with Gene Pitney!!! He's so old my bloody nan likes him!! It proves everything is going to shit.

I feel so weird! Perhaps I should wait for page 2. Oh, I want to be loved. Oh, it's SO CORNY, isn't it?! But I just want to be loved by a bloke that loves ME! I want to feel special, you know. I almost feel guilty for feeling it. Every night I dream about it. Just someone special. I'd still be the same but I am fat and ugly and I don't like pubs and parties where everyone gets pissed and throws up. I just long to be in bed with a bloke. It's not like me but it's how I feel! I want to do it. I want to be loved.

11.50 p.m.
Just done bloody *Paradise Lost* rough plan for tomorrow. How I hate that book. Also had a massive argument with Mum about nothing as per normal. She plays 'The

Logical Song' by Supertramp and sits there looking miserable. It's very difficult to concentrate on Milton's portrayal of Satan when Supertramp are wailing about being a vegetable and asking who they are.

Mum sits there looking pained like she is the one with problems. Her life is a piece of piss – just reading *Woman's Realm* and shouting at me. I know she was in a Barnardo's home as a kid, but come on – that was about 1952 when that happened.

Feel really nothing – confused, angry, peeved, but not depressed. I had planned loads of profound and emotive things to say, but as always when it comes to writing them it all goes to crap.

I don't want to write the next bit – I don't want to bugger up my diary on the second page, but I know what it's about and I will get my revenge on all the people who have brought me down and made me feel small. I have just watched *Dirty Dancing* again and just like Patrick Swayze says, 'No one puts Baby in the corner,' well, NO ONE will put Rae in the corner.

I will make the pretty girls pay.

Wednesday 25.1.89

7 p.m.

I'VE JUST LOOKED AT YESTERDAY'S entry. I think it's pathetic already – what a brilliant start. Oh, today was pretty crap. Guess what English book I had to write about? Paradise Lost. I wrote crap. Didn't even understand one of the questions: 'Milton is a Christian apologist. Discuss.' Went for second question: 'Milton's language is

10

like organ music. Discuss.' I bullshitted for four sides of A4. But all the school shit paled into insignificance today after all the Megan shit came to a head.

Megan has been making herself sick after food for ages. Now she has started to take laxatives. After scoffing two Mars bars today she went to the bog. I went to see if she was doing the fingers-down-the-throat job. Yes she was.

Dinnertime – I had a whopping great roast and Megan had a salad. After everyone else at the table had gone, me and Megan were talking. She goes, 'I feel full up,' and I say, 'I am surprised after you emptied your stomach at break.' Anyway, we went back to the form room and she burst into tears. I gave her a lecture, etc., etc. Oh, Mum is shouting me for tea – I'll come back later.

9.40 p.m.
Sausage stew and a Supermousse is hardly enough – my brain needs more than that to do an essay on Cardinal Wolsey.

Anyway, Megan got to her English exam and walked out about five minutes in. She went home eventually. It's funny – I was going on about feeling fat and ugly and that's what Megan was on about today, yet I would KILL to look like her. Men still do primarily go for a pretty face and figure, etc. I'd like to lose weight but I don't want to get obsessive about it. When you watch things about African war and starvation and that, you think, 'I have got a decent bed, and food,' and you think, 'Stop moaning! They are real people, and how would I feel?'

But watching famine doesn't stop you wanting sex

11

and fancying George Michael. If it did, I would have stopped thinking about shagging after Band Aid in 1984.

Off to hospital tomorrow to discuss lack-of-period situation.

Can't believe Kylie and Jason are still number one – bloody tragic. People are slagging it off at school but secretly I love that song. They reckon they are not romantically involved – yes they are. You can see the way they look at each other. I tell you what – if Kylie don't want Jason, I'll have him.

Thursday 26.1.89

11.10 p.m.

WENT TO HOSPITAL TODAY. THE specialist I usually see wasn't there. I'm pleased about this because it's somebody at school's dad. I know these people have signed a confidential oath or whatever it is but you are not telling me he wouldn't mention that he'd seen me when he got home. I don't want people to know I've got the womb of a middle-aged woman already.

Anyway, I saw this woman who basically said, 'Come back in four months.' And she was on time so I missed hardly any school, which was inconsiderate of her. She said I would really benefit from regular exercise, and did I do PE at school? Of course I don't – I do rounders every summer but the rest of the time I make up some crap and sit it out with the asthmatics. She also reminded me that Ponstan (this tablet that I have) was a painkiller and not a contraceptive ('for future reference'), and suggested I lose weight as I was 'quite badly overweight'.

Why do they always think that every girl under 19 is a raving hussy? I know a lot of people are, but it's bloody annoying when you are desperate for action and you are getting none and you'd love to be down Boots secretly buying condoms and pregnancy kits and pissing on sticks – BUT YOU ARE TOO FAT!!

STAMFORD HOSPITAL WAITING ROOM

Dried up
Tubes tied
Teas from the ladies at the Red Cross in china cups
Endless copies of *The People's Friend*
She tells me that I'm fat
She spent seven years at university to tell me that
Women comparing ovaries
Wishing mine had been troubled by any man
But the only action they've seen is an ultrasound
   scan
To see if the doctors had missed
A cyst.

Apparently Megan is going to see someone to help her realise she is not really fat and that it's all in her mind. I'm pleased she is being looked after but this is awful. I just bloody wish my fatness was in my mind. My marquee clothes and big rugby tops prove that it's not.

Tomorrow I am going to the cinema with Bethany. In fact at fag park (where Bethany always goes for a sneaky cigarette) I poured it all out to her. I told her I was sick of seeing people with boyfriends while I was always on my own and that I was sick of being fat and that I was TOTALLY sick of blokes seeing me as just a friend.

That opened the floodgates. The first thing she said to me was, 'Have you ever looked in a mirror when you eat? You eat like a pig!' Then she goes, 'Men don't like fat girls as it embarrasses them in front of their mates – it makes them stick out in a bad way.' She then suggested I eat less and do an aerobics class like bums and tums. I think she saw me welling up because she tried to make me feel better by saying, 'I'm just telling you the truth. You don't want me to lie to you, do you?'

Cried my eyes out when I got back to my bedroom. What makes people think it's OK to say that sort of stuff to me? Had a traffic-light cake from Chantrel's Bakery but kept thinking, 'I wonder what this looks like. I wonder if I do look like a pig.' Ate it in front of the mirror in the dining room. Yes. I do look like the world's fattest pig. Mum caught me doing it and asked me if I was so vain that I actually like to watch myself eat. Didn't tell her. Can't be bothered to explain. She couldn't say anything to make me feel better. No one could.

It's weird with Bethany, you know. I'm only mates with her because she used to be shy and she seemed like she needed friends. And her dad was the chairman of some enormous company and apparently didn't give her much attention. I felt sorry for her.

I don't now.

Went down the phone box (63401) and rang Mort – she said that Bethany was just a bitch, and why did I bother seeing her, and that she lives on cottage cheese and is a typical only child. I love Mort – I wish she lived nearer. I hate to say it but it is just typical of my life . . . My best friend lives in a village 45 minutes away, with her own bathroom. I don't know if I've even got my own bloody towel.

Bethany has got a point, though – I do need to start exercising. I'll go for a long walk tomorrow by the fields near the Rainbow Superstore. I'm too knackered to write any more. More tomorrow, unless I get too pee-bored tonight, which is possible. I can't sleep at all at the moment. Having Horlicks and malted-milk biscuits by the ton, but that's not working either.

Friday 27.1.89 but technically it's Saturday 28.1.89

00.19 a.m. (only just got in)
THERE IS THE MOST RIDICULOUS rumour going round school. Apparently the Smiths are playing a secret gig in Peterborough on Sunday night. I said, 'Bollocks – everyone knows they all fell out over a year ago, and why on earth would they choose to play Peterborough anyway?' But people are saying they have picked it because no one would ever expect them to play the Fens, and it would keep the national music press 'guessing – and away'. We scoured through NME in the common room – not even a suggestion of it. It's bullshit. The only thing you will see in Peterborough this year is Aladdin at the Key Theatre. And there's more chance of Morrissey coming out of the lamp than the Smiths playing in Peterborough. Still – everyone reckons they are going.

15

I might have to beg Mum for £12 for the ticket.

Trip to the cinema cancelled. Instead – DID SOME EXERCISE!!!! I went for a walk. A couple of blokes on Cambridge Road in a Vauxhall Cherry papped their car horn, leant out the car window and shouted something, then pissed themselves. It was probably horrible, but the great thing about having Suzanne Vega full blast on your Walkman is you don't hear what tossers are shouting. Did about 20 minutes till the bloody machine chewed the tape, then came home. I didn't notice any difference to the way I looked, and my jeans didn't feel any looser. It's a start, though, and I love those fields – there is no one about to take the piss. Then Bethany and me went down the Vaults. She knows quite a few of the blokes from the boys' school, so yes, I am using her basically. Total revelation down there tonight – met some great people (who all talked about the Smiths gig WHICH WON'T HAPPEN) AND DIDN'T GET CALLED FAT ONCE. Brilliant!!

Saturday 28.1.89

EXERCISE!
Borrowed Bethany's mum's *Shape Up and Dance* record with Peter Powell. It's old with really shit cover versions of songs, but I quite like Peter Powell. Well, I used to like him on Radio 1, but after doing this bloody aerobics record I'm not sure. It is sadistic!! During the can-can he starts going, 'Left kick, right kick, left kick, right kick,' too bloody fast, almost like a piss-take. It's bloody hard to do a dance in the front room and avoid Mum's crap ornaments. Even though I

would be doing her a favour if I 'accidentally' knocked over one of her crap bloody china shire horses. I was jumping up and down like a loon so much I ended up making the record jump. There's a massive scratch in it. I'll just give it back and hope she doesn't notice.

Apparently the *Shape Up and Dance* by Lulu is much more sedate so I'll try that. It stands to reason – as Lulu is ancient and probably has rheumatism these days.

Going down the Vaults. I've nicked two quid off my brother's floor. It'll buy a pint of cider if I can get served – I still look like an oversized 12-year-old. Make-up would probably help but every time I put it on I end up looking like Coco the Clown.

Sunday 29.1.89

9-ish

EXERCISE. BUGGER IT.
 I did get served!! Though the landlord asked me my age twice. Ordered a half of cider to be on the safe side. Mum would be furious if she knew – she shat herself when I had a Babycham at a wedding once.

Last night I can tell you – this is why I love Bethany – she knows so many blokes it is unbelievable. They swarm round her. For all her being a cow, she is the best way to meet men ever. Spent most of the night with Harry and Luke, who in turn introduced me to loads of other men from the boys' school. Harry is cute and posh and shy. And, crucially, laughs at most things I say. I can't decide if it's nerves or if he finds me really hilarious. Luke is skinny as a rat and sarcy as fuck. Bethany got walked home by Luke (just as mates – he has a girl-friend). No one offered to walk me home so I just disappeared and came home via Broad Street chippy. Asked for chips with extra scraps. Yes, they are just minute pieces of fried batter, but sod it. I've done more exercise in the past week than I have done in years.

Everyone was wearing *The Queen Is Dead* T-shirts and there are a whole load of people going to the Smiths gig (WHICH WON'T HAPPEN). Mum refused to give me £12, just in case it is true, which shows she knows nothing about music and doesn't care about me. I've never been to see a real concert. Wham! 'The Final' – not allowed. Howard Jones – too young. I even missed out on Live Aid because we had to fly to Morocco to see her husband the next day. She still says, 'Well, at least you saw Wayne Sleep the ballet dancer on the plane, and he said it was a fabulous day.' Like seeing Wayne Sleep makes up for missing the biggest line-up in the history of music.

If everyone comes into school tomorrow holding flowers and talking about the night the Smiths reformed, I am bloody running away.

Monday 30.1.89

HA! HA! TOLD YOU!!! This is priceless. Everyone went off to see the Smiths last night. Everyone paid £12. And, yes, the Smiths did play. THE FAMILY Smith – they are a folk/country band!!!! I asked Daisy at what point did everyone realise the Smiths were not coming on. She said when they did a cover of 'All

Around My Hat' by Steeleye Span. People didn't think they'd have a support band that played that. Then someone looked at the name and put two and two together. And to add insult to injury, the Family Smith said, 'It's good to see so many young faces in the place tonight'! I felt so smug it was unbelievable. Apparently there was nearly a riot. Not surprised. We all know most people who like folk music eat mushrooms, live in sheds and don't wash. I bet the place stank!!

Took this diary to school today and Bethany announced to everyone in the common room that I had it with me. She then grabbed it out of my folder and it got tossed about like a netball till I retrieved it. She was saying stuff like, 'I bet there's not a lot of stuff that happens in it . . . no action . . . Who do you dream about, Rae?' Everyone pissed themselves at this. Bunch of cows. I know my life is dull and manless compared to theirs. Bethany is usually lovely when it's just us, but when we are out in public she takes the piss ALL the time. It's like I'm her comedy punchbag.

I'm SICK of it.

The trouble is, where do I keep this diary? It's not safe at home or in the locker at school. There's already shit in it that if anyone else saw I would die. Just going to have to put it under the mattress and hope. There's NO privacy – there's no place to go in the Fascist State of Mum. SHE still comes in while I'm in the bath and asks me if I have washed properly. Especially (and she always whispers this) 'my credentials'. She means my bits. JUST SAY IT, WOMAN!! She can't even call sanitary towels sanitary towels. She calls them BUNNIES!! It's like the 1950s in this house.

No exercise today. Watched *Alien* on video and it shit me up good and proper. Not going out walking in the dark with the thought of a monster that bursts out your gut.

Tuesday 31.1.89

Late

I AM 17, I'VE EARNED SOME independence, it's time to assert it. On the way back from school, nipped into Wilko's and bought a 49p self-adhesive lock. It had, like, a big sticker on the back so there was no drilling. Before Mum got home I put it on my bedroom door. Didn't hear her come in as I had 'Cuddly Toy' by Roachford (TOP song) on full blast. Next thing I know she is trying to get in. HA!!!! She couldn't. SHE WENT BALLISTIC – ENDED UP FORCING THE DOOR AND BREAKING THE LOCK. Usual speech: 'You used to be so sweet . . . When you pay hotel rates, then you can start treating it like a hotel . . . Who do you think you are . . . ?' And finally the classic: 'I DON'T WANT TO READ THE ADOLESCENT CRAP THAT YOU WRITE.' I said, 'OH, SO YOU DO KNOW I WRITE A DIARY, THEN!' She stormed out and put her Kenny Ball Jazz Band on. I have mates who have their own walk-in wardrobes, a clothes allowance and a video-player in their room. All I want is a bit of privacy. She is so lucky to have me. I am bloody low maintenance. I've never even asked to go on a ski trip. And unlike half the girls at school I don't demand No. 7 lipstick/eyeliners, or have a perm.

Wednesday 1.2.89

6.17 p.m.

FAB AT SCHOOL TODAY. DAISY got bollocked for spelling 'Satan' 'Saturn' all through her essay. And this is someone who reckons she is going to apply for Cambridge. Good luck, love!! Off down pub – write more later.

11.09 p.m.

Just got back from the pub. Had one Diet Coke and NO CRISPS!! Feel so proud of myself. Don't get me wrong, I am now officially starving. The boarders were out. Harry was there wearing a brown cord jacket and jeans. It sounds frumpy and '70s but on him it looked brilliant. We were just talking about stuff and school and A levels. He is basically doing the same courses as me. He still seemed to find me quite funny. I notice this because that's all I've got at the moment till I get my body sorted. If I can make him fall in love with me, then perhaps I have a chance. He bought me a drink – which I was pleased about because I only had 40p for a Coke and it would look tight to nurse one drink all night. Don't want to get my hopes up but I think that he might like me a bit. I'm not sure how I feel. I don't think he's my type but . . . Yes, I am sure how I feel. I just want to do him.

Thursday 2.2.89

TO MAKE UP FOR THE last couple of days of no exercise I thought I would try out games today. I don't know why I bothered. Of course I was picked last for netball by SO-CALLED friends. 'Sorry, Rae – it's just that you're crap.' I mean, they are right and everything, but it meant I ended up being bloody goalkeeper – the most boring bib in netball. I do more exercise avoiding the PE staff and finding places to hide in the school. At the end the teacher, Miss Sarcy-Cow, says, 'Thanks for turning up, Rachel.' Last time I bother. Got back to the common room and scrounged a bag of Hula Hoops. Everyone on about men and when is the right time to lose it. Anytime would be fine with me.

10.43 p.m.
That last bit isn't true. It's got to be someone I care about. Like Harry. Who am I trying to kid? I fancy Harry. Like mad.

Friday 3.2.89

FISH AND CHIPS DAY AND then we went down the market. I watched as Bethany picked up size 10, size 12, size 10. Nothing comes above 14 so there isn't any point trying. Then you get her bleating, 'I'm so fat, I'm so fat,' while grabbing at non-existent bellies and chins. Of course I reassured her. I told her how thin she was. She ended up buying a skintight top with some kind of German symbol on it and a pair of size-10 jeans. Everyone agreed back at school that they would look lovely when she's down town. And, no, I didn't do any exercise. It won't make me thin right now. It won't help me get a boyfriend right now. I'd rather sink my face into a pizza and tell myself I will start on Monday, and this time I mean it.

Didn't go down the pub. No one will notice I'm not there, and Bethany will be like a reed in her size-10 jeans and every bloke will be looking at her arse. Including Harry.

I have got to look on the bright side. Maybe being this big has helped me. There are no photos of me wearing a ra-ra or a puffball skirt or anything. I couldn't fit in them anyway, so I don't wear them. So at least this body has saved me from crap fashions. Except for Deely Boppers and Grolsch bottletops on my Airwear.

Saturday 4.2.89

11.37 p.m.
Probably the worst day of this already crap, crap life in a long, long time.

Thought we'd go to the new Stamford Leisure Pool. Mum had got me a new swimming cossie from Woolies – white and red stripes. Had a few boys call me fat and stuff when I got in the pool but that happens every day. But then Bethany said, 'Let's go on the twisty yellow slide thing.' Started off fine – but then got stuck midway. Everyone was wetting themselves, and one bloke said, 'Shouldn't have got that fat.' Finally prized myself out to a round of applause, sploshed in the pool and realised that part of my swimsuit was transparent. Came home and went to bed at about six o'clock. Been here ever since. I HATE THIS LIFE AND SWIMMING.

Sunday 5.2.89

10.21 a.m.

STILL CRINGING BUT FEEL BETTER after a good night's sleep. Still feel like itchy with embarrassment, like there are people who have seen me in a state of . . . well . . . just in a state.

And I hate the thought that people would have got home and talked about it and today I will be like a joke over the Yorkshire puddings. That just makes me want to sob and sob.

FAT COW. FAT COW. FAT COW.

One thing – bar Bethany, at least no one I know was there. Mum knew I was upset – got a full fry-up this morning. Two eggs and sausages.

Fuck exercise now. I'll start it when I'm thin.

8.40 p.m.

I just wish I could be loved. I just wish someone would lie with me here and make all this shit in my head go away.

Monday 6.2.89

10.01 p.m.

PREDICTABLE. PREDICTABLE. PREDICTABLE.
Of course Bethany had told everyone in the lower sixth. But she had told it in a way that I couldn't be cross with her. Like, 'Oh, it was terrible what happened to Rae on Saturday.' But I saw through it, bitch. It was a good story and made her popular for five minutes. Lots of sympathy, but you know it's like when people want to be shocked and horrified and pretend they really care but all they want is the juicy details. When Bethany got to the bit where the bloke said, 'Shouldn't have got so fat,' everyone went, 'Oh dear,' but you could see 99% of them were thinking, 'Poor fat cow. Thank God that wasn't me.'

It would have been the gossip of the day but lucky for me after the pub on Saturday night Florence Hunter apparently let her boyfriend come all over her face in Tesco car park. She was crying in study room 3 because she was convinced a copper had seen her. Everyone asking is it illegal to let a man come over your face in public. Some thicko in the common room said, 'I don't remember ever hearing a law about that.' Me and Mort were pissing ourselves – of course it's illegal! Otherwise every bloke would be coming over faces in every car park in England.

Mort saved my life today by letting me copy her essay on Ferdinand and Isabella. I couldn't do any work

25

last night. Writing some shit about some Spanish bitch from X amount hundreds of years ago would have finished me off.

Tuesday 7.2.89

Really late (and there is something really crap on the telly)
IF YOU ARE THE FAT ONE, if you are the gobby one, you always get ganged up on to do stuff.

Everyone still pissing themselves today at what you can or can't do in public. The only book our school has got on sex is *Where Do I Come From?* in the Junior Reference Library – so everyone was going to me, 'On your way home, can you nip into Stamford Library and see if they have a law book?' Don't get me wrong – I was laughing too, but actually when it came to doing it things were a different matter. I could hardly go up to the biddies who work behind the counter and say, 'I need to find a book on sex in public.' In this town that would get back to my mum in an instant. Everything I do in this town gets analysed under the microscope. Anyway, I just mulled round in the reference section for ages – couldn't find anything except the *Yellow Pages* for Dorset and thought I might as well look at books that might help me.

Found *What Makes a Woman Sexy* (if anyone needs this it's me) by Julia Grice. Had a woman on the front in a short skirt and stockings – I mean, that's just obvious that blokes go for that. Even I know that! There was also *Becoming Orgasmic*. It's meant to make me love my body. It sticks out a mile, though, because it's got a bloody great flower on the front, so I sand-wiched it between two paperbacks and took them to get stamped. The bloody woman on the counter only showed it to her colleague – 'Oh, look at this, Jean' – and they creased themselves like kids. Pathetic. Mind you, looks like even they are getting it.

When I came out, three completely typical things happened. Firstly the spotty 14-year-olds who think they are hard and who hang around on the library steps started chanting 'Fat cow', 'Jabba' and 'Lard arse'. I went left to avoid them, but THEN I saw Harry going into Stamford Stationers. I didn't want him to see me with a book on orgasms so I walked like the clappers the other way. More 'Jabba, Jabba, Jabba' until I got out of view. Stopped at Pacey and Canham's for an apple – I thought I would be healthy – and what does the woman say there? 'Oh, you are like your mother, Rach – BIG.'

This fucking, fucking town.

I know I don't carry my weight well. I'm not happy or proud of what I am. People say what they like to me because I always smile and I always have a comeback. The man in the paper shop every time I go in there says, 'Here's Stamford's living Weeble – Weebles wobble but they don't fall down!' like he is the funniest bloke in the world.

I hate what I am. I sit here and cry and burn myself with matches because I hate what I am. This place always needs a victim – it always needs someone to pick on – and today it was me. And I hate it. And I hate me.

King rib for dinner at school. Vera the dinner lady gave me two of them. Just fatty pork with sweet and sour on them but they taste like heaven.

Wednesday 8.2.89

SCHOOL WAS SUCH A GIG today. Great chats in the common room and a debate about dangerous dogs with Georgia storming out after Mia had offended her Rottweiler. Then I don't know why but we decided to nick a load of forks from the dining room and put them on Mr Faux's homework shelf. It sounds pathetic but we were weeing ourselves. Brilliant!

Started reading *Becoming Orgasmic*. I'm sick of it already. It starts off with this questionnaire thing to find out why you are not having orgasms. Here's why: BECAUSE I NEED A BOYFRIEND IN THE FIRST PLACE. Perhaps I do need *What Makes a Woman Sexy* or the bloody *F Plan Diet* or something. I need a bloody man, I'll tell you that.

Thursday 9.2.89

11.40 p.m.

AND THIS JUST SHOWS WHY MY MUM IS A COW. I left *Becoming Orgasmic* out in my bedroom. So what?? It's not illegal. Mum was whistling, which always means trouble, and then she brings it up right in the middle of *EastEnders*.

MUM: What's that book in your room?
ME: Which book?

MUM: The book about sex.

ME: It's called *Becoming Orgasmic*. It's not about sex – it's a personal development book.

(MASSIVE PAUSE.)

MUM: Have you finished *Gulliver's Travels* yet?

ME: NO.

MUM: That's fine, Rachel. If you want to end up in a dead-end job like me, keep carrying on the way that you are going.

ME: I have had enough of this. I am going upstairs.

This is typical of her – she doesn't know what it's like to be lonely. She's been married twice. I show a bit of interest in becoming a proper woman and she can't handle it. Well, I'm sick of it. I'm a living, breathing Rae and I need affection. She can't even cuddle me because she says she is not the hugging type. All she cares about is her husband and her mates and me making her look good. GOD, I WANT TO BE NORMAL – I WANT A NORMAL FAMILY. NOT A MUM WITH PEROXIDE HAIR AND A DAD THAT TURNS UP EVERY SIX MONTHS TO SAY HELLO!!!!

And another thing – didn't do PE today either because middle-aged cows are not bossing me around any more.

Friday tomorrow. Might see Harry.

Thoughts bad.

Friday 10.2.89

8-ish

TOOK *BECOMING ORGASMIC* BACK. NOT worth the bother and it's like running before I can walk.

Bob Tex the country-music busker was outside the library. Wish I had his life – just turn up on the High Street, play two choruses of 'Stand by Your Man', collect for charity, and everyone loves you.

Plus, Mum reckons he has had loads of girlfriends, so it obviously helps him pull.

Bethany lent me the 1989 *Just 17 Yearbook*. I think I'm getting a bit old for it but as I am a retard when it comes to boys I thought it might give me some tips. Here is what I have learnt from it:

- Teenage single mums need the support of their families and things are hard for them. (At least they've had sex – look on the bright side.)
- Debbie Gibson doesn't diet. (Bitch!)
- Sinitta is an impulse-buyer. (Who gives a shit?)
- Five-page special on Bros. (Seven-year-olds are too old for Bros.)
- The Complete Guide to Being a Lad. (Basically they know nothing about women.)
- A day out with Simon Mayo (who I LOVE) would be a laugh. (He seems like such a phenomenally gorgeous person, but he has wonky eyes.)

30

- A day out with Patsy Kensit would make me sick because she is sexy beyond belief.
- Two-timing is bad when it happens to you. (See teenage single mums – at least you have a man, even if he does the dirty on you.)
- 1988 was great. (No it wasn't, it was crap. Proof: the second bestselling song of 1988 was by CLIFF RICHARD!)

My stars for the year say I will be attracted to men with humour and intelligence and that my true nature will emerge in July. Didn't say for definite that men would happen. I can wait another year for a snog. I know that.

Didn't go down pub. Harry might be down there. I'm skint, my best jeans are in the wash, and everyone will be down there in bloody Laura Ashley skirts paying for their own booze. Sick of being poor. Mum says, 'Oh well, get a job, then.' She doesn't realise how much schoolwork I do at weekends catching up on essays and stuff. If you want your daughter at university, Mother dear, then GIVE ME SOME SPACE.

Saturday 11.2.89

3.56 p.m.

ANOTHER BORING SATURDAY. I'VE GOT nothing to do, I can't be arsed to do anything, and bloody Grandstand comes on. I've got friends at school who live on farms or in bloody great houses and they come out of their house every morning to a nice lawn and flowers. Sitting at my window I can see Edinburgh Road, all the rubbish bags in front of our house put out for the dustmen on Monday, and Mrs Bark pegging her washing out with a fag in her gob. Totally depressing. Me and White the cat just sit here, wishing we could sail away somewhere. Just cut this bedroom off and go somewhere else. I can see it in her eyes that she thinks the same things as I do. I got so bored I made a showjumping course for her out of old Ladybird books. She wouldn't do it and breathed Whiskas breath on me. Dismantled it. Now just lying here bored out my brain.

Ate so much today – about eight pieces of toast with Flora and Marmite. And that was just for breakfast.

Me and Bethany are going down the pub tonight. So hopefully more later.

12.01 a.m.
No more later. Bethany flirted with everyone. I made jokes at my expense. She made jokes at my expense. Harry giggled. Imogen got so pissed she got thrown out the pub. I came home. Had a kebab. Gave a bit to the cat 'cos she was sniffing at it, but she freaked at the chilli sauce.

Sunday 12.2.89

4.05 p.m.
JUST TALKED TO MORT FOR about an hour from 62929 phone box. She rang me back as I only had 10p. She thinks Bethany uses me to get men interested and that Bethany sees me as safe and non-threatening. This makes bang-on sense as last night EVERY TIME a bloke was near, Bethany changes her voice and starts

playing with her hair and basically acting like a right dumbster. It's pathetic. But it works. It must do, because some bloke was licking her face in the Vaults beer garden before I went to get my kebab.

Still going down the Hole in the Wall with her later. I haven't got any choice - she's the only one around - and like I say, when we are on our own she can be dead sweet. Last night before the pub she told me she used to be fat and feel like I did. She was at a boarding school when she was a kid and apparently she was bullied quite badly. Had her head put down a bog at one point - which used to shit me up when I saw it on *Grange Hill*. I've got to remember that other people have been through shit too and that it has affected them.

11.39 p.m.
Well, Bethany pissed off almost immediately with some posh git from the upper sixth. Thanks for caring. The one good thing about this was it made me speak to loads of new people in the Hole in the Wall. It's another fave jaunt for the boys' school and the girls' school and I met some classics tonight. HARRY WAS THERE. I'd made Harry a stupid card because he said he used to like *Button Moon*, and it was his birthday at the beginning of February. He looked really touched when I gave it to him.

FULL REPORT OF HARRY CHAT

ME: Hello, Harry, I've made you a card with Mr Spoon. Sorry I missed your big one-eight.
HARRY: Oh, Raemondo - that is sweet of you.

Excuse me, I have got to speak to Luke about general studies.

He seemed a bit flustered. Still, short but sweet. Promising, don't you think?!

Monday 13.2.89

I ALWAYS WANT TO BE honest with you, Diary. I made Harry a card because I wanted one back on Valentine's Day. If I don't get something tomorrow I will be mightily pissed off.

Begged Mum for a phone today because for about the 50th time this year I nearly got beat up down 63401 phone box. If I am talking for longer than five minutes the tutting starts. Today was a classic example. I was just chatting to Mort and this woman says, 'Are you going to be any longer in there?' I said, 'No,' and then she says, 'If you can manage to squeeze out of that phone box, you bloody fat cow, somebody else would like to use it.' It's just crap and annoying but she looked rougher than me so I went down 62929. It's in a posher area, more people have their own phones, and it's near the little shop so I can get a Kit Kat on the way there. HATE these new phone boxes, though. They are always smashed in. I know the red ones smelt of piss but at least you got some privacy. And THIS is why me and Mort have come up with a code system. From now on new people in our lives are going to have code names so me and Mort can talk about it in open air and no one is any the wiser. We've already got them for the people I met last night.

Mort chose them and has gone with a chip-shop theme. I'm going to use their new names here too so prying eyes will get NO information!

Battered Sausage
Real laugh. Scorpio. Lives quite near in the posh bit! He's a real lad but we had such a laugh last night. He has nicknamed me Big Razza. It's only affectionate, though – I can tell. Drives a big Cortina he calls Clarence.

Haddock
Battered Sausage's best mate. Mr Rugger-Bugger Star Rugby Player. Mr Sit There With One Eyebrow Raised Looking Mean and Moody. Mr Loves Himself. Mr Don't Say a Lot Because I Am Gorgeous and I Don't Have To. Mr Everyone Fancies Me and I Know It. Mr Ignorant Public Schoolboy Tosser.

Fig (Mort got fed up with chip-shop theme)
Battered Sausage's other best mate. Looks like Captain Scarlet. Really sweet bloke. Walks like a penguin and does the world's best Bruce Forsyth impression.

Dobber
Fig's girlfriend. Really pretty but kept giving me the evils all night. That's her nickname already because she keeps doing dobby, thick things.

We can't be bothered to give the people we already know new names.

I just wish Mum would get a phone – even incoming phone calls only. I mean, it's weird considering her husband lives abroad – you'd think she'd want to speak to him. She reckons, though, she'd have my friends calling up at all hours. It's just another way to make me feel even more crap about my things. If I get piles from sitting on cold phone-box floors it's her fault.

Bloody hell – I've written loads tonight, haven't I?

Tuesday 14.2.89 (Valentine's Day)

MUM GOT THREE. Loads of people at school got one.

One cow got flowers.

Feel bad about calling her a cow. She's actually lovely. I'm just so jealous I could cry.

Of course I didn't get any. You get home and all the way back you are hoping – but no. Not a chance. I hate Valentine's Day. It's like a distorting mirror. It makes you feel even fatter than you already are.

I laughed it off but I close the bedroom door and lose it and I stick it all down here and this is where it all stays. And this is where it has to stay because I am not ending up in the nutter ward again with brown walls and jigsaws, and people crying that their husband left them, and men slamming their heads against walls, and Mum bringing me a mini trifle and a copy of *Smash Hits* like that would make everything better. It didn't. It won't. It can't. Psychiatric wards when most of my mates were . . . I can't tell anyone what is going on . . . Can't write it . . . Can't think about it. Not even here.

So much shit on the radio today too. All love songs

and lots of dedications like 'Boo Boo in Wisbech – I love you – love for ever – Cup-a-Soup Hugger'. WHAT THE HELL??? And love songs all bloody day like bloody 'Evergreen' by Barbra Streisand. STOP RUBBING OUR FACES IN IT AND PLAY SOME STUFF THAT'S REAL. HANG THE DJ!!!

Wednesday 15.2.89

8.17 a.m.
I'm cold. I'm lonely. I've had enough. Only in this house could a battle start
over the pigging radiators. I want to turn them on BECAUSE THERE IS FROST ON
THE INSIDE OF THE WINDOWS. Mum is too tight and says to put on another layer.

Hello? I've got 27 on as it is! I am currently lying here in terry-towelling socks, old school jumper and pyjamas with a baked-bean stain on the trouser. I'm glad there isn't a man in my bed as he wouldn't see the potential hussy in me – he would just see the bag lady.

7.45 p.m.
There was string in the roast beef today at school. I know the council pays my fees, but if I was them I'd ask for a refund.

Yes, that was the most exciting thing that happened today.

Thursday 16.2.89

IT WAS GREAT TODAY WITH the 'crack commando avoid-PE squad'. We discovered if you climb out of the windows of the top study room there is like a roof where you can't be spotted! We could see Miss Sadistic looking for us – it was like being up a turret. I'm sorry – I'm 17 – I'm not a kid. I am sick of being shouted at for not wanting to fling a ball round a pitch with a stick. I'm a bit beyond that. Instead we all had a Creme Egg and a water fight. It was going well till someone picked up a mug of Cup-a-Soup that hadn't been cleared in about three months. I nearly chundered.

It's got round that I like Harry!! Mr I Love Myself Haddock asked Bethany, 'Does your mate with the bloke's name fancy Harry?' Bethany said, 'She might do, why?' Haddock apparently put his eyebrow ten foot up his forehead and said, 'Aaahhhhhh,' and walked off. He's an arrogant tosser. But if he goes back to the school and spreads it and this leads to something, then I'll live with it.

Friday 17.2.89

Bloody late

MY SO-CALLED FRIENDS ARE all a bunch of patronising dill-brains. We were having a conversation today about how we will be remembered after we leave school and what do they come up with? Rae's the funny one . . . Rae's the one with the great personality . . . WE ALL KNOW WHAT THAT MEANS!

Fed up with providing everyone's entertainment – I'm going on comedy strike. No more fat, funny Rae. Just fat – then hopefully slim and dangerous.

BUBBLY GIRL

If you're as round as a bubble
You have to be bubbly
And entertain the crowd
It's as if people don't notice your belly
When you're fun and loud.

But I'm giving up the jokes and the laughs
I'll retire to my den
This body bubble will get smooth and lithe
Then this bubble will nick your men!

My mum bought me the most foul pair of shoes ever today. They are called SunFlairs. (HELLO??? IT'S FEBRUARY!!!) They are green canvas and not a nice green, but '70s wallpaper green. They look like something Boney M would have worn on a bad day. She says they were 'cheap and good for slopping around in'. She says this about ALL the stuff she buys me. She still thinks I'm seven.

Saturday 18.2.89

7.01 p.m.

HAD A GENUINE DISASTER WITH the SunFlairs
but Mum does not believe me. Walking into town,
just by the bottom rec, I stepped in a whole pile of dog
crap. Honestly it was an accident. Of course the
SunFlairs are canvas so I had to abandon them by the
side of the road and walk barefoot to the shoeshop on
Ironmonger Street to get some flip-flops (FREEZING).
When I got home Mum said, 'What's happened to your
shoes?' I told her I had stepped in dog muck but she
didn't believe me. I said, 'Go and check for yourself – I
have left them by the drain opposite the putting green.'
She was furious. I kept saying, 'IT WAS AN ACCIDENT,'
and she kept saying her usual, 'SO WERE YOU!' I said,
'Normally you say when you step in crap or a seagull
plops on you it's lucky – so MAKE YOUR MIND UP.'
That shut her up. It was an accident but it was obviously meant to be!!!

10.43 p.m.

No one is going out tonight. I can't just turn up and
look like Billy No Mates if there's no one I know there.

I couldn't face another Saturday night just doing
nothing so thought I'd do something. I've had the same
wallpaper since about 1983 – red, yellow, green and
white horizontal stripes – so I thought, 'I'll change it.
It's my room, I can do what I like.' Started ripping it

down. And then sonic-hearing old bat Mum tears
upstairs and says, 'I pay the rent – you are not ripping
anything . . . Blah, blah, blah . . .'

There's a load of turf that's never been laid at the
end of the garden. If I could make a hut out of that
and live in it, I would.

With someone like Harry.

I'd obviously need running water installed, by the
way. Oh – and a toilet.

Sunday 19.2.89

L IVING HERE AT THE MOMENT is like living in a
prison camp. I got up for a wee in the night. She
yelled at the top of her voice, 'WHAT ARE YOU
DOING?' I said, 'I'm going for a wee,' then she said,
'WHY??' I said, 'BECAUSE MY BLADDER IS FULL!
HOW CAN I HELP THAT?'

I got my punishment this morning – some radio
station was playing church bells and she put that full
blast on her manky stereo.

Went to Green Lane shops today and got spat on and
slagged off by the twats who sit on the wall. 'Posh fat
bitch – eat another burger.' Fat is one thing. Posh is
another. My room is damp. I live in a council house.
My last proper holiday was Mablethorpe Golden Sands
in 1984. The DHSS bought my bed. I wish I was posh –
then I would be a boarder – away from all this
bullying shit.

Monday 20.2.89

THERE IS SOMETHING GOING ON with Mum. She has started shaving her legs and she keeps listening to bloody Nilsson 'Without You'. I bet you now marriage number two has gone wrong, which is sad and everything but hardly a surprise. He was a school teacher – she ironed the shirts in the same school. He went to Durham University and studied Latin – she went to what she calls the University of Life and studied . . . errr . . . life. As soon as they got married he went abroad to teach. I feel sorry for her, though – it's horrible being lonely and fat. I just hope she sorts it out with him in Morocco and he stays there to teach. I don't want him coming to live here during my A-level year. He's a so-called academic – he should understand that I need space and no hassle.

Tuesday 21.2.89

8.20 p.m.

THERE IS DEFINITELY SOMETHING WRONG. Mum reckons she is doing the Cambridge Diet again. The tub's been stuck in the back of the larder for years – the bottom of it's gone rusty! It's the one where you just have liquid drinks and lose about a stone in two days. Something MUST have kicked it off, though, but I can't get anything out of her. She says she's starting it

Monday. I'll believe it when I see it. She is always starting next week and next week never comes. I tell you what, though – I will not be happy at all if she starts to lose loads of weight. I couldn't handle that – that would do me in. I can't have a mum that's thinner than me – it would not be fair of her to do that.

Shat myself tonight because Mum wanted some gravy granules, which means GREEN LANE SHOPS. WHICH MEANS TWATS. Luckily they were in the video shop – no doubt trying to get some porn or the *Chainsaw Massacre* or some other div film. The bloke in the shop was taking ages to serve me and chatting to his mum in bloody Punjabi or whatever about Kashmir. I was like, 'Fuck India – hurry up and serve me so I can get out and avoid the tossers.' Luckily he did. Sometimes I think the Indians have got it right with arranged marriages. At least no matter what you look like or how much you weigh you are guaranteed a man.

11.44 p.m.
I feel a bitch for writing that last bit. I know arranged marriages can be hell on earth and some women are trapped in them. I saw a thing on BBC 2 once. I can be a cow sometimes.

Can't sleep again. No point mentioning it to Mum. She will either shout at me for waking her up or suggest a bloody Ovaltine.

So lonely this time of night. Thank God for 'Pick Your Poison' on Hereward Radio. If we had a phone I could make a bomb on that competition. Well, I could probably win a Frisbee and a T-shirt, but anything is better than nothing.

43

Wednesday 22.2.89

BLOODY HELL, IT KICKED OFF today!! Bethany apparently has been flirting with Marie Jamieson's boyfriend. It's all round the boys' school because he has been gobbing off about how much they both fancy him, and because they are both seriously gorgeous he is looking like a right stud muffin. Bethany was reading one of Daisy's Mills and Boon bollocks books when Marie came in and just launched at her: 'Who the hell do you think you are? You must bloody love yourself.' Bethany goes, 'I have done nothing.' Marie was like chanting, 'HAVE YOU GOT OFF WITH HIM? HAVE YOU GOT OFF WITH HIM?' Luckily the bell went and Bethany had to go to A-level physics. Marie was crying – everyone crowding round her – and then she says, 'I did it with him last week when his mum and dad were in South Africa. He even used a towel to get the sweat off me afterwards.' Bless her . . . But as I said to everyone later – does she want to go out with a bloke whose parents are racists, anyway?

Bethany called for me later at home. She was bawling her eyes out, saying stuff like, 'I didn't do anything. We were just talking. Just talking!' I don't know if I believe her. I don't care. This is a problem I would love to have. To be the other woman. The dangerous one. The one being talked about and referred to as gorgeous by the boys' school. She kept saying, 'Does everyone hate me? Does everyone think I'm a slag?' I said to her, 'Don't worry – as soon as Marie told everyone she had done it everyone forgot about the row – they were too busy asking her about that. Bethany looked pissed off when I told her that. Don't know why – you think she'd be pleased that everyone has stopped talking about her. Took her to get some chips. Made sure I ate like a bloody fairy princess with dainty bites after what she said about me eating like a pig. I hate eating in public anyway. If I'm eating bad stuff, people stare as if to say, 'Should you be eating that?' Bethany stuffed her face – she was full of snot and her eyes were red raw. Wish all her male admirers could have seen her the way I saw her tonight. Wish Harry could have seen me being so supportive and nice.

I can be such a horrible person sometimes. But I think we all are underneath. Sometimes. I only say bad things here. Never to people's faces. I've had that much crap said to me I don't want anyone sitting in their bedroom feeling shit because of me. Couldn't live with that.

Significant conversation with Mum tonight. About the only thing I did say to her from the time she came in till the time she went to bed.

MUM: Don't get married, Rachel, till you are over 30.
(At this rate I may not have a choice.)
ME: Why?
MUM: Just don't. And make sure you are never dependent on anyone. Earn your own money.
ME: Why, though?
MUM: I've got a headache. Why do you keep going on . . . ?
(ER . . . YOU STARTED IT, WOMAN!)

Thursday 23.2.89

Late

THE TWATS FROM GREEN LANE shops were waiting for me at the top of Worcester Crescent and I knew I was in the shit. I couldn't turn round and run or they would have come after me. I had to face it. As soon as I got near they started singing 'Nellie the Elephant' and shouting, 'Jabba, Jabba, Jabba.' (I could kill the bloke who invented Star Wars.) I felt myself welling up, but if I had cried that would have made them worse. Just walked down the passage and said the first thing that came into my head. And it was, 'You lot want to be careful – my uncle is Reggie Kray.' This is total bollocks of course. They were like, 'Who the fuck? Who the fuck?' but one of them shat himself and pulled the rest off. I was just trying to think of someone dead hard that would scare them. This has only delayed them – when they realise I was lying they'll be back. Legged it home and ate and ate and ate. Then when Mum said, 'You've eaten half a multi-pack of crisps – Rachel, you are going to get ill,' I ate another. Fuck it. I'm the size of a house – what difference is another bag going to make?

Things like this make my brain go bad. End up with the thoughts that I can't get rid of. Then I hit myself and . . . all of it. You know.

Friday 24.2.89

AWFUL TODAY. MARIE JAMIESON CORNERED me by the cloakroom and said, 'Can I have a word?' I said, 'Yeah.' She said, 'For the record, my boyfriend and his family are not racists. They have business interests in Jo'burg and provide employment for black and coloured maids and pay them well.' I was like, 'OK – thank you for telling me.' What could I say? I was rumbled good and proper.

Bet they are racists, though.

Fish and chips, then Wellington fudge pudding, which made things seem better.

Tonight I made the fatal mistake of reading Bethany's mum's *Reader's Digest Family Health Guide*. I swear I have all the symptoms of angina, cirrhosis and Gilles de la Tourette syndrome. Paranoid now that I have permanently damaged my heart. I swear I can honestly feel the cheese, burgers and Wagon Wheels caked in the arteries. I bet no snogging damages your heart. Sexual frustration certainly does.

Big party tomorrow. The theme is '50s/'60s and I have got nothing to wear. The good news is, though, there's a jumble sale at the Congregational Hall tomorrow and it's being done by the Conservative Club. Posh old people with shed-loads of money – it should be a good one. Just hope I can find something that fits.

Saturday 25.2.89

4.35 p.m.
PARTY TONIGHT IS AT THE Angel Hotel in
Bourne. Don't know if I can be bothered to go,
because you just know what will happen. Bethany will
snog someone and I will end up like a total gooseberry.
Plus, I feel like crap. Think I am getting flu from all
those nights when SHE refused to put the heating on.
Got a great jacket from the jumble sale – old suede
thing. Even Mum admitted it makes me look thinner.
She will go mad, though, when she realises I've used
half a bottle of her Opium perfume to cover up the
jumble-sale smell. I'll decide whether or not to go later.

Sunday 26.02.89 (but this is mainly concerned with
SATURDAY 25TH FEBUARY 1989 . . .)

1.12 a.m.
YES! I AM IN A total state of shock! Here are the
full details with background!
   Well, I've felt really achy (probably angina not flu) so I
wasn't going to go to the party. Anyway, at 7 p.m. I
decided to go (it started at 8). Well, HARRY was there.
Everyone was dancing and I pretended not to see him
and he came up to me and put his hands over my eyes
and goes, 'Guess who?' We had a bit of a laugh and then
he came up again because he's good mates with Bethany,

and Bethany conveniently went and we had a semi-cuddle as it were and then he went off again. I HAD MY FIRST FULL CIGARETTE. Perhaps fags make me look more seductive, because then Harry comes up and then –
<u>THE EVENT OF THE DECADE!</u>

We were talking and cuddling and bumping heads, etc., and then, you know, he kept looking at me and he said, 'Well, don't I get a kiss, then?' and I said, 'Well, errrmmm, slight problem – I have never kissed anyone before.' Anyway, he said to me, 'We will try English first,' and then . . . OH. MY. GOD!

I SNOGGED (I hate that word!)
I KISSED A BOY
AND
HARRY!!

Anyway, I said, 'Oh, I'm crap,' and he said, 'I'll be the judge of that.' Then there was an uncomfortable pause and I said (because I did smell a rat), 'Harry, did you do that out of sympathy?' And he said (and good on him), 'Partly yes because a few people said that you fancied me.' And I said, 'You didn't do it completely out of pity, did you?' And he said, 'NO! I really like you but not necessarily in that way.' And I think I really respect him for that.

Anyway, I gave him my Basil Brush badge and then it went a bit weird because 'Fine Time' by Yazz came on and then someone put on 'Hey Music Lover' by S-Express, which is good for raving to but not to have tender moments to. So I just go to him, 'You won't go back to the boarding house and say, "God, that Rae Earl is a silly, fat cow,"' and he goes, 'No! I'm not like

49

that.' I really like him . . . Anyway, he sat on my knee and we talked and we are good mates.

It's brilliant that the first bloke I kissed was really sweet and understanding – I'm very lucky. It's also bloody corny and embarrassing.

By the way, when I say, 'I kissed a boy and Harry,' I mean a boy – and it was Harry. I don't mean I kissed a boy and then Harry – making out he is a mutant.

I also had a puff of a cigar! Unfortunately I didn't do much dancing. Anyway, I am still shocked and happy that someone cuddled me! I'm happy! Thank God for life.

ALL THOSE NIGHTS WORRYING I WAS A LESBIAN ARE GONE NOW.

5.06 p.m.

I got three and a half hours' sleep last night so tonight I am knackered. I can't believe it happened. It's all like a misty dream. I keep getting flashes of Harry and the next minute I can't remember what he looks like. Oh, my Appletiser! To think I kissed him. I still can't believe it. Still in shock. The trouble is, I really like him. Mind you, it's hard to tell – my emotions are in such a COMPLETE AND UTTER MESS!!! Read my stars in *Just 17* – it says this sort of shit was going to happen.

Monday 27.2.89

MUM HAS STARTED THE CAMBRIDGE Diet – she looks totally pissed off with it already. I don't know why she bothers – she has pulled already – she is married and I have proven there are blokes out there who don't care about size. Men who can see through all the thin crap. Men who look beyond looks.

Incredible what Harry's tongue tasted like. It was odd having something of someone else's moving in your mouth. It was like a warm, small animal. But a nice warm, small animal. I wonder what a . . . NO, let's not go there. Can't ever imagine doing that. Think I'd start laughing. Then be sick.

I am such the talk of the lower sixth in the best way ever and everyone is being dead lovely. People are saying stuff like, 'I'm really pleased for you Rae.' I do have a really nice bunch of mates. The only person I haven't told yet is Mort – she hasn't been very well, bless her, and has been off school today.

Saw Harry in the High Street on the way home. I completely fell to pieces. All I really wanted to do was hug him. Typical, though, when I saw him I was downing a giant-size Raspberry Slush Puppie so I had a blue tongue.

Tuesday 28.2.89

MUM IS IN A FOUL mood because of not eating. All my meals are coming from the pressure cooker. It's because it involves minimum preparation time too. I ate half an onion tonight because she hadn't chopped it up properly. It's a bit rich that I have to suffer because she's starving herself for vanity.

I've agreed to do the sound for the school play, *Our Town*. Mort's a big part in it so it should be a laugh.

AND THERE ARE BOYS doing the male parts. Good to see the 20th century has finally reached Stamford High School.

Wednesday 1.3.89

TALKED TO MORT TODAY BEFORE the final *Our Town* dress rehearsal. Told her all about the weekend and she said Harry sounded like a wanker. I said, 'OH MY GOD, WHY?' She said, 'He said he snogged you partly out of sympathy, Rae?? You don't need some public schoolboy's sympathy! You are one of the funniest, sweetest people I have ever known.' I said, 'He didn't mean it like that,' and she was like, 'How did he mean it, then????' I'm sure he didn't. I love Mort – and usually she is right about everything – but we will have to agree to disagree on this one.

It was difficult to take her seriously as she was dressed like a turn-of-the-century American woman, and was having problems with her bonnet.

Day three of the Cambridge Diet and I caught Mum having a bloody MORE cigarette in the back garden. I said, 'What the hell are you doing?' and she said, 'Rachel, it's none of your business – I'm the adult.' Well, act like one, then, Mrs Petulant, and be supportive of me. If she caught ME with a fag she'd go loopy.

I've not told her I've snogged anyone. She thinks you can get venereal disease from loo seats.

Thursday 2.3.89

I'M SO BLOODY CONFUSED ABOUT the Harry
situation. Leah from the year above told me that he
really likes me but didn't fancy me but that he might
go out with me. But then Bethany told me that
SOMEONE at the boys' school had said to her,
'Someone in the upper sixth really fancies Rae Earl,'
and Bethany said, 'Is it Harry?' and this someone said,
'YES!! HOW THE HELL DID YOU KNOW THAT??' So
explain THAT one!

Mort also said you can get venereal disease from loo seats.

First performance of *Our Town* went well. Somebody
had fiddled with my tape counter but I managed to
separate the sound of crickets from the hymn they all
sing in the church and there was a great buffet afterwards. Stuffed my face with fun-size Bounties and dips
for free, crucially with Mum not hanging over me
looking jealous.

Wonder what's happening with Harry. I just don't get
men. Mind you, I don't get me either.

Friday 3.3.89

11.01 a.m.

CURRENTLY IN STUDY ROOM 2. Mum asked me
this morning if I could eat my toast on the way to
school as the smell was making her hungry. I put extra

jam on it as I thought the fog might affect the taste. That's lies – it was just an excuse to eat more.

Sick of Mum's SELFISH diet now. I very nearly got dive-bombed by a kamikaze crow because of her.

10.45 p.m.
Second performance of *Our Town*. Wish I had never said I would do this now. It has stopped me from going down the pub and finding out what the deal is with Harry. Plus the fact it's such a depressing play. The main character dies and goes back in time to live another day of her life. She chooses to be about 16 again, which proves it's total crap because why would you choose living like this? No cash, no love, no sex and no control. Then at the end she decides you can never go back and relive the past because it's never the same and THAT'S meant to be tragic!! It's a good job in my opinion.

Saturday 4.3.89

2.16 p.m.
FINAL PERFORMANCE OF THE PLAY tonight and I'm bloody glad because I want to find out what the hell is going on with Harry. There are rumours everywhere about what he thinks, what he doesn't think, what his mates say, where he was when he said what he has supposedly said. I need to find some truth.

Mum is now even looking at the fruit bowl with big, hungry eyes, so I predict a Cambridge Diet failure in a matter of days if not hours. When I think of it, all of my life my mum has been on loopy diets – yet she is still fat. Soups, grapefruit, hot dogs, F Plan, low fat. But this diet looks the hardest to do – nothing except the drinks. What sort of diet would begrudge you a satsuma?

Sunday 5.3.89

1 a.m.

LADIES AND GENTLEMEN – I HAVE A BOYFRIEND!!! JUST GOT IN FROM PROBABLY THE MOST AMAZING NIGHT OF MY

4.55 p.m.

I fell asleep last night – sorry – so here's the story. I met Harry in the pub after we had done *Our Town*. It went OK but there was a bit where I was meant to play a steam-train whistle. Unfortunately I got the tape mixed up so instead of a train there were chickens clucking. No one seemed to notice, though. Harry looked so cute in the pub I just could have hugged him. Anyway, everybody else went for a chip slap-up and there was just me and Harry left and I put my arm through his and we were walking up the passage near the Animal Health shop. He kind of steered me into someone's front porch and there was this massive uncomfortable silence and he says, 'Actually I'm just trying to pluck up courage,' and I go, 'I know and it's bloody embarrassing and I'm confused because last week you said you weren't partial to me,' and he said, 'Well, I've seen you since then.' So then he says, 'Well . . . err . . . um . . . will you go out with me?' and I go,

'YES!!' And then we had a massive, massive FRENCH snog and I go, 'Why are you partial to me? You could do a lot better than me,' (corny, I know, but you have to find out these things) and he said, 'YOU'VE GOT CHARISMA!!'

I'd rather be gorgeous but charisma will have to do.

This feels like the best day ever. It feels like a relief. It feels like too good to be true. I usually hate Sunday nights but this feels like the beginning of something. Just like the seed of something that is going to make me feel brilliant . . .

I am going round to the boarding house on Tuesday to see him LIKE A PROPER GIRLFRIEND. LIKE A PROPER WOMAN.

Monday 6.3.89

EVERYONE IN THE COMMON ROOM gagging to know what went on on Saturday night. It took one whole study period to go through the entire story. Everybody being so sweet about it – saying stuff like, 'So chuffed for you, Rae,' and they meant it. Bar one person. Bethany. She was saying, 'Let's see how long this lasts first. Don't get too excited – you only learnt to kiss a week ago, and have you met all his friends yet?' Why is she like this?? I haven't nicked him off her. She didn't fancy him. I could see her sat there looking like I had done something wrong. She cannot bear the fact that I am a girl too. And for once it's ME that's getting the love attention. I do not feel guilty – I can't be there for her at her beck and call all the time for every disaster that goes wrong in her life. It's doing her head in because she thought fat girls didn't get boyfriends. Well, Bethany, they do – so those grapes you eat are a waste of time, love!

Spent an hour on the phone to Mort. She is lending me a skirt she got from Black Orchid – the posh shop in the arcade. It's got an elasticated waist so it should fit. Apparently I have also got to put my collar up – bit Sloaney but it's a look blokes at the boys' school go for apparently.

Mum hasn't cracked yet and this is the second week of the diet. I've been willing her to fail. Yes, I am a cow.

Tuesday 7.3.89

TWO HOURS TO 'H' TIME!!! (STUDY ROOM 3) Could barely eat this lunchtime – too excited. And it was sausages! Mort has brought the skirt in and it looks OK. So nervous I could boff.

LATE
Crying my pigging eyes out.
Not going out with him any more.

PERSONALITY

Men say that you have personality
Men say you make them smile
But all that don't mean a thing
When your waist measurement's half a mile.

For men put first the pretty girl
And the size-10 clothes she's got
And charisma is as useful as
A chocolate teapot.

Even my poetry doesn't scan.
   Weird thoughts so bad.
   Can't be bothered to tell you what's wrong because
it's all wrong.

Wednesday 8.3.89

TRIED TO GET OFF SCHOOL sick today but Mum
was having none of it. I could have skived, but
where would I go with no money? And it was pissing it
down. At least you get fed at school. And I ate today.
Don't fucking care. No point in being pretty. You still
get shit on, shit on, shit on.

Yes, Harry thing completely buggered. I went down
to his study in his boarding house. He was acting dead
strangely – showing me his bloody A-level English
essay (it was shit! The first line said, 'All great books
have a beginning, a middle and an end . . .' Errr . . .
yeah, but what's that got to do with Jane Austen?) so I
took the piss slightly only as a joke. Then he got really
odd and asked if I'd always been big. Then HONESTLY
this happened:

   H: I feel like I have been pushed into this but I
   lose nothing by going out with you.
   ME: Pardon?

H: People said that you liked me and I felt pressured into getting off with you and asking you out.
ME: Oh.
(Massive pause.)
ME: OK, then. I'll finish it . . . and I'll ask you out so you don't feel pressured or pushed into anything. Will you go out with me?
H: No. But I would like to be friends, though.
ME: OK. Do you want to meet down the Meadows tomorrow?
H: I don't think that would be a good idea, do you?

And that was it. I walked home up New Cross Road sobbing my eyes out. People looked but no one asked how I was.

Of course news had already got round. Somebody's boyfriend had told them, who had told everyone else. Bethany was looking triumphant and had her 'I told you so' mocking sympathetic smile on – head tilted to one side trying to look like she was genuinely sad. I could see she was gloating beyond belief. Apparently I should not have taken the piss because 'Boys need to feel good about themselves, as they are as vulnerable as us.' Are they hell as like. The rules for them are all different. There's a bloke who must weigh 17 stone in the upper sixth and he still gets women dropping at his feet.

Now I don't fancy anyone. Pretty sick really. Feel awful inside – like all my insides have been ripped open.

I have been listening to 'I Should Have Known Better' by Jim Diamond again and again and again. To be fair, it is about a bloke who has been knobbing around and doesn't exactly fit my situation but sod it. It's sad and wailing and that's how I feel. This will takes ages to get over. This is life-changing stuff.

Thursday 9.3.89

2.46 p.m.
I'M SAT IN THE LIBRARY because I just don't want to hear another story of how great someone's boyfriend is. You think people would have a bit more sympathy. I am going through my first break-up with someone and they are saying how their gorgeous boyfriend bought them a Zodiac Garfield as a surprise present. Whoopee. And then another one says, 'Shall I go on the pill or not?' Like it's important?? And I'm sick of the questions about Harry – I have never been so pleased of the library silence rule in my entire life. You can't even get away from it in my A-level courses – everyone is either in love or doing it.

Theatre arts – we are doing Restoration comedy. EVERYONE is shagging. Even the main character in the play is called HORNER! I'm not making this up.

English – Chaucer's *Franklin's Tale* from *The Canterbury Tales* – all about undying love between this knight that goes to war and his Mrs. She even gets pursued while he is away. And they say it used to be harder for women!

History – Ferdinand and Isabella loving each other in Spain while murdering who they like. Catherine de Medici wearing no knickers and having great parties.

Politics – well, politicians are all at it anyway. Whatever country's parliament we are studying you can guarantee they are at it like rabbits. Even Mrs Thatcher has got Denis.

Going to go home. Eat tea. Go to bed and get away from every person on this earth except the cat. Don't want to see my mum in a chair drinking a bowl of mush looking miserable. She's put herself on this self-inflicted diet torture plan. And she slurps like a horse when she drinks.

It makes me feel sick when I think of Harry. But I still keep eating. Caught in this mess of a body. Can't get out.

Friday 10.3.89

DIDN'T GO OUT TONIGHT. AT lunch had chips and it gave me the world's worst indigestion – I thought I was dying. Plus the fact don't want to see Harry. Don't want to see anyone. Mum came upstairs to bring me my washing and said, 'Look, Rachel, what's the matter?' She sat on the end of the bed and I told her that I had basically been dumped. She said, 'Men don't know their arse from their elbow. They don't know it when they are 17, and they don't know it when they are 70, Rachel. You are going to have lots of these disappointments in your life, because life isn't fair. It never was and it never will be. Concentrate on your A levels and forget men. I am trying to. Now – I'm going to make a macaroni cheese to cheer us both up.' And she did. And we sat down and watched a video of Dynasty as we both love Dex Dexter.

WHY CAN'T SHE BE LIKE THIS ALL THE TIME? I

know she can't hug me or anything but this is fine. This is what I need. Just a bit of support.

Just realised that Mum's off the Cambridge Diet as I don't think pasta with half a ton of red Leicester on it is part of the programme.

Saturday 11.3.89

Late (it's probably Sunday)

MUM HAS BEEN GOING FOR it today food-wise. She has fallen off the wagon big time. There was egg, bacon and fried bread for breakfast. We had a Nelsons sausage roll coming back from town. She sat there fiddling with her hands this afternoon and made herself another sandwich and then she suggested to me that we had chilli con carne and chips for tea. I told her I was going out, and she goes, 'I will save you some for when you get home.' And she has too! There is masses of it.

Just been down the pub ON MY OWN. Thought, 'Stuff it – I'm not waiting for Bethany.' I cannot be doing with her any more. It's like she bullies me in a really clever way. Don't get me wrong – she doesn't hit me or anything – it's just the little comments about my weight, and the way she was about Harry. I'm not being melodramatic but she seems to take real pleasure in my pain.

Anyway, I went down the Vaults and Harry was NOT there, BUT Battered Sausage, Haddock and Fig were!! Battered Sausage yelled across the bar, 'Big Razza, come over here,' and we had a BRILLIANT laugh. We played a drinking game called Captain Birdseye – what a gig. Can't remember the rules but it was funny. Fig was great too – he was showing how he walked like a penguin, but Haddock just sat there looking naffed off with everything and giving me the evils. He said (sorry – grunted) about three sentences to me. Out of the blue he just comes out with, 'What happened with you and Harry, then?' I said, 'I don't really want to talk about it,' and he goes, 'Fine – I don't really want to know.' He is such a moody git. He is gorgeous but he bloody knows it.

Bethany came in looking flustered about half an hour after me. She gave me a right death-stare in the pub but I don't care. She came over and sat on Battered Sausage's knee and said to me, 'Why didn't you wait for me?' I made up something lame. She was so pissed off because I was getting all the attention – even Haddock was pissing himself when I was telling them about the time when I had a body-search at a Turkish airport and the woman customs official thought I was a bloke. Eventually she said, 'I don't feel well – I'm going home.' No one rushed to stop her. Certainly not me.

Walked home via Lord Burghley pub and spotted Luke. He waved at me and smiled. I must say, I really like Luke but I think I probably need some space before I launch into another relationship.

Mum has just stormed in to say that the ding of the microwave woke her up. Did she want me to eat her chilli con carne or not?

Sunday 12.3.89

9.30 p.m.

MUM IS ON ONE. TODAY we had a STARTER with the roast as well as a pudding. I said, 'Mum, we only have prawn cocktails at Christmas!' She just grunted. Something is wrong. Really wrong. She sent me down Green Lane shops for some milk and the usual bunch of pillocks were on the wall. But ever since I claimed I was related to Reggie Kray they have left me well alone. God, I hope they don't write to him in prison and check. When I came back with the milk it looked like Mum had been crying and we had four pints of milk in the fridge already. I said, 'Why did you send me to get some more milk?' She said something stupid like, 'You can never have enough milk, Rachel.' I left it at that. I've got to do an essay on The Tempest. I can't get into emotional turmoil.

Been thinking about Luke. A lot. And been thinking about Bethany. I do need to be more understanding. Perhaps I was a bit harsh last night.

Monday 13.3.89

11.40 p.m.

I CANNOT BELIEVE WHAT HAS HAPPENED today and I am telling you, Diary, I just wish you could talk.

I went down town at lunchtime to meet everyone for

a jacket potato. Bethany was there surrounded by a crowd of people. When I got near I could see that Bethany was crying a bit and everyone death-stared me and someone said, 'Why are you being such a bitch to Bethany?'

Bethany had told everyone the following:

1) I stood her up on Saturday and left her in the rain.
2) I told Battered Sausage Bethany was an ignorant cow.
3) Ever since I'd had a boyfriend I'd 'changed'!!
4) I am jealous of her because of her fast metabolism.

Only no. 4 is true.

To stop a riot I said, 'Look – let's go down the Meadows and have a chat.' So we ended up feeding the ducks while Bethany grilled me with loads of questions. She knew what she was doing. She soon cheered up when we were on our own.

B: Why have you fallen out with me?
ME: I haven't.
B: Why didn't you want to go with me to the pub?
ME: I just wanted to go on my own for a change.
B: I felt really hurt and embarrassed and it was obvious you had been slagging me off to Battered Sausage.
ME: I had not!! We'd been playing a drinking game.
B: I have always supported you and tried to help you. Is it too much to ask that you wait five minutes for me?
ME: No it's not.

So eventually I completely backed down and apologised for NOTHING. She instantly was fine – surprise, surprise. We walked home with her telling me about all the men that fancied her and topped it off with a talk on what hairstyles suit bigger girls like me.

I think I might be doing a lot of mock A-level revision these next two weeks.

At least she is mates with Luke. That's one thing in her favour.

Tuesday 14.3.89

10.57 p.m.
SPENT ALL DAY AVOIDING SCHOOLWORK and Bethany! Cleaned out my big cupboard and found a load of old annuals. Read Judy from about 1979 (great Dial-a-Boyfriend game and a poster of the Carpenters – poor woman – she died of thinness), Mandy from 1980 (bit disappointing) and The Smash Hits Yearbook from 1984, in which George Michael was going on about how his mum still got him up for work! Now he's all grown up and singing about wanting sex he won't want to be reminded of that. AND in the bit where it said watch out in '84 for these new artists, it says MADONNA. Which seems bizarre now. Mind you, it also says watch out for a group called Physique, who I have never heard of – so they weren't all right.

Before I knew it Bethany was calling for me to go down the pub. I was going to ignore the door but Mum answered it and shouted me down. (I'm sure she knew I was hiding.) On the way there Bethany was asking me who I liked. I said Luke. As quick as a flash she said, 'No chance – his parents are loaded.' Then she said (as a joke), 'You could be his bit of rough, I suppose.' I also said in a strictly physical sense I fancied Haddock but this was in much the same way as I fancied Nick Kamen from the 501 adverts and David Sylvian from Japan. Bethany pointed out both Haddock and Luke have girlfriends. Fuck knows who goes out with Haddock but she must have the patience of a saint to put up with that grumpy git. Anyway, I left it there. Or rather she did. Apparently a bloke from Stamford College has asked her out for a drink on Saturday and she wanted to tell me all about how he had got talking to her in the pub and what he had said. He does car mechanics, wants to specialise in high-performance vehicles, and she reminds him of Belinda Carlisle. Why does she think that is interesting to me?? Anyway, I tuned out and went with my fantasy of Luke into dreamland.

Down the pub. No one was out. Bethany talked at me for three hours. We came home. I had a Kit Kat.

Lonely. Feel lonely. And empty.

Wednesday 15.3.89

WAS ON THE WAY TO call Mort tonight when I passed a toddler who turned round to his mum and said, 'Mummy, why is that girl so fat?' I raced by – I saw his mum smirk half embarrassment/half amusement. What could I do? I can't threaten a toddler with the fact that I am related to Reggie Kray, can I?

By the time I rang Mort I was crying. She was so

sweet about it and said, 'Kids say stupid stuff all the time,' but it hurts even as I am writing this. It's like everywhere I go I am pointed out and stared at by EVERYONE and it's like my weight is there to be discussed and laughed at. But if I was in a wheelchair they wouldn't do it. If I had terrible scars they wouldn't do it – but it's OK to do it to me. Because they know. I caused this. This is self-inflicted. This is lazy, stupid, careless, crap, fat me. And the only way to make myself feel better right now is to punch myself as hard as I can . . . cry, cry, CRY . . . not tell anyone . . . and pretend everything is brilliant because no one gives a shit. Sorry if this doesn't make sense but that's how it is right now. That's how it is. No one is coming to save me. This is how it's always been. It's like the Alarm song where they go on about leaving all the pain behind by running away from it all. But I can't. It's here. It's everywhere. In a room with a door that doesn't close properly. With a mother who hates me. With a belly that looks like a ton of dough stuck to my body.

Thursday 16.3.89

Late

NOTHING TO TELL YOU. DON'T want to go out. I just get stared at. I'd rather stay inside my bedroom – just me and the cat – and listen to Simple Minds.

Weird thoughts all over the place and just crippling.

Friday 17.3.89
Made myself go out. I still hurt a bit but not as much.

HARRY CAME INTO THE PUB. Bethany told him that he broke my heart and he said, 'Is that good or bad?' I felt like saying you can't break wrought iron. I disliked him intensely then. But in a way it was more like 'Why don't you fancy me, Harry, you bastard?'

Luke was in!! He came over to talk to me and Bethany and for some reason me and him got into a food fight. He threw a packet of Skips at the back of my neck, so I shoved a packet of peanuts in his face. If I like a bloke I just end up ripping the piss out of him rather than being nice. Now he keeps reminding me that we are due a fight. I can make such a good impression, can't I?

I really want to go out with Luke. I really do. I bloody fancy him, and more importantly I LIKE him. Unfortunately several factors point towards this being yet another let-down:

1) Luke probably does not fancy me.
2) According to Bethany he has got a girlfriend and she's gorgeous.
3) Apparently he is not really into 'heavy relation-ships'. What's his definition of 'heavy'?
4) Even if he was, his A levels are approaching.
5) Just going back to no. 1 – I think we can quite confidently swap probably for definitely.

Saturday 18.3.89

11.53 p.m.

MET UP WITH BETHANY'S DATE at the pub tonight. He seemed a bit dim but I have to admit he was attractive in a pretty-boy way. Anyway, they were asking each other stupid questions like what's your star sign (he's a Leo). Bethany said, 'Oh, the proud lion, and you've even got a thick mane of hair.' He wet himself at this utterly crap non-joke, so I went and sat with Battered Sausage and Fig, who are just lovely beyond belief. I told Battered Sausage I slightly fancied Haddock in a physical sense and Luke in an altogether sense. He pissed himself at this but promised not to tell either of them. Haddock came in later with his usual pissy stomp, but tonight at least he asked me how I was – even though by the time I answered he was at the bar. Battered Sausage said I should give him a chance because he is 'really all right underneath it all'. No he is not. He is a typical rugger-bugger lad who probably does anal-chugging with beer and talks about tits till he is blue in the face.

Left about 10.45. Bethany was snogging Pretty Boy. I snogged a burger.

Sunday 19.3.89

BETHANY CAME ROUND TO ASK me why I didn't wait for her last night. I mean, what am I? Her bodyguard? She can piss right off. She said that Pretty Boy and her were full on and that this could be serious. She says that about everyone. She's just gagging to lose it. That's the problem.

Monday 20.3.89 (holidays)

WENT TO SEE NAN TODAY. She is completely blind now but still lovely. Mum is looking after her and bathing her, and Mrs Berridge across the road in Edmund's Close is making her meals. Mrs Berridge always laughs at everything I say and calls me a Dutchman for some reason. However, she always redeems herself by making me an extra Eve's pudding and custard so I'll let her off. Mr Berridge was doing his usual – moaning about the Japanese in the war and telling me to buy British. I told him my Lloytron personal stereo was British-made. Secretly I would love a Sony one – at least it would have a bloody rewind button. I wouldn't say that to him, though – him and his flat cap would have a fit.

Nan asked me if I was courting. I said no. She said, 'Plenty of time, Rach.' Then she tells me about running the post office in Wittering during the war and the great times she had. God, she loved her husband. It must be terrible to lose someone after so many years of being married to them. I can't imagine. That's perhaps because I can't imagine a time when I will ever be married. Who'd have this gob on a blob?

Incredible that Nan is no relation to me at all. She feels like it. She is just a lady that lived next door to us and we got friendly with her years ago – but absolutely know she IS my nan. She has also never got angry at me – except for the time I tripped on her emergency cord and Mrs Houston the warden shouted, 'Everything OK, Mrs Clements??' It was a bit embarrassing but piss funny too.

I love Nan. She never judges me and she never comments on my weight.

Tuesday 21.3.89

JUST REALISED FROM LAST ENTRY Nan can't comment on my weight because she is blind.

Feel bad talking about Nan and sex in the same entry but Bethany is already talking about going on the pill for the Easter weekend as Pretty Boy's parents are away, and could I go to the doctor's with her for moral support? I said to her, 'Isn't this a bit quick?' She said even though her and Pretty Boy have only been together for four days there is a connection. An almost freaky thing! Oh yeah, of course there is, dear. He just wants to get his end away. She's booked in tomorrow and I am going with her. Got nothing else to do. Except revision. And I can't face the Ottoman Empire right now.

Wednesday 22.3.89

12.53 p.m.
JUST BEEN TO THE DOCTOR'S. Bethany got a right grilling! She thought they would just give her the pills, but the doctor wanted to know how many partners she has had, how old her current partner is and how many sexual partners he has had. The doctor suggested the barrier method may be better. I had to ask what that was – he means johnnies. Bethany then told him that she hadn't used condoms before and he told her to prac- tise on a banana! HELLO!!!! What do these people think we are?? He gave her the pill in the end with a huge lecture about AIDS and sexually transmitted diseases. Like there is AIDS in Stamford. Come on – it's Lincolnshire. We only got the wheel 50 years ago.

She went into Boots and got them. Honestly, she looked so proud of herself. It's only sex!

10.20 p.m.
Who am I trying to kid? I would love to be having an Easter weekend of doing it. As it is, I'll be lucky if I get a Smarties Easter egg.

Thursday 23.3.89

10.45 p.m.
SOMEONE SAW ME IN THE doctor's and Mum cornered me and said, 'Why were you in the doctor's yesterday?' I said I was just waiting for someone. She goes, 'Rachel, I would like to think that if there was anything important happening in your life, you would tell me.' AND YOU COULD TOTALLY SEE SHE WAS THINKING SHAGGING.

It's great, though, that my mum thinks I just might need contraception. I said, 'Look – I'm 17 and I think it's OK that some things are private.' She walked off then, pulling a right face. There is something going on but I can't get to the bottom of it. I did have a poke around in her bedroom but the only suspicious thing was a bloody Open University book on child psychology. You won't understand me that way, love, 'cos I ain't no kid no more!

Just looked out my window. Mrs Bark across the passage was washing up and laughing with her husband. They looked really happy. Even though he was wearing a white vest. Well, off-white. Perhaps true love is blind.

Good Friday 24.3.89

HOT CROSS BUMS. HURRAH! HA! Meant to write buns!! I must be obsessed.

Bethany is gutted because she has to take a week of

pills for them to work, and they can make you put on weight . . . OH YES, YES, YES – there is a God! PLEASE let her pile it on.

Actually I wouldn't wish this on anyone, even people I can't stand.

Mrs Bark has just death-stared me and closed her kitchen curtains in a really pissy way. Oh, get over it, woman – I don't want to be living on top of you either.

Saturday 25.3.89

11.52 p.m.
I JUST HAD A VERY INTERESTING Saturday night in the Vaults. Firstly Bethany has told me she is not going on her pill just yet as she is worried about weight gain early on in a relationship. It's like she fears being fat – being me – more than anything. Thanks.

Later I was sat with Battered Sausage, and Haddock's girlfriend came to sit with us. She is lovely – I don't know what she is doing with him. Well, I do – he is fit – but he is also bloody moody and she is a right laugh. She is good mates with Dobber, Fig's girlfriend, who was also brilliant tonight. It worries me I can get people so wrong. Haddock came in later – he put 'Convoy' on the jukebox – that shit CB radio song from the '70s. No doubt it's a rugger-bugger in-joke thing because he sat there smirking to himself. I said sarcastically, 'Good choice, Haddock – you should be a DJ. With that mumble-grunt you could be on Radio 1, mate.' This made everyone laugh except Haddock, who just sighed into his beer and glared at me. If he can't take it he shouldn't give it.

75

No Luke. Good job. I was wearing an old sweatshirt. Not very feminine.

Bethany and Pretty Boy disappeared to his house at about 9 p.m. – probably to do it. She has said she is losing it tonight. Another virgin bites the dust. I looked around the table tonight and I just knew I was the only virgin there. I'm so behind. I look 12. I feel about 12. Only my figure looks middle-aged. I wish I was like everyone else.

2.25 a.m.
Just discovered a note on my windowsill from Mum. 'Don't look into Mrs Bark's window. She has mentioned to me you are staring in.'

So while Bethany is having the best weekend of her life, I am being told off for LOOKING. You couldn't make it up.

Easter Sunday 26.3.89

TWO EASTER EGGS. ONE DAIRY Milk egg. One Double Decker egg. One china mug with hollow egg and chocolate-flavoured footballs (not counted).

Gagging to know how Bethany is getting on. She is due to come round tomorrow to tell me all about it. I feel sick. Don't know if it's because I have scoffed two Easter eggs or if it's because I am so jealous – almost aching with jealousy of Bethany. Just to be loved and cared for and WANTED. I can tell you, Diary, but I can't tell anyone else. Just to be held. Just to be needed. This stupid body. It stops everything, everything that I want. I'm like a blancmange – wobbly and good at parties, but inside all this fat I'm a girl. I want to be a normal girl wearing clothes that fit and . . . Oh, what's the point? If I turned up in a skirt and make-up everyone would laugh and I couldn't take it.

Just listened to the charts to make me feel better. Some great songs about:

- Texas – 'I Don't Want a Lover'. Yes – forget love, I do just need a friend.
- Poison – 'Every Rose Has Its Thorn'. Basically a song warning blokes off pretty girls.
- Bananarama and Lananeeneenoonoo – 'Help'. Piss funny.
- Madonna – 'Like a Prayer'. Brilliant.
- I even have to say I love that Paula Abdul record.

Please notice every woman in the charts is thin. Bar Dawn French in Lananeeneenoonoo – but that's not counted.

Easter Monday 27.3.89

4.10 p.m.

> Bank holidays mean nothing
> Just *Disney Time* and such,
> A Bond film, a hero,
> A dream at which I clutch.

77

Just someone who can see through it,
Through fat and come what may;
Just someone who can stand up to
What his mates might say.

A someone who won't judge me
Who'll understand, not tut;
But for now I'm like the shops today
I'm well and truly shut.

BETHANY HASN'T BEEN ROUND. SHE must be staying over longer. If I had a phone of course she could have rung me – but I haven't. It's not 1989 in this house, it's 1959.

Tuesday 28.3.89

7.09 p.m.

HELLO, DIARY. WHAT A GREAT day. Can you sense sarcasm in my voice? I have spent all afternoon listening to Bethany describe losing her virginity. Of course it was perfect. He made her a cheese sandwich after the pub. He got two brandies from his dad's drinks cabinet. They drank them on the sofa. He then picked her up and CARRIED her to bed. 'He even bumped his head on the beams.' YES, Bethany – we know you lost your cherry in a barn conversion. He undressed her. It hurt a bit the first time, but not the second, third, fourth or fifth time (pretend embarrassed laughter). They slept in each other's arms.

The condom split but it didn't matter. I said,

'Bethany, you need the morning-after pill.' She said, 'You are jealous – just trying to spoil it.' I said, 'Look, Bethany – I have read *Just 17*'s problem page for five years – I know when a johnny breaks you need the morning-after pill.' She then called me a baby that had fallen for adult propaganda. There's no telling her. They are meeting each other for a pizza tomorrow. But it's love. BIG love and she is no longer a virgin.

Yes, the 'fell asleep in each other's arms' bit did make me jealous. I can't imagine being naked in front of a man. I've only had one shower after PE in the past six years because I can't bear the thought of people looking at THIS.

Wednesday 29.3.89

I AM SICK OF HOLIDAYS NOW. Just spend all my time avoiding work and watching crap on telly like Gardening Time and Rainbow.

Walked to the Vaults with Bethany tonight. Pretty Boy had bought her a necklace – black cord with a silver disc. He reckoned he had made it himself at college. It was vile and you could see she thought it was too, but she put it on and rubbed his hair and said, 'Vroom, thank you.' I pissed! Apparently 'Vroom' is her pet name for him because he mends cars!! When I laughed she said it was because I am just jealous. Now normally I would say she might have a point – but for the record I never want a boyfriend called Vroom!

LUKE was in the pub unfortunately – he was with a girl and a group of people I didn't know, so I sat with

Fig and Dobber (Fig's girlfriend). Again we had such a laugh – they never make me feel like a gooseberry and Fig always buys me a drink because he knows I am skint. Dobber asked if I fancied an afternoon and evening sesh on Saturday as Fig has got his proper A levels in two months and has to revise. I said yes. This is brilliant. She only lives by the rec, and crucially – unlike Bethany – is lovely.

Feel bad about the last Bethany bit. She is OK. She just loves feeling better than me.

Thursday 30.3.89

11.?? (digital clock has broken so can't see the minutes)
BETHANY IS REALLY RUBBING MY nose in it – I'm sure she doesn't mean to but she is. Why do I need to see that Pretty Boy has bought her a double love album? Why do I need to see that he has customised the song titles on the album sleeve to suit their relationship? For example, for 'It's Heaven When You Lie Your Body Next to Me' he has written in biro in brackets 'Bethany, you know it's true.' I pretended to retch (and it is vomit-making) but it still makes me wish . . . wish I wasn't so ugly and big. I don't want albums, but . . . I don't know.

Had two Twixes tonight and shoved the wrappers down the side of my bed. Don't want to put them in the bin or Mum will see them and have a go. I know it's crap but right now it makes me feel better.

Friday 31.3.89

IN *TV GUIDE* THIS WEEK THERE is a competition to win a part in *Neighbours* where you get two weeks in Australia, £500 spending money and a cameo part in *Neighbours*. That programme needs a fat girl on it – every women who has ever been on it has been thin. Charlene – thin. So-called Plain Jane Super Brain – thin. Even that ancient Helen bloody Daniels woman is thin. In the same mag Paula Yates (still gorgeous after having kids) is going on about how much she fancies CLIVE JAMES – old, fat bloke. Yet again proof a man can be fat AND sexy – but it don't work the other way round, does it?

Saturday 1.4.89

10.45 p.m.

KARATE KID IS ON TELLY. Wax on. Wax off. The love interest of *Karate Kid* – a girl called Ali – is skinny as anything. I have seen this film a thousand times. In the end it does not matter that the Karate Kid is bullied because he beats everyone. Classic American fairytale lies. I'd like to see him tackle the blokes from Green Lane shops in a kilt when they are calling you every name under the sun.

Just got back from a major session with Mrs Classic Dobber. Only a bit ruined with Bethanbitch. Write tomorrow as too knackered and beered.

Sunday 2.4.89

12.10 p.m.

THINK I WAS A BIT PISSED last night.
Have a hangover, but what a night. Met Dobber
outside Tesco at four and then we walked to the shop on
Scotgate run by the Maltese guy where she can get served.
Got a massive bottle of Diamond White, a big bottle of
lager and a bottle of Ribena. Ended up down the Meadows
(till the Vaults opened at seven) making our own snakebite
and black! Dobber is lovely – she was telling me how her
parents are getting divorced and stuff, and things have
been hard for her – but she is such a laugh. We then
stumbled on to the Vaults where we met up with everyone
and we had a TOP night. The only crap thing was Bethany,
who came in with Pretty Boy and said, 'Can I have a word
with you?' Once we were sat outside the girls' toilets
upstairs, she said, 'I've been talking to Luke tonight in the
Hole in the Wall and he says he really likes you and really
wants to go out with you.' Honestly I nearly died – I was
going off my head until she said, 'April Fool!' I think she
realised she had gone too far because . . . well, I welled up
a bit really but I told her it was OK and pretended to see
the funny side. When I went back downstairs Haddock
said, 'What's up with you?' but I couldn't tell him . . . He'd
just take the piss something chronic. I know I play practical jokes on people, but I'd never do anything like that.
Bethany thinks she is a right Jeremy Beadle.
God, it hurt.

Monday 3.4.89

RANG MORT AND TOLD HER about Bethany. She thinks it was a cow thing to do and I am not being hypersensitive. I know you think I am overreacting, Diary, but . . . Oh, don't want to think about it any more. Don't want to think about men any more or anything about love or anything. Because while I am like this it won't happen. With anyone. Even a blind man could feel my gut.

Listening to 'Like a Prayer' by Madonna loads. Madonna is looking so bloody brilliant as a brunette. This is probably my favourite look of hers since the 'Live to Tell' video. The cassette I bought stinks of patchouli oil, which is weird. I don't know if Madonna had it specially scented or something. She can do what she likes because she's Madonna.

She tells men to jump, they say, 'How high?' According to *Smash Hits*, Madonna and me are the same height. She weighs under nine stone. God knows how much I weigh.

How long would it take me to get to her weight? And would I change? Perhaps I'd be like Madonna – all hard-faced and don't mess with me. I'd like to be that. I would, however, never dance round burning crosses in the middle of the Fens wearing a nightie like she does in the 'Like a Prayer' video. Even she would get the piss taken out of her if she did that round here.

Tuesday 4.4.89

SHIT. BETHANY CAME ROUND – SHE IS LATE and BRICKING IT. Didn't know what to say at first. I said what we need is a Brook Advisory Clinic because that's what Melanie in Just 17 always recommended. Of course there isn't one in Stamford. She kept saying, 'It was only once – it was only once.' I could hear Mum in my head saying, 'That's all it takes – that's all it takes.' If she is pregnant it will be a disaster. She'll either have to have an abortion or leave school. Our place doesn't do pregnant schoolgirls. Bethany kept gripping her stomach saying, 'I know I am – they say you just know.' She wants me to go and get a pregnancy test for her. But I can't. Someone would tell Mum and I can't cope with that amount of Gestapo interrogation. She is only two days late anyway – I told her worrying about things would make it worse. She hasn't told Pretty Boy yet as 'Vroom wants to keep things casual.' In other words he is a bastard shag-about who wants to sleep around. I told her this but she doesn't want to hear it. He, according to her, is a bad boy – which, according to me, means he is a twat.

Bethany left about 20 minutes ago. Mum came straight up and said, 'What's wrong with Bethany?' I said nothing. She said, 'If she is that upset, Rachel, she should tell her mum.' I can guarantee it – she has been listening through the door and she knows, and THAT IS CRAP. The walls are so thin in this house. I should know – I've found out so much stuff through these walls it's unbelievable. Like when I found out my parents were getting divorced.

Wednesday 5.4.89

7.17 a.m.

JUST WOKE UP THINKING, 'WHY is this bed so uncomfortable?' One of Bethany's huge earrings was sticking in my backside. Even when she is not here she is winding me up.

9.23 p.m.
Sat here trying to make sense of it all. Rang Mort about Bethany. She won't say anything to anyone. Mort doesn't think she is pregnant and thinks she is just being a drama queen. She does agree with me, though, that Vroom sounds like a total pranny. I rang Bethany after Mort – she couldn't talk properly because the phone is in her front room and her mum was watching *Coronation Street*. She could give me one-word answers, though. She hasn't come on yet, she still thinks she is pregnant, and she is going to do the test tomorrow.

Really feel for her. I know she winds me up but she is a good friend really and I hate falling out with people – I hate the atmosphere.

Thursday 6.4.89

11.02 p.m.

BETHANY IS NOT PREGNANT. GENUINELY relieved for her. She did the test in Red Lion Square toilets because she didn't want to risk doing it at home! She also showed me the carpet burns on her back she had got from doing it on Pretty Boy's parents' en-suite shower-room floor. 'They only have a thin carpet.' Then she was moaning about her clothes, saying the last time her mum had bought her a new coat it was for the school ski trip to Val d'Isère, and even then it was from C&A.

God, my life is so boring. Just telly and crisps in this room, and other people's stories. I'd love a boyfriend. I'd love these dramas.

Oh, stop being pathetic, Rae. I piss myself off.

Friday 7.4.89

11.35 p.m.

WELL, I'VE BEEN TRYING TO get my work done with little success. I've nearly done my theatre arts but that leaves US politics (massive!!), British politics, British history and English.

Just been down the pub with Dobber. Brilliant – a total smash and everything. But I still don't seem to be getting much interest from the boys. Dobber suggested my suede jacket from the Congregational Hall jumble sale is a bit musty and off-putting. Musty, it may be – it was also only 15p. She was just being kind anyway. I know what is putting men off. And I can't just take it off when I get home. I have to live in it.

Bethany and Pretty Boy had a row towards the end of tonight. It's not exactly clear-cut but it looks like she told him she'd had a pregnancy scare and he freaked out big time. Not that badly, though, because they were eating each other's faces by the end of the night.

Mum has refused to get a home phone again. Cow.

Saturday 8.4.89

4.10 p.m.

MUM GOT A LETTER THIS morning – and she announced that she is going to Morocco to see the husband in June. Which means – FREEEEEEEEEEEEEEEEE house!!!

BRILLIANT!!!!

And just in time for the first week of the summer holidays!! YES!!!

It's weird, though – she seemed a bit upset. Actually more angry than upset. She usually shoves letters behind the clock on the mantelpiece but this one she put straight in her bag so I couldn't examine it. As predicted by me ages ago, I KNOW something is going on.

Going to the pub later with Dobber.

Read my horoscope. It said, 'Meet the chaos head on. You are short of cash on the 12th.' When am I NOT short of cash?

Sunday 9.4.89

EastEnders omnibus is on so . . . 2-ish?

NOT LONG GOT UP. GOT in late last night. Great in the pub with Dobber, Fig, Haddock and Battered Sausage. Then we all went back to Dobber's to watch TV. Ended up watching *The Hitman and Her* with this bit in a club where the men rate the women out of ten and vice versa. The boys were playing along at home and giving really low scores to some of the women on there who were a lot better-looking and thinner than me. They were saying stuff like, 'She's a ten-pinter.' I mean, what do these blokes want? It was totally depressing. Battered Sausage gave me a lift home in Clarence the Cortina. I got in, made some toast and watched pages from Ceefax until Mum shouted at me to stop eating and come to bed. It all went really flat at the end. If blokes give women scores, fuck knows what mine is. Don't want to think.

No Luke last night.

7.14 p.m.
Mum just showed me the Great Universal Catalogue, trying to get me interested. What's the point? Everything in there only goes up to size 14 – nothing fits. And the week she can't afford the payments it will be me who goes to the door to say she's not in, even when she is. There's no point buying new nice clothes till I am a size 10. It's pointless dressing nicely now. It'd be like putting Chanel on a turd.

88

Monday 10.4.89

10.20 p.m.

I JUST CAN'T GET MY BLOODY A-level work done.
I've put it off for yet another day. Just can't be bothered
with it. Sat in my bedroom with me portable telly. Just
broke the on/off switch so having to turn it off and on by
prising the knob out with nail scissors. Sometimes it feels
like everything is going wrong. Even with the things that
are wrong already. I'm the only girl at school that still has
a TV with a DIAL to find the channels rather than buttons.
Waiting for *Come Dancing* to come on at 11.

I want to write more. I've got that mad feeling. It's
weird. I really want to go out with Luke but it's not
likely to happen. That's life – it's cruel but it's life. I'm
not making the same mistake of getting totally infatu-
ated and making a complete fool of myself. I do feel a
picture of the legendary Luke is in order. Actually scrap
that. I can't do him justice with a biro.

Why is he so attractive? He is sarcastic, bitchy,
funny, affectionate. BUT I'M NOT GETTING MY HOPES
UP. I can't believe I ever fancied Harry. I can't believe I
went out with him – he's just not my type, whatever
that is. So quiet – I just fell for that sweet Aquarian
face . . . but I shan't do that again.

11.45 p.m.

Here I am watching some telly. To think that not long
ago there was no night-time TV. Now there's *Prisoner*

Cell Block H, then the *People's Choice Awards* – whatever that is.

I wish someone was here with me now. Just beside me, holding me – giving me that warm feeling and really meaning it. I wish I could take it and give it back. I completely know I could – to the right person. But it'll have to be someone I really trust with my heart – and he will take some finding.

I never want to end up in prison. Especially in Australia. They are all lesbos. And the only job you get is in the laundry doing whatever the 'top dog' wants you to do.

Tuesday 11.4.89

11.45 a.m.

A STRANGE TIME TO BE WRITING, I know. I've just cut up my diary (old one). It looks so weird. A part of my past wrapped up in yesterday's edition of the *Daily Mirror* and tied in a dirty shoestring. Now I'm going to burn the bloody thing. Appalling. Let me quote one line: *'I'm too busy with a commitment to Tom Cruise to bother with a boyfriend.'*

In proper talk that means 'I have to fancy a film star because no one fancies me.'

Ahhh . . . the fragrant joys of bullshit.

Sad thing is, two years on nothing has changed. My boyfriends are still imaginary.

Wednesday 12.4.89

1.23 a.m.

WATCHING MORE TV.
     Not the best evening. Forgot I had written my
old diary on that paper that doesn't burn very well.
Used the old Qualcast mower's metal grass-collector to
burn it in. It created an unbelievable amount of smoke
and you could still read half the stuff in it. Then Mum
came home from Nan's and went mad. Usual crap.

     Then just went for a late-night walk, and Mum killed
me and grounded me. I only went for a quick midnight
walk – it's not as if I'm taking heroin! She is so lucky
to have me.

     Had good conversation with Bethany today. I don't
feel loved by anyone basically, but I hate pity. Actually
if pity helps me lose my virginity I will live with it.

     Bethany doesn't think I'm 'fertive' enough. That's her
term for tarting. Flirtation never was my thing, was it?
Things will start to heat up once we are back at school
hopefully.

     I know the real reason. The weight. Everyone skirts
around it but pretty girls at school don't have to flirt. If
they just stood there gutting fish, blokes would still
want to do them.

The BBC close-down has just come on. They always
have a classic public information film – oh no, it's the
one about Rabies! No! No! It's 'BAG IT AND BIN IT'!!

     I know this routine like the back of my hand. The

announcer will say, 'That was a public information film.' YES, DEAR, WE KNOW AND, YES, I ALSO KNOW THAT YOUR COLLEAGUES AT RADIO 2 ARE STILL THERE THROUGHOUT THE NIGHT!!! What's your name? Something David? I bet you are going home to someone – even though you have a beard and wear corduroy.

National Anthem! Marvellous! Can't be bothered to stand up.

I know this routine back to front because I can't sleep. Stuff races through my head.

Weird thoughts bad today.

Tuesday 18.4.89

SCHOOL WAS A BLOODY NIGHTMARE today. Everybody seemed to be in a state about exams. Lots of comparing of revision timetables. I have done basically fuck all. It's only mocks. All the people who are going to apply to Oxford and Cambridge (aka not me) seem to think their lives will end if their predicted grades aren't any good. Mort is applying to Cambridge. I hope she gets in – but what if this changes her, and changes our friendship? I hope not. They say people who go to Cambridge come out arrogant.

Bloody minestrone main meal for lunch. Don't know what it's meant to be but it's slop in a bowl. Everyone comparing diets too. Daisy is on one peanut-butter roll a day because she thinks she has a fat backside. It's not big – just big compared to the rest of her.

Had more chats with Bethany about men and sex. My worst fear is recognised. Well, not my worst probably, but on its way. Apparently boys find ME intimidating! I over-power them. According to Bethany I am too much. Can't be fagged to write any more. All shit.

Wednesday 19.4.89

6.20 p.m.

TODAY AT SCHOOL WE HAD to watch the spec-tacle of Daisy eating her one roll a day in the common room. First she licked the peanut butter off bit by bit. Then she dabbed her finger and got the flour off the cob. Then she basically ate the bread crumb by crumb. It was pathetic and watching her put me off food. Georgia Manton kept wafting a packet of barbecue-beef Hula Hoops in front of her face, which was a bit cruel. Daisy was saying stuff like, 'Honestly I am not hungry' – but with a waft of roast beef from the canteen you could see her drooling big time.

I don't think I could ever diet. I can't imagine life without crisps, roasts, chocolate and Primula cheese.

Thursday 20.4.89

LISTENING TO 'BAT OUT OF HELL' by Meat Loaf. That song was written for poor sods everywhere like me who are stuck in crap little towns. A town that you are desperate to get out of – even if it means dying in the process.

Actually I am not that desperate now but there are times when I have been.

Daisy gave in today and ended up eating two help-ings of angel whip – the school's cheap version of Angel Delight. It seemed bizarre as it's actually total crap and not worth having a big arse for.

Tomorrow is Friday, believe it or not, fact fans, and I feel there may be a distinct possibility of seeing a lesser spotted Luke if one goes to the regular jaunts – i.e. the Vaults or the Hole in the Wall – over the weekend. Then again, maybe at the next major party. Why on earth didn't I confront my distinct fancy for Luke at the onset?

Well, I would say there is as much chance of me getting off with Luke as there is of Arthur Scargill getting off with Margaret Thatcher. Nil.

Friday 21.4.89

6.47 p.m.
I HAVE MOVED ON THIS YEAR. Things HAVE changed. So, romance-wise, ladies and gentlemen, what have I learnt so far this year?

1) Be 'fertive' – entails everything from mild conversation to caressing of legs, arms, knees, necks, ears, etc.
2) French kissing is the widely acceptable getting of a kiss, and not as previously thought restricted to married couples of over 50 years. (Call me old-fashioned.)
3) Men don't like to be overpowered or intimi-dated.

94

4) Men don't like it when you tell them you'd like to marry them.
5) I am capable of mild romance.
6) Infatuation on an individual basis is not a good idea.

However, key dates where love action MAY be the order of the day:

7 May – big gig at the Scotgate pub with the bloke from Stamford School who thinks he is Howard Jones. Crap music but everyone is going, and apparently a two-year-old could get served in the Scotgate.

12 May – party. May not get invite, though – depends on various connections.

Luke, it is speculated, will attend both. Bethany is here now so I'm buggering off – might be back later. She sounds chesty. Too many fags. She reckons they keep her thin.

I need love like LL Cool J!

What that has got to do with Bethany sounding chesty I don't know.

Saturday 22.4.89

JUMBLE SALE AT SCHOOL RAISED about £500 for *Blue Peter* or someone. Everyone was doing it for their Duke of Edinburgh Award because it counts towards the Bronze. No, it doesn't mean anything to me either. The best thing is, I got this fantastic tweed jacket. Smells a bit fusty but after a couple of days in the chest of drawers with lavender bags it will be fine.

Went pub tonight. Started off in the Hole in the Wall and SAW LUKE. Stuck my tongue out at him and he stuck it back. I HAD HOPE! Luke then was seen 'fertively' caressing his girlfriend's back as he led her out.

Pain. Agony. Heartbreak.

Then went to the Vaults. Usual crowd in there including Dobber, Fig, Haddock and Battered Sausage. Battered Sausage has started calling me 'Slug'. He claims it's nothing to do with my weight but it makes the other lads laugh and it makes Dobber scowl. I went in a bit of a stomp and Haddock of all people told Battered Sausage to stop it. He is an arrogant prick but he has his moments. He then went off and argued with his girlfriend all night. It's all they seem to do. Luke came in later with his girlfriend and they sat there looking at each other. All bloody night.

Came home a bit pissed and a bit pissed off. I hate fancying people who don't fancy me back – i.e. everybody. And I fancy Luke even more now. IT'S NOT FAIR.

Sunday 23.4.89

10.45 p.m.

I DID FEEL EXTREMELY PISSED OFF today. Eventually went to Film Society at the boys' school. Watched *The Blues Brothers*, which was aceamay. Cheered up immensely with sighting of Luke. Conversation went like this:

ME: Luke, you floozy!

LUKE (acknowledgement of greeting): Hello, Rae, pregnant with promise! (This relates to a joke that we have about a Cardinal Wolsey A-level question.)

ME (then I got nervous and said something that defies sense): Have you got a safety pin? My trousers are falling down.

LUKE: No, sorry, dear, I haven't.

WHY DID I SAY THAT???

Anyway, later down the pub Bethany said to Luke, 'Do you like Rae?' Then he said, 'We have a laugh, but I'm going out with someone else.'

Typical!!

I can't expect wonders, I know.

Off to London tomorrow for A-level politics trip to see Tony Benn, Paddy Ashdown, Norman Tebbit and David Owen. Should be interesting.

Monday 24.4.89

10.46 p.m.

BRILLIANT DAY. ME, MORT AND everyone got the back seat – I know it's like we are 12 but it's a tradition. We ate our lunch stupidly early, so we were starving by the time we got to London, even though Jessica Dunford had bought 27 bags of sweets. When we got into the place we were the only ones with bloody school uniform on, and MISS STALIN DEPUTY HEADMISTRESS BYRON had come on the other bus so we had to sit there like something out of Enid Blyton. The thing itself was brilliant except for hundreds of public schoolboys with fat wedge haircuts jeering Tony Benn. It was great, though, when someone yelled from the back of the auditorium, 'TWAT!' when John Selwyn Gummer was talking. I could see Miss Byron grimacing during Tony Benn. You don't get to be headmistress of a private school and not be a Thatcher love-child. She wants to try two weeks in a shitty council house and then see who she supports. Thank God for Ben Elton opening my eyes to it all. My mum votes Conservative – FUCK knows why. It's almost like habit.

Wonder if I should consider politics? 'Now here's a broadcast by the Fat and Needs a Snog Party!' My manifesto would be 'If you take the piss out of a fat person you should be force-fed until you are a whale, and then see how you like it.'

Tuesday 25.4.89

5.58 p.m.
CAREERS DAY AT SCHOOL TODAY. Everyone trotting back to the sixth-form block with prospectuses and brochures and HOPE. I go along there. Teacher asks me what I would like to do. I say children's TV presenter, like Caron Keating (funny and pretty). She looks bemused, then says, 'Well, go to university and get a degree – that's a good start.' (WHY???!!!)

Then she suggests I think about GOING INTO THE ARMY!!

WHY? WHY? WHY?

I HATE getting up early, I HATE being yelled at, and I HATE short hair. Do these people KNOW me? DO THEY CARE?!

Wednesday 26.4.89

9.20 p.m.

UNBELIEVABLY MUM AGREES THE ARMY would be good for me. PARDON??? For fuck's sake! Is that all I am good for? Marching in a scratchy jumper? I've been with all girls for the past six years – why would they want to put me in ANOTHER lesbo atmosphere? I don't want it. I am just written off constantly because I am fat, skint, mad and loud. For all these people know, somewhere in my brain could be the cure for cancer. But OH NO – I have just got to wear navy blue all my life and do what other people say.

BOLLOCKS. It stops now. I do stuff my way. This is a state of independence.

Mum just came in then with an ironed shirt for tomorrow and said some shit like, 'The choices you make now will make a difference to your future life.' REALLY???? I NEVER WOULD HAVE GUESSED. Do these people think I am brain-dead?

Can't be doing with schoolwork any more. Going to put the Cure on and forget I exist.

11.08 p.m.
Can't lie. Listened to Gloria Estefan instead. Soppy but I love it.

Thursday 27.4.89

9.25 p.m.

JUST AS I THOUGHT – MUM admitted that life in the Forces would probably get my body in better shape. So that's what it's all about – being thin. I knew it. Dug out my Which Way Now? careers guide booklet from about 1986, and pointed out to Mum that cinema usherette looked like a great job, as the positives listed were that you 'got to see the latest films for free', and the only negative was 'unsociable hours'. She said, 'You are capable of so much more than that.' Yeah, yeah, yeah . . . Well, love, I quite fancy a job in the dark with King Cones and Kia-Ora on tap.

Friday 28.4.89

11.45 p.m.

TOTAL DISASTER – MY PORTABLE TELLY is broken. I'd rather not watch telly than sit down-stairs with Mum.

the pub tonight I had an in-depth chat with Luke by the fruit machines!! He told me that people called him 'ratty' sometimes because he was so thin. He reckons everyone gets stick from time to time, and that when people call me lardy and fat I should just let it wash over me. Then he gave me a little hug and left. What a sweet bloke. God, I fancy him. God, I like him.

Spent the rest of the night with Battered Sausage and Haddock. I was being a bit charming to Battered Sausage, calling him a shit-stirring bastard. Mind you, he was giving as good as he got. When I said, 'I'm going to get my brother on to you and he's nearly 20 stone,' Battered Sausage said, 'Well, so are you.'

I had to laugh.

But it hurts.

Luke. Luke. Luke. Luke. Luke.

Saturday 29.4.89

11.50 p.m.

I WAS DOWN TOWN WITH BETHANY tonight when I saw Luke in a car with his girlfriend – snogging. Hurt, hurt, hurt, hurt. I stuck my Vs up at him. He must have clicked on to the way I feel about him – he must have. He stuck his Vs back and smiled. Ended up coming home and eating half a pack of sponge fingers because it was the only thing in the larder. I shove it in and it makes it all better. I'm a bulimic without the being sick.

Sunday 30.4.89

9-something . . . I don't know

THE BULLSHIT IN THIS HOUSE. Apparently the sponge fingers were for a trifle. WHEN?? Mum last made a trifle in about 1977 for the Jubilee. It's just another excuse to play the same record – moan at me for 25 minutes, then watch *Last of the* pissing *Summer Wine*. It's the same routine every Sunday. The only way to get through it is to eat and forget and fantasise and to pretend that this shell I am stuck in is different. And to avoid mirrors and windows – I don't want to be reminded.

OH MY GOD. MY TELLY JUST MENDED ITSELF. BRILLIANT! Only it can't get Channel 4. Fine – can't stand *Brookside* anyway.

Monday 1.5.89

10.15 p.m.

TIME MOVES ON. DO I diet or do I not? I don't want to change my personality and that often seems to happen when people lose loads of weight. It will go against every principle I've ever had. You know – 'personality before looks'. Right – I'm staying as I am till next week. This weekend is the crunch time. If I don't get a man (preferably Luke) before the end of the weekend, THEN I'll diet.

Trouble is, the Friday after that it's Welly fudge pudding at school, so I can't diet then. Perhaps I'll leave it till the start of June.

I'm pissed off with being fat, but don't want to go against my principles. I just need a cuddle and a snog and someone to give affection to. I'm not special – I need to be hugged and told everything is going to be all right. I'm no different to any bugger else.

I'm nearly in the middle of Volume 1 of this diary and so much has happened. Nothing happened in the last one. Yet in this one a lot has happened. Well . . . one snog. Nothing else, though. Actually, take it back –

nothing has happened. I'm still fat with no boyfriend. SAME OLD SAME OLD.

Watched *Dr Zhivago* this afternoon. There was no happy ending. Good. Makes it more real.

Tuesday 2.5.89

7.23 p.m.

EVERY TIME I THINK I'VE got problems someone comes along with far worse problems than me. Got into the common room today and Mort marched me straight out and warned me not to piss about with Amy Healer as she'd had a nasty shock but she couldn't tell me. It took me till the end of double politics to get it out of Mort. Amy had been doing it in her bedroom because her parents were in the Lake District for the weekend. They'd come back early and WALKED IN THE BEDROOM MID-SHAG. I honestly can't think of anything worse. The thought of my mum seeing me even acting like a girl makes me shiver. Anyway, she has been gated till about 1991, and the school nurse has been brought in for a 'chat'. It's the shittest punishment on record.

10.25 p.m.

Mum has just come up to ask why I ate all of the stew that was left in the pressure cooker. When I replied, 'Because I was hungry,' she called me a 'selfish cow of a girl cow'. Now not only does this sentence make no sense, it's also bollocks. I didn't know the other bit was for her. I did not know that she had not eaten. I just thought I was eating leftovers.

Why can't she just rustle up some soup for herself or something? Oh no, I am an easy target – come and have a yell at me, everyone else does. SICK OF IT. All that over pissing braising steak – it tastes like shoe anyway.

Wednesday 3.5.89

7.28 a.m.

RAN AWAY LAST NIGHT. JUST had enough. Just packed a bag and went. Got round the block once, went and sat in a playground on the slide. Got death-stared at by a pensioner who must have thought I was a mugger or something. Had a go at the monkey bars but couldn't get my feet off the ground. Stared at all the lights for ages. Then got cold and went home. Thought no one would notice, but she guessed – SHE was on the stairs – she slapped me round the face and it hurt. But she was worried – I could see it. Good. I am glad. I know that makes me sound evil but I am going off my head here and no one has bloody noticed.

Have to go now. It's school, and if you are late you go in the late book. Another piece of tradition designed to make our lives miserable. I don't even think anyone looks at it. It's just another guillotine hanging over my head.

10.02 p.m.
Came up straight to bed. I'm not apologising this time. She can for a change.

Thursday 4.5.89

7.07 p.m.

MUM HAS JUST BEEN UP – no apology. Instead, a suggestion from her. She suggested the old chestnut 'If you are not happy you can go and live with your father.' No I can't. She told me he didn't even turn up to the custody hearing years ago – so I know when I am not wanted. More to the point – he lives in Ipswich! Suffolk is more dead than Lincolnshire.

When I said, 'Don't be stupid,' she said, 'I am going to get some chips. Do you want some?' I said, 'No, thanks – I have got chips at school tomorrow.' She closed the door and said, 'That's not stopped you before.' Yes, well, it's stopping me now because I wouldn't have to sit here night after night if I had someone. I could sit with them. And nibble them.

Friday 5.5.89

10.16 p.m.

EVERYONE IS JIBBING ON THE beer tonight so I am sat here on my bed watching a documentary about penguins. Sound down. Smiths on. 'How Soon Is Now?' My song.

The song that sums everything up. How fucked off I am. How I feel inside. How I always hope but my hope always turns to shit.

I wish I could say I wrote it. But it's Morrissey. It could have been me, though, because it's everything I think. Everything. And you're left alone in a room full of Twix wrappers shoved in sheets. And he's singing what you are thinking. And that's all.

Saturday 6.5.89 •

11.45 p.m.

IT'S THE GIG TOMORROW SO there was no one out tonight except me and Bethany and Pretty Boy Vroom (tonight in stone-washed jeans – EEK!). When Vroom went to the toilet Bethany told me that she was getting a bit annoyed with him because he was insecure. She still loved him and everything but he wants to see her more than she wants to see him. Vroom came back from the bogs and obviously knew we had been talking about him. He kept putting his arm round Bethany and his hand on her thigh and squeezing it. It was like watching my mum when she feels all the fruit in Tesco. It was making me queasy so I said my goodbyes.

I don't get Bethany. All men go for her but she is not that great-looking. It's like she believes she is gorgeous and everyone just invisibly agrees with her.

Came home from the pub early tonight especially to watch the end of the *Eurovision Song Contest*. Bloody YUGOSLAVIA won! It beat our entry by seven points, and I'm not being biased or anything but it is an utter pile of turd. 'Rock Me' it's called. Utter bollocks. The lead singer (who looked like the woman who used to sing with Matt Bianco) was wearing fashions that

106

looked like something from about 1983. Horrible red batwing thing. Honestly the people who voted for that pile of poo want their bloody ears syringing out. Proves yet again that the world isn't fair. The world doesn't reward talent – but if you are a fit bird in a short skirt with half-decent legs you could persuade the whole of sodding Europe to vote for you.

PREDICTABLE. PREDICTABLE. PREDICTABLE.

Sunday 7.5.89

Late

JUST GOT IN FROM THE gig to find this message from Mum:

> Rachel,
> This is not a hotel, it is MY home. I asked you to be in by 10 p.m. and at the time of writing it is now 10.45. Please leave your front-door key on the kitchen unit as I would like a spare. Have you looked into a summer job yet?

Oh, PISS RIGHT OFF. Just feel like scrawling the word NO all over the house.

Actually, it's been quite a good night tonight. Only got one comment about my weight from some prat who said I looked like a walrus when I clapped. I think he meant a sea lion. The rest of the night I got left alone. To be honest, people could have been saying stuff but the gig was so loud I could not hear them. Wish it could be like that every day.

Yes, I did see Luke tonight. No, nothing happened.
Do you think, Diary, I'd be telling you about the walrus
thing if anything had happened with him?

Monday 8.5.89

TALK OF SCHOOL TODAY WAS the gig last night,
and I have to say that the gig last night WAS
incredible. I have always been very dubious about the
Scotgate and most of the music that comes from the boys'
school but last night I was proved wrong. I went with
Dobber and met Battered Sausage, Haddock and girlfriend,
plus Fig and Bethany there. Getting served in the Scotgate
is easy beyond belief. At the bar it looked like a Brownie
meeting at one point. The gig started with a group called
the Mysterons. They mainly did Bauhaus covers, and there
was some indie dancing near the stage by some girls in
the fifth year, but fuck all else. Then Stamford School's
answer to Howard Jones came on and blew everyone
totally away. His songs were just there, if you know what I
mean. He played a song called 'Take It as Read', which
apparently is about his ex-girlfriend two-timing him. He
played it twice and everyone was singing the chorus:

Take it as read
When all is said
You'll be sorry you did what you did.

It just summed up what a lot of people have gone through.
    After the gig everyone was just milling around. Luke
wafted past me (he looked GORGEOUS tonight) and said

hi. He disappeared with his girlfriend. Then bloody
Haddock started the most bizarre conversation with me
ever about the Harry situation – totally out of the blue:

H: You do realise that Harry partly went out with
you to prove a point . . . ?
ME: What?
H: Well, the rumour was that he was a poof, so he
went out with you to prove he wasn't. And he felt
sorry for you because you are really nice but a bit . . .
ME: Why are you telling me this?
H: Because I think you—
ME (INTERRUPTING): No – because you are a
nasty prick with an attitude problem.
H: Well, fuck you, then.
ME: No – fuck YOU, then.

I stormed off. Battered Sausage told me off and said
Haddock was just trying to get to know me better. No
he wasn't – he was just trying to shit-stir. I see right
through it.

The way Haddock tells it, Harry makes me sound like
a dare. Bastard. Mind you, I wasn't even a dare. I
wasn't even that. I'll forget I ever kissed anyone.
Nobody has snogged me. It's not counted. It wasn't
real. Harry, I will do my level best to forget you. I must
snap out of it. It's just the thought that the only bloke I
went out with only went out with me because of pity.
WANKER!!! I hate that – I hate that so, so much!!

Battered Sausage was really pissed last night. I was
being a bit fertive. Bethany said, 'You are getting in too
deep.' I pointed out I'm young and I can do what the

hell I like. Battered Sausage is brilliant, but not the one for me. I just want Luke's heart and soul!

Tuesday 9.5.89

8.47 p.m.

SUNDAY NIGHT WAS INSPIRING FOR lots of us. Loads of talk about starting bands. Daisy in the common room suggested a goth band that does All About Eve and Mission covers. She can't be in it herself because she lives on a farm and her dad won't drive her to band practice. Someone suggested the name BLACK LETTER. I volunteered to do the band logo as I really want to be a part of this, but I only play the recorder – and 'Oh, Susanna' on the harmonica – because Mum was too tight to pay for music lessons. Got shit-bored today in British politics so had a go at songwriting too. Got as far as writing this about Luke:

> You don't know love's hard to do
> But I seem to be in love with you.
> There's someone in the world
> (Der der dum dum).
>
> They say you're attached but I don't care
> Let them say what they dare
> There's someone in the world
> Because love changes everything
> From fools to kings.

Can't decide if this is brilliant or total crap.

11.55 p.m.

Just watched this thing called *Take Me Home* where
this ancient taxi driver (who is the old bloke from the
sitcom *Duty Free* and looks like my dad) starts an affair
with this gorgeous twenty-something. What is it with
the BBC? It's like middle-aged men propaganda! THIS
WOULD NOT HAPPEN IN REAL LIFE. Then Mum comes
in and says, 'Goodnight. Did you just watch that
thing?' I said, 'Yes – wasn't it crap?' and then she says,
'No. Loneliness does funny things to people, Rachel.'
Maybe – but not that funny.

Wednesday 10.5.89

4.55 p.m.

REALISED MY SONG NICKS A bit from Climie
Fisher 'Love Changes (Everything)' but the rest of it
is original, I am sure of it. Looks like the band is off
anyway, because people at school only play the violin,
piano or the bloody clarinet – there are no guitars,
drums or anything else. Plus the fact apparently Black
Letter is a type of condom that goths use. God knows
why goths need special condoms – perhaps being
miserable makes . . . Oh no, won't go there.

Going to the pub tonight. It's the last time mid-week
before A levels start in earnest. Battered Sausage is
picking me and Bethany up from mine at seven.
Bethany is trying to avoid Vroom because she thinks he
is getting too possessive. She does not know how lucky
she is.

Oh God – please let me see Luke. Let me see him

111

and let him fall so madly in love with me it consumes
every part of him.

Thursday 11.5.89

11.23 a.m.

WRITING FROM STUDY ROOM 4. Last night was
so uncomfortable. Bethany confessed that she was
going to chuck her boyfriend, Vroom, as he was
'pathetic'. Now, Diary, I do not like the boy but I felt so
sorry for him. First of all he turned up in the Vaults on
the off-chance that she would be in there. He was
carrying with him a cuddly pig with a big heart on it
(Bethany collects pigs). He raced up to her, gave it to
her and clung on to her like a limpet. He must have
known it was coming. Then she suggested they go for a
walk down the Meadows.

Battered Sausage and me sat there waiting for her to
come back. He is such a good laugh – we were talking
about A levels and music and where he wants to go to
university and how much we both secretly love Dusty
Springfield's 'Nothing Has Been Proved' and Spandau
Ballet. He put 'Through the Barricades' on the jukebox. He
said, 'Rae, this can be our song. We drank our beer on
wasteland and through . . . the barricades.' I was pissing!

Eventually Bethany came back in tears and said,
'That was so hard, so, so hard. He was gutted.' Apparently he called her a 'fucking slag', told her she was a
bitch, burst into tears and stormed off. Battered Sausage
said that that's what blokes do when they are 'dead
hurt'. Bethany cheered up with this, and spent the rest

112

of the night talking to Battered Sausage about losing it. Apparently he lost it in an alleyway in Castle Bytham. I went to the toilet like I always do when shagging comes up. It avoids the inevitable question 'What about you, Rae?'

No Luke out last night. Apparently he is worried about his economics exam. HOPE he is out on Friday or Saturday. I need just a glimpse.

Friday 12.5.89

3.15 p.m.
THERE IS A NEW CODEWORD going round school. DFS. It means 'desperate for sex'. It sounds like you are talking about the furniture shop. For the record, I am certainly DFS. In fact I am permanently shopping in DFS with no hope of getting out the store.

Going down the pub tonight, but I can't see this changing.

11.50 p.m.
Pub tonight was traumatic to say the least. Me and Bethany were just sat there waiting for everyone when Vroom came in. He just started yelling, 'YOU BITCH. YOU ARE A USER. A FUCKING USER.' Bethany tried to ignore him but he came up to our table and started yelling, 'WHO IS IT? WHO IS IT? TELL ME WHO IT IS. TELL ME NOW.' Luckily Battered Sausage came in with everyone, grabbed hold of Vroom and said, 'C'mon, mate – time to leave it.' Fig grabbed his other side and kind of marched him out of the pub.

113

Bethany wasn't in tears this time – she was FURIOUS. But I could see part of her was loving it. And who wouldn't? Battered Sausage and Fig were like male bodyguards that just sprang to attention. Only Haddock sat there and wouldn't do anything – all he could say was, 'I've been there, mate, I know how he feels.' OH, SHUT UP, HADDOCK – no you haven't. You have got no idea what it's like to feel crap about yourself and hate your body and feel totally alone, because you are Mr Gorgeous My-Body-Is-a-Temple Sportsman. I hate people who try to make out that they know how it feels when they so obviously don't. Haddock really needs taking down a peg or two. And I will do it one of these days.

Luke was there. Came over and talked, then went back to his girlfriend. I didn't look at her – it hurt too much. Later on it looked like they were having a row. Battered Sausage reckons it has been rocky for a while. OH, PLEASE LET THAT BE TRUE . . . AND PLEASE LET HIM LIKE MEATY GIRLS.

May I just give you this little table?

Now, there may be something in this. Perhaps the lack of success with men is not because I am fat and ugly – it's because I am going for totally the wrong star signs. As a Sagittarian, I need FIRE and AIR signs – NOT water!!

COMPARATIVE ZODIAC SIGNS OF PEOPLE
I FANCY (OR FANCIED)

MAN	YEAR AT SCHOOL	STAR SIGN	COMMENTS	POTENTIAL
Luke	Upper sixth	Pisces	Is renowned for his bastard two-faced side, only I haven't seen it yet. Affectionate, sarcastic, good-looking but not much hope.	3.10 Likes me but doesn't fancy me. Not much hope as he is going out with someone
Haddock	Upper sixth	Aries	Bloody grumpy but gorgeous. Unfortunately everyone fancies him. No hope.	0.10 Only one person he really loves – Haddock
Battered Sausage	Upper sixth	Scorpio	Weird. Friendly, sarcastic, malicious, nice. Re: star sign!	1.10 Going out with someone. Adored by literally tons.
Harry	Upper sixth	Aquarius	Well legendary! Very sweet and quiet. Gorgeous. I still have relapses!	Minus 1,000.10 It finished the first time.

Saturday 13.5.89

5.50 p.m.

ANOTHER BORING SATURDAY. WHAT DO other people do on a day like this? There is nothing to do without money. No, Mum, I do not want to go to the library to get a book out. I want to be sat here with someone. But there is no one, and only Speedway or a John Wayne film on the TV. So I sit here with two slices of cheap white bread, a packet of Walkers prawn-cocktail crisps and a glass of full-fat milk. I put the crisps in the bread to form a sandwich, seal the edges by crimping the crusts and dunk it in the milk. Yes, I know it sounds disgusting. And I hate myself for doing it – but while I am chewing and licking and swallowing it all feels nice. Without these things there would be no pleasure. There is no Knight in Shining Armour coming to save me. I'm on my own. I have to find ways to make things OK.

Pub tonight. If I can be bothered.

Sunday 14.5.89

12.35 a.m.

I'VE GOT SO MUCH TO WRITE. I'll probably forget things, but here we go!

Well, I went down the pub and I was thoroughly peeved off. I really felt lonely, as if I didn't fit in anywhere. Bethany kept going on about how she was depressed

116

without a man. She has been without one for all of two minutes. Luckily Dobber came in with all the lads and we had a right laugh. I love Dobber – she is just so . . . Well, she doesn't make little digs like bloody Bethany does. Like every time I eat something bad, Bethany always says, 'Should you be eating that?' I get sick of it.

BUT FORGET BETHANY AND BUGGER HER, BECAUSE LISTEN TO THIS:

There was no sign of Luke tonight but LUKE's girlfriend – who I have never, ever spoken to before – came over to me and said, 'Well, Rae, me and Luke are finishing – so you can have him.' I was like, 'PARDON?!' and she said, 'Look, Rae, everyone knows you like him. Well, you are free now because we have finished. No hard feelings.' I don't know why but I denied it and said, 'Look – I am not interested.' She just smiled at me and walked off. OH MY GOD. OH MY GOD!! Battered Sausage said there is someone Luke has been hinting about. I daren't hope – but it MUST be me. It has to be. SURELY?! Bethany was like, 'Oh, that's right, you're going to be with someone and I will be left here on my own.' But she said when she next sees Luke she is going to do some digging for me.

This time next week I could be writing all sorts of stuff here. SOME ACTION FOR ONCE!

Had chips on the way home. Sod it. I think I may have broken up a relationship, so I can't be that bad.

5.18 p.m.
Unbelievable. Vroom just turned up at my house to ask ME why Bethany dumped him. I said, 'Look, Vroom – it just wasn't working out for her. It's not because you are nasty

or anything.' He said, 'Watch her, Rae, she is one nasty piece of work. You want to hear some of the stuff she says about you.' Then he disappeared in his dad's Volvo.

Bethany can't say anything worse behind my back than she does to my face. At least you know where you are with her.

7.20 p.m.
Bet she calls me 'fat bitch' or something.

11.25 p.m.
Been down pub. I'm pissed off with myself. When I like men – when I fancy them – I just start ripping the piss out of them. WHY?? Luke came over to speak to me and Bethany. I was like, 'Hello, Luke. FANTASTIC stripy shirt tonight – don't go to Yarmouth, someone might sit on you.' It's not even funny. WHY do I do it?

Anyway, we had a little chat about A levels and stuff, and then he said he had to get back to do some more A-level revision. We did NOT talk about his girl-friend. But in a genius masterstroke Bethany has agreed to meet him for coffee Monday lunchtime to find out more information. Love her for this because I know she is feeling really cut up about the Vroom situation.

Hate myself for the nerves I get when blokes are around.

ME LIKE THE MAGNET

> Men I like, I repel
> Like a magnet do
> So if I'm nasty

Then you know
I probably fancy you.

'It's defence,' the shrinks would say.
'It protects against a fall.'
It's impenetrable this fence of mine
It's like the Berlin Wall.

Monday 15.5.89

6.19 p.m.

BEEN TRYING TO GET HOLD of Bethany all night.
She met Luke for coffee this afternoon. I have
walked down the phone box about 50 times, but
according to her mum she is still out. Spoke to Mort at
school – she is really excited for me and reckons the
Luke situation sounds positive but told me not to get
my hopes up as 'Men can be bastards and act in ways
you can never predict.' I know she is right, but I cannot
help thinking that there might be something in it.

On the way back from 62929 phone box I had a
Wall's Feast. I am telling you now that the chocolate
bit in the middle of the ice cream has shrunk unbelievably from last summer. I am not having it. I have
borrowed Mum's typewriter and I have sent them a
letter accusing them of reducing the chocolate and
therefore swizzing us. I know I'm right. Mum said I was
daft for getting so het up about it – but we all need to
stand up for what we believe in. NOTHING gets done
without pressure. FREE NELSON MANDELA!!!! I've got

the T-shirt and bought the record. We have to keep the pressure on South Africa and the other people. It's an ice cream today, but it could be a country tomorrow.

Tuesday 16.5.89

9 p.m.

BETHANY AND ME SAT DOWN today and analysed the coffee session with Luke yesterday, and she reported back the following:

- Luke is undecided about the whole relationship issue.
- Luke likes me and thinks I am a good laugh but thinks I am a bit insecure.
- Luke feels under a lot of pressure to do well in his A levels, as he would like to be in marketing.

She said that reading between the lines, she does not think he wants something serious – and still seems quite hung up on his previous girlfriend. In fact they aren't even completely finished – just 'taking a break'.

OH, LUKE . . . JUST SEE THROUGH THE LOOKS AND LIKE ME. BUGGER THE A LEVELS – YOU CAN RETAKE.

Exams fuck everything up.

Just listened to 'O Superman' by Laurie Anderson in the dark and really freaked myself out. It just makes me shiver when she is going on about planes coming and she's going, 'Ha ha ha ha ha ha haaaa.' I don't even know what it's about but it messes with my head. So freaked out I had to put on 'International Rescue' by

We've Got a Fuzzbox and We're Gonna Use It straight on afterwards to lighten the mood.

Thoughts awful tonight. I know no one I know thinks this way. God, who would want me? I'm a mess.

Wednesday 17.5.89

1.55 p.m.

JUST HAD FIVE YORKSHIRE PUDDINGS and then rhubarb crumble. Bethany just had a yoghurt today and took an apple for 'later'. She says now she is single again she has to be 'really careful'. And then I swear her eyes passed over my belly, and I feel . . . Oh, if I was thin! If I was thin, all this would end. Why can't I have discipline? Why am I so out of control? I've been chubby since I was . . . I can't remember. I've always felt chubby. I always felt big and clumsy and not like a girl. When they sent me to the child psychiatrist she kept asking me about stuff. You know . . . Oh, I don't want to write it here. The really bad stuff. But she said that had affected me and made me scared to be feminine. But it doesn't make sense. Why, then, am I so desperate to look nice and go out with someone?

Child psychiatrists talk shit anyway. She made me draw a picture of a garden, then she said the gardener I had drawn looked disinterested, and what did I think that meant? How the fuck should I know? She's been to university, not me.

Oh, Luke . . . just like me.

Going to see *Hamlet* tonight. I really don't want to. We are not even studying the play – it's for theatre arts

A level. They want us to take note of the staging. I can tell you now the only good things will be the bus trip there (as long as we get the FULL back seat) and the ice cream in the interval.

Thursday 18.5.89

9.45 p.m.

RUSSELL GRANT'S STARS SAID THIS week would basically be CRAP and he was right.

Luke HAS finished with his girlfriend, but he wants me to know (and the rest of the world) that he's not available. He's not available because he's after bloody Bethany – who dropped the bombshell this dinnertime, which ruined the particularly delicious chicken curry I had just scoffed.

Yes – Luke rang Miss Bloody Perfect Bethany up, walked her home, and is generally making advances in that direction. So I wrote Luke a letter which apparently made him feel guilty. While I am left here extremely pissed off. Because the fact is – there goes another one. I am very bitter. As a friend, I comforted Bethany and helped her out. It's like a punch in the face – people progress and I get nowhere. Why? Because I am fat and ugly . . . and Bethany is neither.

She wasn't going to go out with him but she will. She is meeting him tomorrow. But Luke has reassured her that he doesn't want to avoid me – OH NO!!!! – I'm a good friend! Yes, I'm a good friend to everyone . . . As Miss Bloody Perfect Arse Bethany says, 'She'll understand.' Good old dependable me. Well, it doesn't stop the fucking hurt and the pissing pain, does it? NO IT DOESN'T. OR THE RESENTMENT!!!

Every pretty so and so gets a man. When will I find one?? God, at the moment I could just lose three stone and walk into a party with nothing on and just get off with everyone regardless – that's how I feel.

It's worse with Bethany – SHE'S MEANT TO BE MY MATE! If she does go out with Luke, I'll be hurt. If she doesn't, Luke will hate me and resent me because he fancies her.

MEN!!!! They just can't see through, can they?? I feel so ANGRY!! It's not like me to feel so extreme, is it? Dear Diary, what the hell am I going to do? What about when they are down the pub? Shit – what if she gets all smug? I'll get so angry. Megan is another one who keeps going on about her looks . . . SHUT UP, SHUT UP!!! YOU ARE A SIZE 8, FOR GOD'S SAKE! DON'T BE SO SELFISH! AND DON'T CALL ME SELFISH, BETHANY, BECAUSE I AM HUMAN!!!

I'M SO CROSS!! Everybody's probably laughing at me and feeling sorry for me.

Oh well . . . They're probably not . . . Calm down. What's the best plan? Play it cool and not be bothered. It will be hard, but I've been kicked before. Come on, Rae – you're tough, baby! Fight it! Fight it!

Superiority. That is the thing. Get it sorted out here in this diary – it's safe.

Luke does not fancy me.

So . . .

He fancies my friend.

So . . .

He goes out with her.

So . . .

I act not bothered. Still act the same. 'Do what you will.'
THEN . . .

I GET OVER HIM!

I still feel a little resentful to Bethany. I mean, it
wouldn't be so bad but she was my confidante in all this
and I helped her out in a rut. I DIDN'T EXPECT
ANYTHING! Just seems a hard lesson to learn, that's all. I
know we are all FREE. I'd probably convince myself
everything was all right and it was an OK thing to do.

I just feel betrayed.

When will things really get better? When will I get
that kind of affection? When? I bet Bethany will probably marry Luke, knowing my luck.

SO WHEN?

> Another couple interlock
> Clenching surface and soul
> This time a friend is in the double with
> Him
> So when
> When do I find the key to my lock?
> Jealousy like a duvet smothers me
> Others find love and I am left to brood
> So I turn to crisps and other food.

(I'll probably piss myself over that poem tomorrow. Still
– it suffices for now.)

I don't think my mood is helped by sitting in a 1
cm^2 pissing seat from 7.30 to 11.30 yesterday watching
a crap production of *Hamlet*. I wanted to yell out,

'JUST BLOODY KILL YOURSELF AND FUCKING YOVIK!!!'

Friday 19.5.89

9.23 a.m.

I'VE HAVE JUST GOT TO school and I'm literally spouting fire!! CALM, RAE!!!

11.06 a.m.

Bethany has told everyone that I don't mind her going out with Luke and that I have given her my approval. This is partly true because she said, 'Rae, look – I won't go out with him if you don't want me to, but he really likes me and I really like him.' What could I say? I had to do what I normally do and say fine. I said, 'How long have you felt this way?' She said, 'Since the coffee on Monday.' Mort death-stared her across the common room and has told everyone what she did. I said, 'Mort, do you think I need to lose some weight? She said, 'If it makes you feel better, darling, yes.' This is a lovely friendly way of saying, 'I can't lie to you, your weight is putting people off – but let's pretend you are doing it for yourself.' But I wouldn't be. I'd be doing it for men. I'll admit that to you, Diary. I am.

Have come into the toilets for a cry. I am not doing bloody PE today. It's trampolining, but my bra is crap and everything bounces out.

Not going out tonight either. Can't face seeing Luke and Bethany. Oh, it even sounds good . . . Luke and Bethany. Luke and Bethany. Bet she practises signing her name with his name. Bet they have this enormous wedding with Bo Peep bridesmaids and an announcement in a posh paper.

Eat. Eat. Eat. Eat.

Saturday 20.5.89

Late (who cares?)

TONIGHT WAS EXTREMELY DEPRESSING FOR several reasons:

1) Luke/Bethany situation: yes, he is going out with her. Well, it was on the cards, wasn't it? I was out with Dobber (who admitted she didn't like Bethany, and that even at Stamford College where Dobber goes she is known as a man-stealer) when they walked in. They nodded hello to me. Later when we waved goodbye I went over and said goodbye properly, and he was ruffling her hair and stroking her back and . . . well, I smiled through it and it was all very happy, but inside I was . . . dying, basically.

2) Battered Sausage told me that if Bethany wasn't going out with Luke he would be making a serious move on her. Even though he was in a drunken stupor, this counts. What the hell is the big difference between me and Bethany? Except for about four measly pissing stone??

Had a pizza on the way home. All to myself. Fuck it. Big fat pig. Don't care. I love the night. No one can see.

Sunday 21.5.89

I BLAME MUM FOR SO MUCH. She denied me a *Girl's World* as a kid so I have absolutely no idea how to apply make-up. The Christmas I wanted one I think I got Connect 4 instead because she said *Girl's World* encouraged an unhealthy interest in the external appearance. The feminine side of me has been completely played down. Sometimes I could just wear a boob tube and mini-skirt and do everybody's head in. If it wouldn't show off the massive spare tyres round my waist, I would.

Now sat in one of the fields on the way to Tolethorpe, listening to 'Messages' by Orchestral Manoeuvres in the Dark. Just beautiful. The lyrics just say it all. This song was written for beautiful evenings when you are in bits.

And I am in bits. Falling apart. Have to keep it together. Can't end up losing it again, because no one knows what to do with you – you just get . . . you just get . . .

I can't write it.

Monday 22.5.89

9.45 p.m.
B ETHANY TOLD ME TODAY THAT after I went over to say goodbye to them on Saturday night, Luke said to her, 'God, Rae has got balls. That must have been so hard for her.' Bethany simpered this to me

127

like I should be grateful for this. I'm not. What did he expect me to do – plead for him to go out with me? Even I have got more self-respect than that.

Haddock apparently told him off for leading me on. I don't need the pity vote from Haddock, thank you very much. Now there's a man who won't ever know what rejection feels like.

It's the talk of the school of course. Walked into the common room today and there was a debate going on about 'If your mate fancies a bloke and that bloke fancies you and not your mate, is it OK to go out with him?' The general consensus was no. Someone tell Bethany that. Someone tell Bethany that when someone does that to you, you feel so angry you want to punch every skinny woman you see on the street. Because however nice I am, however funny I am, I will never beat them.

Mum made macaroni cheese tonight. Perhaps she realises how totally pissed off I am. Ate it watching *Coronation Street* – Audrey Roberts and Don Brennan bought a greyhound called Lucky. I don't know why I am telling you that. I do know why – it was funny, and probably the best thing that happened today.

10.42 p.m.
Mum just said she is starting Slimming World on Monday, so she is having naughty things now. Oh great. Another diet. Another week when my bag is checked at the front door for 'nibblies that might tempt her'.

Tuesday 23.5.89

8.19 p.m.
BETHANY HAS JUST BEEN ROUND. She told me
Luke was getting on her nerves. He has come on to
her too heavy. He wants to take her to 'his folks' place'
in Tuscany. He wants a year off with her building a
community centre in Uganda. He wants her to meet his
parents over Sunday brunch. She is like Medusa – these
blokes just fall for her like lambs to the slaughter. She
was moaning, though – emotionally she said he was
clingy and acted too adult. Plus the fact – and listen to
this – after Vroom she realised she needed to hold back
more so she didn't give out the wrong messages!! She
said, 'In 1989 I am about discovery.' Yes, I very nearly
did piss myself at that bit.

So it looks like this relationship won't last long.
Good. I fancy Luke, but I actually don't think we would
be right together – even if he did fancy me, which he
doesn't. I don't want to go to Uganda for a start.

9.50 p.m.
Just been thinking about a year abroad. Somewhere
mad actually might help me lose weight. They surely
don't have Boost bars in Africa.

Wednesday 24.5.89

10.35 p.m.

WELL, I HAVE HAD QUITE a brilliant day.
Bethany chucked Luke. She did it before most
people got into the pub, and Luke ended up talking to
ME about it by the men's bogs.

He started to cry and say things like, 'I am such a
sensitive git.' I pretended to care but inside I was
laughing my head off. Seeing him so pathetic really put
me off him.
Eventually he disappeared and Haddock and girlfriend,
Fig and Dobber and Battered Sausage came and sat
with us. Battered Sausage was taking the piss out of
Luke, and Bethany was joining in. They kept chanting,
'Uganda! Uganda! Uganda!' in Luke's slightly annoying
public-schoolboy voice. And apparently Luke is not his
real name – it's Colin! Luke is only his middle name.
You can see it on all his report cards!

I know it shouldn't have done, but it really has put
me off him. But I hate that in me. I know what it's like
to be teased so much that you go home and sob – I
shouldn't laugh along. Haddock didn't – but I think this
is more to do with him being a grumpy cock rather
than some moral point he was making.

Me and Battered Sausage are getting closer and
closer. Surely it's just a matter of time? Apparently he
said to Bethany, 'I love Rae – she's the girl I love being
with the most. But I don't fancy her.' But perhaps he

can *learn* to fancy me? One thing's for sure – I am not telling Bethany how I feel. She'll jump on top of him before I can finish my sentence.

Came in tonight to Mum playing 'Requiem' by the London Boys full blast. Shouldn't it be ME doing this? She is not meant to like the London Boys – she is meant to like Engelbert Humperdinck. She said to me, 'Oooooohhhh-hhhh, Rach – I like the one in the leather cap!' Like I need to know that? And when I don't respond she says, 'Have you revised the Constitution yet?' No, I haven't, Mum, and I won't be when you have two blokes on full blast singing and you are flinging yourself around the living room like a 12-year-old. ACT LIKE THE PARENT.

Thursday 25.5.89

6.25 p.m.

I HAVE TO DO REVISION. I MUST start tonight.
 Bloody French-exchange students are at school, and bloody French girls are gorgeous. They hang around together like they know it too. Daisy's is called Jeanne – and she was making everyone piss today with stories of her boyfriend, Claude. Apparently, when they went skiing together they made love in the chalet while his parents were in the next room. This girl is five months younger than me. Look at the life she has. She makes love regularly, and everything she wears is from Benetton – even the little jumper tied round her neck. She referred to me as the '*grande fille folle*'. I know '*grand*' means 'big'. At least 'big' is better than being described as 'fat'. A bit better.

We are taking them out for a coffee with a load of

blokes tomorrow. I don't think we should let them loose – they all have tans and they all smoke cigarettes in a way that if I spent the next 50 years practising I could never do. They are sexy as hell.

8.23 p.m.
I am not a lesbian, by the way, and I only fancy men. Just read that sexy bit back and I sound a bit weird.

Friday 26.5.89

6.01 p.m.
GREAT USE OF EXAM STUDY leave this after-noon. We took the French girls to the Meadows to meet the boys' school. Battered Sausage was all over Jeanne and she was lapping it up. Bethany did NOT look happy. She was being upstaged brilliantly by someone who could flirt for Europe. Battered Sausage for some reason was smoking CIGARS. I said, 'What the fuck do you think you look like? You're not Winston Churchill – just a twat from Lincolnshire.' The French girls found this hysterical, and so did Battered Sausage – who told the French girls to call me 'La Big Razza'.

We are great friends – why can't it go all the way? I mean, I don't massively love him, but you can build a bit on fancying.

Just getting ready to go out again. I know I should be revising but they are only mocks, and if I don't know it now I never will. Battered Sausage is leading the way – he has got an actual A level on Monday but he is out all weekend. He says there are always retakes.

Saturday 27.5.89

5.02 p.m.

REALLY WEIRD NIGHT LAST NIGHT. Basically, peer pressure got the better of my emotions. Dobber pointed out that the way Battered Sausage looked at me meant that he fancied me. So we arranged to find out. I conveniently tailed off with Dobber, and Bethany asked him and he said, 'No.' So much for the body language, Dobber!

Then me and Battered Sausage went for a soda and black in the Vaults, then walked home and he told me that he loved me and poured his heart out. I told him I'd miss him when he buggered off to university, and he said, 'We'll have fun all summer!' But it's weird – because like in the High Street today when he was with his mates it seemed as if he didn't want to know me. Then later when Kieran Wren chucked me in the river down the Meadows, Battered Sausage said, 'Don't worry, everyone, she's like a buoy – she'll float.' While I was in the river, I caught Battered Sausage looking at Bethany. She looked like a swan – I felt like a big fat water vole.

Bethany and Jeanne also got into a right slanging match in the Vaults pub garden. Bethany said to Jeanne that women who lead men on in this country are called slags. Jeanne said something really fast in French and she just flicked her fag and said, 'You are green,' and smirked this incredibly gorgeous grin. Bethany just walked off – she was beaten by a better woman, and she knew it.

Even the mole on Jeanne's top lip suits her.

133

Going out tonight and staying at Bethany's. Her floor is like kipping on concrete, but at least you can go for a wee in her house in the middle of the night without the Spanish Inquisition of Mum.

6.16 p.m.
Just read that back again and just want to say again I <u>do not</u> fancy women. I can just see that Jeanne is beautiful, from almost a bloke's perspective.

Sunday 28.5.89

2 a.m. (in Bethany's bedroom)
YOU CAN TELL BY THE location that it's a bit dangerous to write. In Bethany's bedroom, and Bethany is going out with Battered Sausage. She told me tonight. I was due to be staying at hers and it was too late to go home. She has been a total, total cow. She is now covered in yoghurt because she says it helps her spots. You'll need to raid the European dairy mountain with your zits, bitch.

FANCY UPDATE

Battered Sausage: slight outside chance – like a donkey in the Grand National, but at least it's running.

Haddock: not a chance. Mr Grumpy Arrogant Rugger-Bugger . . . Everyone bloody fancies him. Plus the fact you'd only want to snog him – going out with him would be torture. You could have better conversations with a tortoise.

There's no one else I fancy at the moment.

And no, I am not a lesbian.

11 a.m.

Bethany's mum only provides muesli or Weetabix for breakfast. She says there is no need for a full breakfast, and doesn't want Bethany to get 'un-athletic' (aka fat). Weird how many people eat breakfast at a specially laid table. Weird how many people are so frightened of getting fat. Actually, it's not. This is hell. They must know it.

Tell you one thing, though – I didn't feel that hungry anyway after last night's revelation. Bethany seems to have a radar for anyone I like. Lying in that sleeping bag last night listening to her breathing I just wanted to scream at her. But let's be honest – if it wasn't her going out with him, it would be someone else. Just not me.

Listening to 'The Power of Love' by Frankie Goes to Hollywood. Makes me cry like a baby. Don't know why.

Feel bad about the zits comment. It's not Bethany's fault she has bad skin.

10.40 p.m.

I have just had such an odd evening. Went down the pub expecting to see Battered Sausage and Bethany all over each other. Bethany wasn't there, but Battered Sausage almost jumped on top of me when I got in the pub. He bought me a drink and said, 'You do realise that Bethany and me are not actually together . . . ?' He went on to say that he reckons he will not go out with anyone at all until after the exams. I went, 'Errrr . . . that's good to know.' Then we talked about how he once got dumped by a girl and now he has to be 'careful', and how women come and

135

go but good mates are like herpes – once you have them you can't get rid of them. What he is saying is: women he shags mean nothing to him but I mean more. Yes, but that's no comfort to me at the end of the night, is it? No mates of mine get into bed with me to stroke my hair and tell me everything is going to be OK and that I'm not really a ten-ton Tessie. That's what I want.

He is such a bastard in the boyfriend sense, yet probably the best boy -mate I've ever had.

I don't think I do fancy him. He is going bald and he is only 18.

Like Lloyd Cole says, 'I'm just looking for a brand-new friend.'

I fancy Lloyd Cole. Even in the polar neck he wears.

Monday 29.5.89

JEANNE THE FRENCH-EXCHANGE STUDENT caused outrage in the common room today. She reckons most French girls lose their virginity at about 14, and there's a trend over there to have sex in rain-coats. We were all thinking what a bunch of frog weir-does, until she explained that 'raincoat' is the French slang for 'condoms', and 'having English lessons' actually means 'teach me the art of lovemaking'. I think I will remember the French word 'impermeable' for ever now. Hopefully one day it will come in useful. Though I doubt it with French boys – they are used to thin. All the French girls are like rakes and leave half their lunch. They must be trained to do that somewhere.

Tuesday 30.5.89

8.10 p.m.
A VERY STRANGE PHENOMENON – BETHANY and Battered Sausage have just been here. I don't fancy Battered Sausage. Oh, I don't know . . . I love him. I get a bit miffed with women near him. It was weird having him in my bedroom – it felt wrong. *The* bloody *Dairy Book of Home Cookery* was by my bed. I have just been using it to lean on, as this diary is flimsy as anything, but it must have looked like I read rice-pudding recipes to get to sleep. I don't, by the way. It just looked like such a cliché – fat girl reads food as well as eats it. I can tell what people are thinking. I could see Bethany had clocked it. She only reads Jilly Cooper and Jackie Collins, and her dad's copy of *Forum* that he thinks he is hiding beneath a box of tissues in his bedside table. Perv.

It was a really odd conversation:

BS: Hello. We are going down the pub – coming? (He was rubbing her back.)
ME: No – I've got to revise.
BS: Oh come on, Big Razza, we'll have a snakey B and then a sound bit of sausage and a battered flange. (This means fish – yes, 'flange' does mean a woman's part – he thinks it's funny to go into chippies and ask for this.)
ME: Nah – you two go . . .

137

BS: Suit yourself. Don't say I don't do anything for you.
BETH: See you at school.

And they went. They didn't beg me to come. They didn't fight. In fact, they were visibly relieved. And all the time Bethany is giving it the doe eyes . . . Slight glance downwards . . . Butter wouldn't melt . . . I KNOW YOUR GAME, BETHANY.

Being called Big Razza doesn't normally bother me, but in front of Bethany it's different. She does this crap little giggle and sniggers and looks embarrassed, like somebody has broken the big taboo: REFERRED TO MY WEIGHT.

But I stay quiet like I always do. Because it doesn't bother me. Me and Battered Sausage are just friends.

I wonder what Bethany and him have been up to all night?!

Oh yes, I do fancy him, Diary. Why am I lying? Nothing would make me happier than him kissing and hugging me. I hate her near him – she's got men after her left, right and centre. Why can't she be satisfied?! PIZZA-FACED COW.

I'm so possessive over him. Why? I've never felt this way. I can't tame him – he will always go for pretty bitches.

Now I'm unhappy, and I still haven't revised sodding *Paradise Lost*.

Playing 'The Story of the Blues' by the mighty Wah! Pete Wylie sings it like it is. 'They' take every emotion you have. Then you realise there's nothing left inside of you. You are just empty and dead inside. I've been there. I'm there now.

If it wasn't for music, Diary, I would be done in by all of this. At least I know other people have felt like shit.

Wednesday 31.5.89

7.15 p.m.

LAST ENTRY WAS A BIT bloody psychopathic, wasn't it?

Just did three hours' panicked cramming, and the alarm is set for 5.45 a.m. That's why I'm not writing much, because I'm having to learn irrelevant nonsense like HENRY VIII'S DOMESTIC POLICY – WHO GIVES A MONKEY'S?! I now know that the Court of Augmentations made £25,000 in its first year from the dissolution of the monasteries. But WHO CARES??!! I can't imagine a time when this fact will EVER be useful.

Why can't they teach us something useful? The French girls were telling us today they have make-up application and deportment lessons as 11-YEAR-OLDS! Their parents even rub Gorgonzola on to their gums as babies, so they appreciate fine flavours. No wonder the boys' school are queuing up to do these women. They are *women*.

Avoided Bethany all day. Don't want to know what went on OR what's going on.

Thursday 1.6.89

8.30 p.m.

BETHANY COULD NOT WAIT TO tell me today that Battered Sausage tried to get off with her the other night down the Meadows. I swear this is all punishment, you know – for all those times I have thought, 'Well, Bethany is not that amazingly pretty.' I remember thinking in March that even I had a boyfriend for all of three days and that I would have another one immediately after that, and NOW everyone is dropping at HER feet! It all bloody fits!

Bethany told Battered Sausage that she is not interested until after the exams. He 'understands'. But after the exams there's a whole summer stretching ahead of long nights and short skirts and shagging in fields. I hope Bethany's hay fever makes her snot like a baby with a cold.

I wish I could wake up tomorrow somewhere else. As someone else.

Weird thoughts so bad today. As bad as it gets. Took 22 minutes in all. And even then I had to come back to the house.

Friday 2.6.89

After 11 p.m.
HAD A BRITISH POLITICS EXAM. Bollocked on about voting behaviour for four sides. Five minutes before the end we all got done because Jasmine Bobs did one of her legendary comedy sneezes. She sneezes like a horse. We all creased up – and the invigilator went loony going on about how serious it all was and how our future partly depends on the outcome of these exams. THEY ARE MOCKS, WOMAN!

Just been down the Vaults. Left early tonight to avoid Bethany coming round. Sat with Dobber and Haddock's girlfriend because Battered Sausage, Fig and Haddock were having a bloke's night and being lads. No women were allowed. There was lots of loud laughter, and later in the garden they were talking about anal-chugging. Rugby players do it because they are hard. Well, not in Haddock's case – because he was spewing by the barrel-shaped flower pots before ten o'clock, after only about three pints. He tried to save face by claiming it was a 'tactical chunder' that would allow him to take in more lager. I shouted that he was a lightweight across the pub. He then marched over and slurred the following:

HAD: What's your problem with me?
ME: My problem with you – and the other members of your gang – is that you are public-schoolboy prats who even have your own made-up dance to Salt-n-Pepa's 'Shake Your Thang'. Dancing like you've had a stroke is not funny. And, when everyone else was dressed like James Dean and Marilyn Monroe, YOU went to Nathan Thompson's fancy-dress dead-celebrities party as a member of the Space shuttle Challenger crew: a) the victims were not celebrities, and b) they had families, and that is not funny either. You don't give a shit about other people's feelings because you are a prick. (Massive long death-stare pause.)
HAD: I have NEVER called you Slug.
ME: So???

He then walked off. Swearing. Bugger him, two-dimensional tosser.

Me, Dobber and Haddock's girlfriend had such a top

141

night tonight. We have decided to call ourselves 'the Gads' – it's a girl version of the lads. We have even written our own song to the tune of 'Do They Know It's Christmas?'. I do feel slightly bad because that was a song for famine relief in Ethiopia – but I bought the single five times and wanted to go to Live Aid, so sod it.

It's summertime, there's no need to be afraid.
At summertime we don our shorts and we don our
    shades.
And in our world of beer we can spread a smile of
    joy
Put your arms around a Gad at summertime.

But say a prayer
Pray for the jibbers
At summertime, it's hard but when you are having
    fun . . .

That's as far as we have got writing it. We just skipped to Bono's bit because that's the best bit. Dobber screamed it, and was well embarrassed because everyone in the pub seemed to have a lull in their conversations at exactly the same time. Dobber is a great laugh and NEVER puts me down. We've agreed to have an all-summer sesh, but just for the record: the Gads will not be doing ANY anal-chugging.

I had a great night tonight. No names. No feeling uncomfortable. I'm sorry, Diary, I have to link that up to the fact that there was NO Bethany. I'm honestly not being a cow, and it's so difficult to explain to you but she is horrible in ways that I don't think about till

142

afterwards. Things she says are like bombs that have a timer and go off later in my head. Little comments, digs – I am not being hypersensitive – they exist. She must know what she is doing.

The kebab I had on the way home has made my breath so bad that White the cat just went for me. Deal with it, cat – it's only garlic. You eat moths and lick your own arse.

Saturday 3.6.89

2.45 p.m.
I HATE EXAM TIME – BECAUSE EVERYTHING in my head gets worse and I end up having to do all the stuff I need to do to make everything OK. And I eat. All the time. Toast – slice after slice after slice. Fat. Butter sliced on. Marmite so thick it makes my gum tingle.

I'm eating it now. Big greasy stains all over me.

It's all kicking off in China. Students are protesting for freedom. I remember when Wham! went there – the crowd weren't even allowed to dance. In fact . . . indirectly, perhaps George Michael has caused this. Brilliant!

Yes, it does make my fat problems seem ridiculous.

11.50 p.m.
Just got back from the pub.

NO BETHANY again. Battered Sausage was asking where she was. Like I should know? I said, 'Ring her yourself. In fact go round her house and call for her if you are that bothered – she doesn't live that far away. I'm not her keeper.' He looked pissed off and made up

143

some bullshit excuse why he needed to see her – something to do with some revision notes of his. Shut up, Battered Sausage – I can see right through it.

Mind you, it's good to see blokes getting pathetic over girls. I hope they hurt too. I hope they get home and think about all the things that have been said. I hope they have to write it down and go to sleep worrying about it.

Revision notes?? I don't think they even do the same subjects. I bet what he wants to revise does NOT get taught in schools!

The French students were out tonight. Jeanne and me had quite a long conversation. Out of the blue she goes to me, 'Bethany talk to you shit.' I said, '*Vous dites* that *parce que vous deteste* Bethany.' She said, '*Vrai*, but she talk to you shit.' Thing is, Jeanne does not need to speak English to know how Bethany treats me. You don't need words sometimes. I like Jeanne, even though later on Battered Sausage was all over her asking her if she wanted a pizza – he has never offered me so much as a chip. But then at the end of the night when he was really pissed, he out of the blue said, 'Rae, come here,' and gave me a massive kiss on the forehead, and said, 'Love ya,' like I had been his wife for 20 years. How are you meant to read all this???

Sunday 4.6.89

3.28 p.m.

EVERYTHING HAD GONE TO CRAP in the world. I have been so excited recently because it looked like there was going to be this massive revolution in

Communist China. There have been these students wanting freedom and democratic rights. One bloke even stood in front of a tank – just him on his own with his carrier bag, against everything. It will make the greatest poster ever. But now the soldiers have rolled into Tiananmen Square and started shooting and people are dying. Just so depressing. Everything stays the same. Nothing EVER changes.

Everywhere in the world there is repression and cruelty, with the older generation hammering down the young.

All the Chinese are very thin. Not an ounce on them. Surprising – considering all their food is done in batter.

5.09 p.m.
Listening to more about China and the Tiananmen Square demonstration. And I have made a decision. It's time to distance myself from Bethany. If people my age can protest when they are getting shot, then I have to grow some balls. This weekend has convinced me.

I don't want to fall out with her. I don't want a big row. But I don't think I can get better when she is around. She makes me eat more. She makes me feel like I will always be the donkey with all of the racehorses. And I realise now I actually really don't enjoy being with her at all. The thing is, how do I tell her? With a letter? With a phone call? She will call round for me and I have to be honest with her. She deserves getting a straight reason for it all.

6.30 p.m.
Just rang Mort. She thinks it's absolutely the right move. She says if I send Bethany a letter she will end up showing it to everyone and it could even do the

rounds at the boys' school, and I can't risk that. She thinks a face-to-face meeting is totally the best idea. Feel sick thinking about it, but I know she is right.

7.12 p.m.
Bethany just called for me. I ignored the front door and turned my music right down. When I peeked through the bedroom curtains, I saw her walk as if she was going into town. A group of lads were staring at her and one whistled. I have to do this. I will never get a bloke when she is around.

Monday 5.6.89

Late (time doesn't matter)
EVERYTHING ALWAYS GOES TO SHIT. From the crap that's going on in my life to what happens in the world.

Bethany cornered me today by the computer room and said, 'Can we have a chat?' My stomach was doing flips but I said yes. She started spurting out such shit:

B: You cling to me. We need some distance. You make me feel guilty when I am with boys because they don't fancy you.
ME: Thanks . . .
B: But you won't do anything to make it better. You have seconds every day. And then you accuse me of taking Battered Sausage off you.
ME: I said that once when I was pissed.
B: But I can see that's what you think ALL the

time with everyone. That's why I didn't come out at the weekend.

ME: OK. Well, I was thinking exactly the same things actually, so . . .

B: And stop telling people that I take people off you. I have never taken anyone off you. You are so immature. If you don't like the way you look, then DO SOMETHING ABOUT IT. Every time you come round my house and sit on the sofa, the first thing you do is pick up a cushion and put it over your belly to try and hide it. And you're always going on about what you will wear when you get thinner. How about trying to look good now? Stop wearing rugby shirts and dirty jeans. Wear a skirt!!

ME: Oh yeah – that's really me!!!

B: I am meeting someone for lunch. I've got to go.

I cannot believe the stuff she came out with. It shows what she was thinking all along. So much for the kind speech I had planned. I thought I would be really upset, but I just feel angry that I even put up with her. She is obviously a robot with no feelings.

So that's it. But I'm not that bothered. Mort is a great friend – and I know Dobber and all her gang now, so I have someone to go to the pub with.

Should I wear skirts out, though? Wouldn't everyone piss themselves laughing if they saw me trying to be sexy? I can't even imagine it.

Tuesday 6.6.89

10.53 p.m.
I'M WATCHING AN EXTREMELY BRILLIANT programme on nuns. There is always that option if I flunk the exams, I suppose.

11.30 p.m.
The nun thing is a complete non-starter. For one – chastity. Plus I do not want to wear another uniform after seven pigging years of having to wear a hat and KILT!!! And nuns are always meant to be quiet, and I think that's out of the question.

I wish things would change between Battered Sausage and me. I wish he wouldn't think with his dick and just see me as an adequate proposition – aka a woman he wants to SNOG!

Got to revise *The Tempest*. Wish Shakespeare had got a bloody medieval life and written less.

Mum has been up twice to complain about music being too loud. Have played Smiths' 'How Soon Is Now?' over and over and over again. When I feel down I always do it. It says everything. It's like I sat down with Morrissey in the pub and told him all the shit and he sang it.

Wednesday 7.6.89

7.50 p.m.

I HAVE HAD A RESPONSE FROM Wall's Ice Cream!!!! Can't believe it. I wrote to them to complain that the chocolate in the middle of Feast ice creams had shrunk. They claim that the chocolate had actually merely changed shaped and still weighed X amount of grams . . . and as a 'gesture of goodwill' they enclosed a £2 voucher. I went straight to the shop and blew it on Cornettos. Mum was cross that I had spent it so quickly, till I gave her one. Amazing how a mint Cornetto can stop nagging almost immediately. I must remember that.

Just watching *Coronation Street* – Lucky the grey-hound is pregnant. They thought she was 'just getting fat'. Even a dog comes under scrutiny for sticking it on.

Thursday 8.6.89

9.15 p.m.

G OT UP EARLY TO REVISE. Got to school at 8.30 a.m. Went to queue for exam – and it was in the afternoon. Bloody typical. Hung around the library but couldn't concentrate on work, so looked at the pictures in French *Elle* and thought and dreamt. Usual stuff: brilliant jobs, massive wage packets that buy lovely clothes for my new model figure, Tom Cruise as a boyfriend. Usual stuff that has sod all chance of coming true, but passes the time.

There was this one model in French *Elle*. I can't imagine what it must be like to be her. She was brunette with big thick lips and was wearing this tight navy dress by Azzedine someone. She was so beautiful; and the choices she must have, and . . . Oh, I would give it all up just to have been born that way because her life will be so easy. She won't have to think, and men will fall into her lap and . . . It's all unfair and I don't want to even write it. It will never change, and no one wants to admit it but being thin and pretty is the best thing a woman can be.

All shit.

Friday 9.6.89

10.35 p.m.

TOLD MUM ABOUT THE WOMAN in *Elle* tonight because I went to look at her again today and I just can't get my head round it. Mum said her usual nonsensical phrase: 'You talk more random than duck's shite.' She reckons most of those models eat about one carrot a week, chew cotton wool like race-horse jockeys to keep thin, and smoke cigarettes. Apparently, they all look crap by the time they are 30, and go out with the 'wrong' sort of men (any men would be right right now). I said, 'You have edited *Vogue* and know all this for definite, do you?' She said, 'Rachel, I have moved in circles that have allowed me to get this information.'

Let's see, shall we?

150

Born in 1942 as a result of her mother's affair with a Canadian soldier.

Lived in Hastings and Leicester with her granddad. Or in Barnardo's homes.

Married Dad. Had first baby at 18. Lived in Ketton. A village the size of a thimble in Lincolnshire.

Worked in a factory sewing knickers.

Worked cleaning offices where they made blood bags for hospitals.

Started ironing shirts in the boarding house of the boys' school. Admittedly, she reckons at one stage the drummer from the Police's son was there.

Divorced my dad. Married the Latin teacher.

Went abroad to see him in Turkey and Morocco.

Now lives in a council house in a small town – looking after my nan.

Where in that list would you gain knowledge about haute-couture and the fashion world, precisely?

She talks crap. Howard Jones said it years ago in 'Look Mama'. She has to let me get on with it because she does not know it all. This is my life, not hers!

Saturday 10.6.89

6.16 p.m.

HAVE TO BE HONEST WITH you, Diary – I have been thinking all week about what Bethany said about me wearing different, sexier clothes. I got out the free booklet from *Looks* magazine last night – 'Dress to Suit Your Figure'. I found my figure shape. I was described as 'You know there's a bit to lose'. It suggested

151

no big patterns, bold accessories and lots of black.

So I have just been to Peterborough. What a depressing waste of time. Every shop I went into I was greeted by coat-hangers that only went up to size 14. So I went to Evans, which is meant to be for bigger ladies, and it was full of clothes for the only people they think are fat right now – women over 40. Row upon row of kaftans and dresses the size of marquees. It's like all the shops were saying, 'You don't deserve nice clothes, fat cow – do something about it.'

Eventually ended up in Burtons men's shop trying on men's large trousers. They fit and everything but there was massive extra space in the crotch. I can't walk around looking like I have a penis. So thought, 'Fuck it.' Bought some Japanese Wash Grains from the Body Shop and some big T-shirts from the market. Yes, they hang off my breasts, but by that stage I just felt so finished by it all.

Meant to be revising. Sod it all. If bloody *Beadle's About* is on tonight that will just top a totally shit day off.

Sunday 11.6.89

10.23 p.m.

JUST BEEN DOWN PUB AS it was the French-exchange students' last night. There was a really uncomfortable moment at the end when Jeanne went to give me a hug goodbye. She obviously hadn't been told I don't do hugging. Even when I tried to bat her off she grabbed hold of me and said, '*Bon chance* and love Sausage.' Battered Sausage doesn't need any loving from me – he was too busy sticking his tongue down the throat of some girl from the fifth year. Bethany looked well pissed off. She was with her 'new friends' from Stamford College. I sat with Dobber and Fig.

SAW LUKE TONIGHT! He hasn't been out in ages. Exams, he says, and I imagine he wanted to avoid seeing Bethany. I upset Luke for the most ridiculous reason today. He was wearing that bloody white jumper that he always wears EVERY time he is out, so I go, 'Luke – that white jumper is becoming famous – is it true that it is going to open a branch of Sainsbury's all on its own?' He got really mardy about it. Definitely right off him. Mind you, was I ever really on him? Still, that's life. Full of the emotional fibs that you tell yourself.

Can't sleep at all at the moment. Feel like a zombie. Going to do a quick bit of revision.

Monday 12.6.89

12.20 a.m.

HAD ENOUGH OF REVISION. IT'S so weird: I'm worried sick over an exam, but someone I used to go to school with is worried sick because she is about to give birth to another human being. The rumour is that Chloe is just about to drop the baby, and she is really shitting herself about it. Actually, 'shitting herself', according to Mort, is an apt term – because apparently you do when you give birth.

Anyway, it puts exams into perspective.

Got to go – up at 4.20 a.m. to cram.

Tuesday 13.6.89

7.24 p.m.
ALARM WENT OFF AT 4.20 a.m. but put it on snooze and fell back asleep. Woke up at 7.30 and there was no time for any cramming at all.

So tempted to cheat in these exams but I can't work out a safe way to do it. You do the exams in either the gym or the main hall and the teachers patrol them like the Gestapo. Also, normal desks are so full of graffiti you can go into the classroom before the lesson and hide stuff like historical dates and French vocabulary in the graffiti. Exam desks are a different matter. Green and plain with nothing on them. Bastard desks.

I thought the exam went OK today but then everyone got out of the gym and started discussing how they had answered certain questions, and I'd answered nothing like everyone else. I'm not too worried, though, as Daisy admitted that she had a total mental brain collapse and had forgotten how to spell the word 'why' – so just wrote the letter 'Y'!

I hated being in the gym. The bloody vault and beam were in there. I didn't even get BAGA Award 4. Everyone had an award patch on their leotard except for me, even (and this will sound really bad but it's true) Sharon Teeg – who was in a wheelchair. Who decided flipping on a plank should be a sport, anyway? It's bollocks.

Wednesday 14.6.89

8.15 p.m.

L AST TWO EXAMS TOMORROW and Friday.
Currently making a 'Chartform' compilation tape.
I'm up to Chartform Volume 10, but I am thinking of
packing up the series. I can't be bothered to sit around
taping the charts on a Sunday any more. Anyway,
Bethany's mum buys her every *Now That's What I Call
Music* tape that comes out – so I'll just copy hers.

HAH!! Just realised that I may still have to tape the
charts after all. I can't really just turn up at Bethany's
house and ask to borrow her records now, can I?

9.32 p.m.

Mum has just been up to ask if 'NEEE-NAARR Cherry'
is helping me revise. I said, 'It's Neneh Cherry – get it
right – and yes it is.' I don't need to be nagged by a
woman who has never taken an exam in her life. Every
time I say that to her, she says, 'I was in the Girl's
Naval Training Corps, and never had the chances you
had.' Then she started to give me a lecture on how she
is going away for two weeks and she does NOT want
the following:

- girls she doesn't know staying round
- any boys AT ALL staying round
- any parties (she reckons she will 'know')
- loud music

- smoking
- drinking
- funny stuff (she means shagging – chance would be a fine thing).

I agreed to all these but I don't intend to stick to any of them. Actually, some I will probably have to stick to because I can't imagine losing it over the next two weeks. I don't think I could do it in my bed or her bed, anyway. And if I do have a party I will be making damn sure no one else does it either. I don't want people having a better time than me in my own house.

Bloody love Neneh!! 'Manchild' – WHAT A SONG! You could shout it at so many blokes. She's another one with a kid that looks totally beautiful. And I'm not being lesbo or anything but she's gorgeous.

Thursday 15.6.89

6.20 p.m.
EXAM WENT OK BUT THEN, God knows how, I have been roped into being the Scarecrow and have to do the choreography for the sixth-form play *The Wizard of Oz*. I know I have been practising dancing for years in my bedroom but they must be desperate if they are picking me. None of the serious drama people want to be associated with it because they think it is going to go to shit. This is a chance to show a different side of me, and prove them wrong. For a start I have picked these songs:

156

- Kylie's 'Hand on Your Heart' – for the Tin Man because he wants a heart.
- Smiths' 'The Boy With the Thorn in His Side' – for the Scarecrow (me). I thought there could be a vague scarecrow/plant/tree/thorn reference in it, and it would please the indie fans.
- Guns 'n' Roses' 'Paradise City' – for when the Wicked Witch is talking about Oz, and to please the metal fans.
- Feargal Sharkey's 'A Good Heart' – for the Tin Man again. I already have a dance for this, which I developed in 1985.
- Tight Fit's 'The Lion Sleeps Tonight' – it's the only song I could think of that involves a lion.
- 'The Time Warp' from *Rocky Horror*, which has got nothing to do with anything, but everyone knows the dance so I have shoved it in.

Mum is currently packing. The sound of her wardrobe being emptied is a lovely noise!

Just playing Beastie Boys' 'Fight for Your Right (to Party)'. I don't really like it but it makes the point!!!!

Friday 16.6.89 (end of exams)

EXAMS FINISHED!! OVER!! GONE!! GOOD RIDDANCE! GET LOST! PISS OFF! PLUS MUM IS OFF TO MOROCCO TO SEE HER HUSBAND – FREE HOUSE! FREE HOUSE!

It's the day we thought would never arrive! Just been to Oliver's nightclub! They had a special ska ten minutes. Completely went mad when they played 'One Step Beyond' by Madness. Hadn't heard it in ages. A drunk bloke at the bar said to me, 'You move fast, considering your size.' I ignored him. If it was an insult it was crap.

If it was a chat-up line (some hope!), it was even crapper.

Battered Sausage was a total git; but when one thing goes right (i.e. exams finishing) another thing has to go badly in return. Apparently, he is 'well in love' with his new girlfriend. Well, I have got shit-loads of parties over the next few weeks, so I cannot be bothered to think about him or her. If he wants to ignore me so he can give his new floozy loads of attention, then so be it. Wanker.

It was a right laugh tonight, a damn good boogie, and Mort is currently staying over. We have just been talking about blokes. She thinks Battered Sausage is a wanker but also charming. She fancies Fig and has told me never, ever to tell Dobber, and she thinks Haddock is very good-looking but arrogant. We both agree that Haddock is such a good dancer it is unbelievable. Tonight he was dancing to Yazz 'The Only Way Is Up' and it was honestly like watching a professional. Don't get me wrong, though, he is still a cock – but a hand-some cock. I love Mort: we have a great night, and then we can talk about the night for another two hours and it never gets boring.

Saturday 17.6.89

LATE – IT'S PROBABLY SUNDAY – NO MAN ACTION SHIT NIGHT. Just been to Lewis Deede's party. It was weird. I felt really unloved, and I was drunk. Sat in the field behind the hall and cried. This crying was disturbed by two people shagging . . . I was concerned at first, as I thought by all the heavy breathing someone was having an asthma attack. They were at it. Everyone was at it. A girl from the year below was doing it in the cloakroom. The music was shit. There were too many goths there. I mean, there was a bloke with zits and a distressed leather jacket, customised with 'Fields of the Nephilim', and even he was snogging a plain girl from Stamford College. If all the dos are going to be like this, I would rather stay in my room for the rest of June!

Sunday 18.6.89

2.12 p.m.

I LOVE MUM BEING AWAY. I can play everything FULL BLAST.

Feel crap. These are the songs that are making it better:

• 'A NEW ENGLAND' – KIRSTY MacCOLL. Fuck Shakespeare. This is one of the best songs ever

159

written. It's about how you think people are brilliant but in the end they let you down. At the end she is by the phone waiting for someone to call and help her. No one does. I don't have a phone at home but I know it would be the same for me if I did.

- The whole of 'MEAT IS MURDER' – THE SMITHS. Morrissey for prime minister!
- 'PARTY FEARS TWO' – THE ASSOCIATES. It's mad, but it's brilliant. It's about feeling nervous before a big party; and I will tell you now, however much I am looking forward to going to a do, I am always so worried about that first moment that people see me because I know loads of them will be thinking, 'FAT COW, HOW DID THAT HAPPEN?'
- ABBA. Yes, it's embarrassing. But I love them.
- 'SHOUT' – TEARS FOR FEARS. SAYS IT ALL.

Dreading tonight. When I am on my own at home, my head goes more weird. So I am forcing myself to go out. Can't cope with my head going again. Ever again.

Monday 19.6.89

1.14 a.m.

THAT WAS MORE LIKE IT!!! Charles Leigh's do at the Danish Invader pub tonight was brilliant. The invitation was either to dress in pyjamas or as Hawkwind. I went in pyjamas, as I didn't have a bloody clue what Hawkwind was. When I got there I was relieved, as Hawkwind is a band that the bloke from Motorhead used

160

to be in. Lots of leather and long hair. It was all a bit Quo. Good laugh, though. I STILL got no man action, even though my pyjamas were a teensy bit see-through.

5.14 p.m.
We are in trouble with *The Wizard of Oz*. And I found out tonight there are blokes coming to see it. Which worries me no end. Jasmine looks stupidly gorgeous as the Good Fairy – she is wearing a basque. Every man will get a stiff – it is almost certain. I can't begrudge her it, as she is lovely too. But I am here stuffed full of straw on top of my, errr . . . 'natural padding'.

Mind you, some poor cow has got a baked-bean can on her head to be the Tin Man, so I really can't complain.

The director is having a breakdown. She called me over to the back of the hall in tears, saying, 'Everyone is having a go at me, Rae – I can't cope! My boyfriend is going to university to do sports science, but they don't do religious studies so I can't go there, and now the Munchkins are moaning that their knees hurt, and the trees say they have nothing to do!!' (I have shortened the dance routine for the Munchkins, and given the trees more branch/arm waving to 'Hand on Your Heart'.)

I never thought the hours of dancing in my room would have ever paid off, but they have. Everyone commenting that I am a natural when it comes to dancing and, being honest, I have long thought I am. When the bedroom door is closed and I am going mad, I can move fast and in time. The routine for Kylie Minogue is particularly good. I tried to do something extra for the trees with a routine based on Madonna's 'Express Yourself', but most of them can't do a spin like

I can. To be fair, their cardboard trunks do stop them.

How many things would I be brilliant at if I wasn't carrying this spare tyre? Dancing? Three-day eventing? (Don't get me wrong – I have never done it, but I have always thought that if I was from a loaded family I could be a superb horsewoman.) Pulling? Snogging?

Everything.

Been eating even more shit than normal since Mum's been away. I'd never admit it to her, but I miss her really. I miss her cooking.

Tuesday 20.6.89

Late

I AM VERY PISSED OFF. I thought I had been invited to every party that was happening this year, but in the common room today an invite slipped out of Amber East's folder. It was for a party I have never even heard of. Now, I am good mates with her, and her boyfriend is meant to be a mate of mine too. When I asked her why I hadn't been invited to his special HBI do, she started pissing herself. I don't know if it is a secret posh society or some other bullshit, but it just proves that rich people stick to their own groups. God knows what other stuff I am missing out on.

Wednesday 21.6.89

10.30 a.m. (lower-sixth common room)
SOMEBODY HAS JUST TOLD ME that Harry is going out with someone, and I'm bloody upset. Well, what a ridiculous state of emotions. Apparently, she is in the upper sixth. Why the hell do I feel like this? It's bloody ridiculous. I only snogged him twice – and that was nearly four months ago.

11.23 p.m.
Turn up for the books. Battered Sausage turned up to take me out for a drink. When I asked him if he had been invited to the HBI party, he started to piss himself too. Maybe it is a posh clique thing, because he comes from a council house too. He said, 'I don't think there's many people going to that, my old battered flange.' Then Haddock turned up. He was grumpy because he had argued with his girlfriend (AGAIN).

And that was when I had the most embarrassing conversation of my life probably ever. When Battered Sausage went to the loo, just to make conversation I asked Haddock if he had been invited to this HBI party . . . This is the full doom conversation that followed:

ME: Have you been invited to this HBI party?
(MASSIVE DEATH-STARE WITH ONE EYEBROW IN THE AIR.)
HAD: Are you taking the piss?

ME: What?

HAD: Are you saying I am a poof?

ME: No – I just asked if you had been invited to Amber East's boyfriend's HBI party, as I have NOT been invited.

HAD: You are serious, aren't you?

(He started grinning at this point. Yes, nice smile, but he was in full piss-take mode now.)

HAD: Rae, 'HBI' stands for 'hot beef injection'. He was inviting her round for a shag.

(MASSIVE PAUSE. I WAS DYING.)

ME: But it was a proper invite and everything . . .

HAD: Well, mate, he obviously needed a proper shag.

ME: Would you like a drink?

(I had to do something. It was even worth buying a round for. Honestly I could have died.)

HOW COULD I NOT KNOW THAT?

I didn't mention it to Battered Sausage when he came back from the toilet. And to be fair I don't think Haddock did either, or I know Battered Sausage would have taken the piss all night. When Haddock left, though, he did wink at me. He knows now he has got something MAJOR over me. I'll have to redress that balance.

On the way home I told Battered Sausage how I felt about Harry. He said that first loves always hurt the most. After he lost his virginity down that alleyway in Castle Bytham, his girlfriend dumped him. He said he even cried a bit. Like it was the worst thing ever. I told him women liked it when a man cried, as it showed sensitivity. He said, 'Only the nice ones, Rae. Only the nice ones.'

Feel so ugly and lonely tonight. No HBIs for me for the foreseeable future. Why do blokes always call their cocks after something you would find in a butcher's shop? Beef injection, pork sword, love sausage. They all act like they are 12.

Thursday 22.6.89 (actually it's Friday)

1.54 a.m.

EMMA'S PARTY TONIGHT WAS BRILLIANT. They played a lot of good crap, if you know what I mean. We did 'Do the Conga' and I got sandwiched between Battered Sausage and Fig, who were doing daft dancing. On nights like this I do fancy Battered Sausage a bit, which is a real shame, because a) he only fancies slim blonde things, b) he sees me as 'one of the lads', and c) he's buggering off to university soon, if he gets his grades.

He is staying the night tonight. Don't get excited, we are in different beds. Fig came round too. He stayed until 1 a.m. Battered Sausage is in Mum's bed. I can hear him snoring.

I love him so much it hurts.

Fig reckons any future husband of mine would be hen-pecked. This is bollocks. It would have to be someone with a stronger personality. I can't bear weak men. I always go for people with big personalities.

3.14 a.m.

No I don't. Harry could barely speak. Some pigeons have a bigger personality than he does.

Friday 23.6.89

11.30 p.m.

FIRST FULL DRESS REHEARSAL FOR *The Wizard of Oz* was a total and utter disaster. The Tin Man's paint would not come out of her hair. Jasmine fell out of her basque when she was doing the 'jump to the left' on 'The Time Warp'. I am telling you now – her figure is amazing. I just can't relate to it. She is a size 8 to 10. She even smells nice all of the time. Then the Wizard of Oz's curtain dropped prematurely. The director in tears again – I told her not to worry as Battered Sausage had told me only spods and people's boyfriends are coming from the boys' school, so who gives a shit about looking like an idiot?

Saturday 24.6.89

11.56 p.m.

I MADE BATTERED SAUSAGE TOAST THIS morning and he moaned that I hadn't spread the Flora properly. I don't think I could marry a man with an attitude like that.

Went to Peterborough today. Used some of the food money Mum had left me to buy two PHENOMENAL records:

    1) *THE QUEEN IS DEAD* – SMITHS. I only had a
       taped copy and it was getting knackered. 'There

Is a Light That Never Goes Out' is a song –
well, it's about ME.
2) *RAW LIKE SUSHI* – NENEH CHERRY. It is
BLOODY AMAZING. This is honestly the best
album I have heard in years. I would love to
look like Neneh Cherry. She is so bloody
gorgeous – even in crap cycling shorts.

Alone in the house. Sounds like it should be wonderful,
but it isn't. Hypochondria creeping in nastily. Feel bad
all over. Some people are doing Ouija boards at school
but I'm not touching that shit. Knowing my luck,
bloody Jack the Ripper would try to get in touch.

We have all decided not to rehearse *The Wizard of
Oz* any more. We can't be bothered and some of the
costumes are already coming apart. The trees are
looking ever so tatty.

Sunday 25.6.89 (FIRST PERFORMANCE)

10.55 p.m.

*W*IZARD OF OZ WENT BRILLIANTLY! In the end –
due to budget constraints – I had to source my
own costume. Hence the fact that my favourite suede
jacket (that the lads have nicknamed 'Dennis Waterman'
because apparently he used to wear one in *The
Sweeney*) is now stuffed with straw. The dance routines
went dead well – especially Kylie Minogue's 'Hand on
Your Heart' (everyone got their hands on their heart at
the right time) and Guns 'n' Roses' 'Paradise City'
(though Jasmine reckoned she had got a migraine

through head-banging). The Wizard missed her cue, but everyone creased when I said in a scarecrow voice, 'I don't think the Wizard is quite ready yet.' The director's boyfriend said, 'Rae, you were really funny,' which was sweet – but let's be honest, he does sports science – and is attached. How much can one person know about PE??

School seemed to enjoy it. Wish some blokes had been there to see it. I mean, I looked like crap but perhaps if they had seen me performing then they would have seen me in a whole new light.

Monday 26.6.89

6.14 p.m.
A. C. C. U.

GOT MY EXAM RESULTS TODAY. Yes, they do mark them quick – they have nothing else to do. Yes, I was pleased about English. Politics and history OK. Yes, history was an unmitigated disaster, but I knew it would be. Form teacher said, 'Altogether good, but what about history?' I said I would work harder. But I won't. I can't be bothered. Nazi Germany would be worth learning about, but not Elizabeth I. Me and her have got a lot in common, though. We are both gobby and confident, and we are both virgins. But I am telling you now – I AM NOT DYING ONE!

But it all scares me. I can't imagine doing it with a bloke. I just think he'd laugh. I wouldn't know what I was doing.

168

Midnight-ish

Pissed and knackered. Just got in from a party. Another three hours of the same songs from the Leo Mobile Disco that everyone hires. If I hear 'My Boy Lollipop' and 'The Final Countdown' by Europe one more time I swear I will punch someone.

And what else was the same about this evening? No snogs. Four sodding months to the day. All work. No play. Shit. Tonight, one girl said – and I don't think she meant it nasty – 'Does it bother you being so big, Rae?' and I said, 'No, I don't often think about it.' What could I say? Yes – every moment of every day? Burst into tears when I got home. They can't know what it's like. But it's hell.

Tuesday 27.6.89

11.10 p.m.

I WANT TO WRITE BUT EXAMS and performing have left me feeling totally exhausted.

Second and final performance of Wizard of Oz tonight. It went really well, though there weren't many people in the audience. Then we went down the pub in costume for a laugh. It says everything that the Tin Man got more attention than me. SHE WAS SILVER, FOR FUCK'S SAKE.

Do you know what, Diary? I am sure you are sick of me feeling shit about myself, and I am sick of going on about it. Why don't I just do it? Why don't I just look on the bright side? I am clever, people think I'm funny, I am predicted good grades for my A levels. The only bad things are fat and men.

Wednesday 28.6.89

9.56 p.m.

HAVE COCKED UP ROYALLY ON the money Mum left me for food. Stupidly have spent £7 of it on an Enya cassette from Stamford Music Shop. Great field and thinking music – but now there's no food in the house. Polly came round tonight with an emergency bottle of milk and a Frey Bentos steak-and-kidney pie, but I'm still in trouble. Won't starve, though, because of dinner at school, plus the boarders will sneak me out breakfast if I ask them.

I could even see it as a really quick way to lose weight. Just eat one meal a day at school, and spend the rest of the time listening to Enya and OMD in the field by the Rainbow Superstore. It's a nice thought; but the farmer gets well narked if he sees you near his sprouts.

Thursday 29.6.89

4.15 p.m.

I HAVE AGREED TO SOMETHING THAT might go so wrong I may be grounded for life.

Battered Sausage asked today if him and a load of his mates could stay at mine tonight. I thought it was because I was dead popular, but I discovered it's because they want to use my house as a good 'base' for their end-of-term/school big stunt prank. Battered Sausage would not tell me for ages what it was about, but finally

170

I got it out of him. It is unbelievable. They have got the shell of a bright-pink Mini, and they are going to put it in Stamford School hall. One of them has managed to get hold of a key. It's light because it hasn't got an engine, and it's hidden behind the cricket pavilion. I have told Battered Sausage that I cannot be implicated in the plot in any way. It's a risk, but I am going to be the only girl with about ten blokes in her house – so it is worth it.

Friday 30.6.89

9.32 p.m.

I HAD THE MOST WEIRD NIGHT last night. But I have done something shit. I have got someone so wrong – said something so bad. It was because I was drunk, but I made someone cry last night. I made a bloke cry. I have never done that before. And I can't stop thinking about it. I have cried loads of times when writing in this diary because of what people have said to me. Last night I did just the same thing to someone else. I was a bitch, and I have made such a mistake and I am a cow.

Anyway, Battered Sausage, Haddock, Fig, Luke and a load of others came round mine until about 2.30 a.m. All the lads decked themselves up in camouflage gear, and over the gas hob they burnt wooden pegs that they spread over their face. It's apparently what they do in the army.

There was a lot of piss-taking because they spotted the big television in the lounge that has a 50p meter on the back of it that pays for the rental. That was it, then. They went and found that just about everything in our house has a meter on it. Because of this, my nickname is now 'Rita Lovely Meter Maid'. (Apparently, it's a Beatles song.) Then they left to wheel the pink Mini into the main school hall. They managed to do it, but the caretaker was on an all-night practical-joke watch, so he wheeled it out again.

Then a load of them came back and stayed the night. I was having a real laugh with all of them and they were all being dead sweet. But then . . . Oh, I don't even want to write it.

Haddock asked for a drink and called me Rita, and I just thought, 'You arrogant public-schoolboy prick – I am going to teach you a lesson.' Ages ago Battered Sausage told me something about Haddock and swore me to secrecy. It was something private. Anyway, I said it to Haddock. And the moment I said it, I knew I had gone too far.

Oh God, it was awful. It was awful. He just went pale, and said, 'What?' But he knew what I had said. I said, 'Look, Haddock . . .' and went to grab him, but he just legged it out the front door. I caught up with him, and said, 'Haddock, I am so, so sorry – I'm just pissed.' But he just said, 'It's OK, it's OK,' but he was filling up. Fucking hell, it was horrid. It was like I was talking to another person. And then he ran off. I couldn't catch up with him – he's a rugby player.

Everyone was asking where Haddock had gone, and I said, 'Oh, he has just gone for a walk.' Everyone was so pissed they believed it.

I was sitting there worried out of my head for a few hours, then the front door went at about five in the morning. It was Haddock. His eyes were red raw. He just looked at me like I was . . . It was awful. And he just said, 'Get Battered Sausage.' So I did, they went off for about an hour, and then Battered Sausage came back and said, 'Nice one, Rae. He's well upset.' I then burst into tears, and Battered Sausage didn't know what to do and just said, 'Don't worry, Razza – he'll get over it.' Then he told me Haddock isn't rich at all, that he doesn't think much of himself really, and that when he comes across as arrogant he is actually just being shy. When I went to argue, Battered Sausage just said, 'Think about it.'

I've read back a bit on this, Diary, and perhaps loads of times I was being a cow to him when he was just trying to be nice.

Yes, I feel like shit. A total shit.

Battered Sausage eventually left about 8 a.m. Haddock. How wrong can you be about someone? I thought he was just another rugger-bugger meathead, but actually he has depth. I feel so guilty because I gutted that bloke, and it was a deliberate attack. But honestly – I have never read someone so wrong in a long, long time. He isn't the cock I thought he was.

I just assumed because he is so good-looking he would be a cock.

I am a twat.

All that happened at school for end of term was someone had drawn a big knob in the lawn with bleach.

Haddock. Just so sorry.

Oh God . . . I may have to face him tomorrow night.

Saturday 1.7.89

11.44 p.m.

JUST BEEN DOWN PUB. SPOTTED Haddock in the Vaults. I went up to apologise again and he just turned away. Battered Sausage says just to ignore him and it might be OK. But it is making things so difficult. He won't sit at a table with me, and so all of us have to sit in separate groups. I bought him a drink but he wouldn't even accept that. He looks at me like I have done something so terrible. And the honest truth is I have. And all those times people have called me names. This is how it feels to be the one that caused all the pain, and I feel sick with it. It's like I'm the bully. Ridiculous in this case, because he is Mr Gorgeous Untouchable and I'm just the fat gob. It's like a caterpillar having a go at a lion. Or something else big.

I can't think about it.

Right . . . Time for a massive end-of-school-year emotional update:

The thing about all these parties is, there's only so many times you can listen to bloody Jennifer Rush's 'The Power of Love' and watch endless couples snog. In fact, seemingly every other person on the earth snogs, and you are left propped up by the bar, or hiding in the toilets, or stood by the DJ swaying your hands jokingly in the air, singing along badly and laughing – but inside feeling crushed up like a can – WISHING, WISHING, WISHING that your big fat body would shrink – like those Shrinkie Dinkie things you used to get free with Weetabix.

In conclusion: I'm losing weight. I'm doing it for myself. Time to shock – but inside stay the same. Quite frankly, I want to be done senseless by a man. This is all a bit strong, but that is what diaries are for – strong, passionate, secret emotions. No one is ever going to see this.

So here we are at the end of the lower sixth. It's been a brilliant, eventful year – here's to the rest of '89!

Just found this!! Me and Bethany were passing this note to each other in English AGES ago. Mrs Matthews was going on about Geoffrey Chaucer, and I was looking pissed off because even in *The Canterbury Tales* they were getting it. Bethany asked me what was up.

Here is the note:

What's up?

When will I stop hurting? When will I find someone? Is it because I'm a fat cow? I seem to be permanently in a rut – when is it going to stop?

If you are worried about the way you look, or that fat affects the way men like you, then only you can change that. Pigging out is not helping you and you know that. Where has the old Rae gone? Is she lost for ever?

Don't YOU start. What do you mean? Please explain! Are you saying that I'm getting obsessed? PLEASE be honest!

175

Maybe not obsessed . . . but you used to be so cheerful and now you seem sad all the time.

It's . . . I don't think you can comprehend . . . Here at school all the girls like and love me for what I am, yet men all hate me for the same thing. I can only attribute it to the way I look.

Only you can change that, if you feel bad about it. Men always judge by first appearances. And most like 'ladylike' women. But do you want to change into something you don't want to be? The choice is yours.

I don't want to change, but I'd like some love. Perhaps I should run away and become a hermit.

If you want love, then perhaps you need to change - or have to change. Don't run away and become a hermit. Perhaps you come on a bit strong, then they get scared and run.

But I'm not a flirt!

I don't mean flirting - but throwing yourself at everybody in a friendly sense. Men don't like it.

But that's me – I like to be at the centre of every-thing. I can't help that, that's me! Most men don't mind. They just don't fancy me. Do men dislike me? You are with them more . . .

Men don't hate you - just think you are a bit OTT.

Have you heard them say it, then?

YES!!!

Who??!!

Lots of them!

What do they say? Be honest!

That you are a bit loud ... overpowering ... too pushy ... Like shouting about in the pub ... throwing pints on the floor!

That was an accident. There was a jam in the doorway going out to the garden in the Vaults. I'm a wide load – I got stuck.

Sunday 2.7.89

6.20 p.m.

PISSED. BORED. SICK OF MY head. And if this is what diaries are for – passionate, secret emotions – then you might as well have it all because it's too much in my head. No one is ever going to see this. Fuck it. Let's talk about what is really going on.

I want to tell you how my mind works. I think part of me is completely and utterly mad. Every day it takes me about 20 minutes to leave the house. I have to check every socket, then the gas fire, and then I get stuck. I can see that it says, 'OFF,' but I look at it and I look again and again. And then when I have finished checking that, I check the gas hob again and again. I count all the knobs: one – two – three – four – five – six. I can see they all say, 'OFF,' but I go back and back. I think if I don't do all this the house will burn down, or Mum will die in a plane crash when she comes back from Morocco, or I will become possessed or something terrible like that.

But it's not just that. A few weeks ago I had a terrible feeling that bloody shit Sinitta song 'Right Back Where We Started From' might make it to number one. So my brain said, 'Touch the windowsill 25 times and it won't.' I did. And it didn't.

And there's other stuff from the past . . . I know I sound off it, but by doing all these things I think in 1986 after the Americans bombed Tripoli, I helped to turn back the Russian warships that were sailing towards Libya. And after that bloody nuclear war programme *Threads* was shown on television, I think I helped to stop nuclear war. I am crying as I write this because I know I can't do all these things but my brain says I can do all these things – and I have to try because if I don't terrible stuff will happen. I can't risk it.

But I know it's not consistent, because I have been doing all this checking to get a man for days and THAT still hasn't happened. (Mind you, I haven't turned into a lesbian either, so it must be working a bit.)

When I read that back it sounds totally mad. I was locked up for less than that. I can't tell anyone this or I will be back in ward 4 of Edith Cavell Hospital in Peterborough. I will be painting pictures of things that are meant to mean something, with Mum visiting me and bringing me a mini trifle and a copy of *Smash Hits* like everything is normal.

Nobody must ever see this.

It's worse when there's nothing to think about. Summer holidays are totally crap. I reckon I have seen every episode of *Champion the Wonder Horse* at least 15 sodding times. Especially that one when Ricky discovers ice cream – BULLSHIT.

Monday 3.7.89

7.55 p.m.

SORRY ABOUT YESTERDAY. I WAS feeling a bit down. In fact, I was feeling flat as a pancake.

Mum would say I was over-tired, so all I have done all day is lie on the sofa and read and watched telly. Read some of Mum's women's magazines. Lots of 'I did it!' articles about women who have eaten nothing for six months and lost 12 stone. 'My husband loves the new me' etc., etc., etc.!! Didn't he like the old you? Recipes for cheap, affordable stews. Problem pages about affairs and people who have shit husbands. Articles on Andrew Lloyd Webber. In *TV Guide* there was a competition to win a date with Stefan Dennis – aka Paul Robinson from *Neighbours*. Why would anybody want to win that?

Nobody has been round. I have eaten three bags of crisps. Everywhere you look there are women moaning about men. On telly, Deirdre has just finished moaning about Ken in *Coronation Street*. There's this song out called 'Superwoman' where this woman is moaning that she does her husband a fry-up early in the morning but he never thanks her. It makes me wonder if they are worth it. But they are. They are. Anything is better than being left here without anyone – or anything – but a bloody multi-pack.

Tuesday 4.7.89

4.01 p.m.

RANG MORT. SHE IS GOING to Egypt tomorrow. I know she is my best mate but sometimes I am so jealous of her family. Her parents are like mates to her. They talk to her like they really actually like _her_. She gets her own space, but she gets her meals cooked for her too. It's like a perfect world.

While I was in the phone box I saw the twats from Green Lane shops that used to chant, 'Jabba,' at me. I papped it because I haven't seen them in months, and I knew they would have been saving it up. They have probably forgotten I am (NOT) related to Reggie Kray. Luckily they didn't spot me – they were too busy taking the piss out of Ralph, the old bloke who lives in the flats, and his tartan shopping trolley. I feel guilty saying this but I'm glad he was there to deflect the attention. He can hold his own. He always shouts at people, 'I killed three Germans with my bare hands.' At least that's what we think he's saying. It's hard to tell – he is originally from Cornwall.

11.20 p.m.
Went down the pub tonight and this will just show you how things have changed. I sat with Dobber and Battered Sausage. Battered Sausage told me that Bethany had come round and said goodbye to him, as she is going INTER-RAILING. France, Spain, Germany and Italy with her new friends. God, I felt jealous. I get

180

a panic attack going to Leicester, and that is less than 30 minutes away.

I would love to go round Europe, though, where no one knows me, where I am not Diane's daughter, where I am not Rae Rent-a-Clown Rent-a-Gob.

Have to wait another year. I should lose some weight before I go. The amount of things I will do when I am thin it's unbelievable. It will all be different.

Wednesday 5.7.89

8.45 p.m.

MUM IS BACK TOMORROW SO I just had a massive clean-up. It's a good job that I did because I have just found the following:

- three burnt pegs from down the back of the sofa. I thought I had put them all in a saucepan of water. I got so paranoid I even put the matches they used in the sink. This could have started a fire, I know. But more to the point – they could have started the biggest row EVER if Mum had found them.
- a balaclava
- a Stamford School blazer IN MUM'S BED! (Battered Sausage!!)
- four branches used for camouflage from the bush in the back garden. These were stuffed behind the washing on the dining-room table.
- a copy of *The Eight-Legged Groove Machine* by the Wonder Stuff (brilliant, and I haven't got it so I am nicking it).

I have spent about three hours hoovering because our hoover is a pile of crap and won't pick anything up. The house now looks tidier than when Mum went away, which will make her suspicious, but sometimes you can't win. I am damned if I do and damned if I don't.

Goodbye, Freedom. You've been fun.

Thursday 6.7.89

9.40 p.m.

UNBELIEVABLE TURN OF EVENTS!
You won't believe this. Actually, you will. Because in my life, shit like this happens. According to Buddhists, the shit you get in this life is because you have been evil in a past life. Well, I must have been Genghis Khan, Stalin, Hitler and every other nutter in history. Because LISTEN to this!

Mum is back from Morocco, where she was meant to be seeing her second husband. She came back carrying pictures of a bloke called Adnan who she says is 'just a friend'. He is in his twenties. He is the champion body-builder of Morocco. He is Mr North Africa. He is a champion kick-boxer. And MUM – AGED 46 – HAS PROCLAIMED THAT HE MAY BE COMING OVER TO *STAY*.

Apparently, the marriage to number two is over, as – wait for this – HE IS A HOMOSEXUAL!

You heard right! Mum's second husband is gay!

Now, don't get me wrong, the signs were there – silver trousers, Sister Sledge albums, the 12-inch of 'I Feel Love' by Donna Summer – but this is still a shock. That is one thing. This Moroccan person coming to stay

182

is quite another. Why can't that be IT now? Why can't she just say, 'My best days have gone, I will settle down now'? Why must I be forced to share my home with a BODYBUILDER? She says he is very nice. She already has a photo album full of pictures of him. Why can't I have a mother who just wears sodding aprons and bakes cakes?

If this new bloke turns out to be her new 'boyfriend', I am living down the Meadows, I am telling you now.

And then she has the cheek to ask, 'How are you sorting yourself out a summer job?'

HELLO!!!!!!???

And I didn't even get a present. No perfume from duty-free, or novelty camel. Not a flaming thing! For the record, a copy of the Royal Air Maroc in-flight magazine DOES NOT COUNT.

Friday 7.7.89

11.10 p.m.

I'VE WORKED OUT WHY I have been so down. It's a mixture of:

1) The end of a brilliant era and 'not fitting in'. Last school year from January to July was unbelievably and phenomenally brilliant. It was gorgeous. I mean, I bathed in it. Now all the decent blokes are going, and we are left with total twongos from the lower sixth who think jokes thrown at me across the room like 'Mind that chair, it might split with all that weight' are

hilarious. Well, they are not. They hurt like hell.
But I smile through it. I feel like Glenn Close in
Dangerous Liaisons when she goes, 'I learnt to
smile at a dinner table when I was sticking a
fork in the back of my hand.' That's how I feel.

2) Mum pressuring me to get a job. I have nine
GCSEs, woman! I did not learn how to say,
'They are very expensive – have you got a
cheaper pair of curtains?' in French just to
grade peas at Christian Salvesen or chop
sodding lettuces at Bourne Salads.

3) I don't know where I'm going. I want to be
famous but I don't know who the hell Rae Earl is.

4) Well, let's be honest – lack of boyfriend is
becoming a major, major issue. Why can't my
love life be like one of those Jackie or My Guy
photo love stories, where everything turns out
OK? Because they never feature fat girls. You
never see a speech bubble coming from a bloke
with the words 'What you look like doesn't
matter – it's your personality that counts.'
Because that's lies. That's the lies they tell girls
like me so life seems to be fair. But it's not. A
sexy face and body can jump queues, be wined
and dined, cuddled and stroked and loved.

I'm the clown. They tell me the appeal of that
will last far longer than a great pair of tits. But
at the end of the night, when a thousand
couples are snogging, my jokes feel like big,
deflated, sagging balloons.

I'm so jealous of the choices being pretty
brings. I know girls in my class who start

184

conversations with sentences like 'I don't know if I want my current boyfriend any more' nearly every week. But half of these blokes they are talking about are smashing – I'd have them. They'd be bloody perfect.

I'll have the cast-offs. I understand the cast-offs and the way they feel.

I'm watching Mistral's Daughter starring Timothy Dalton. He is so horny . . . Well . . . perhaps not so horny when his hair descends into that middle parting.

I'm full and totally empty all at the same time.

Oh, I bloody well hope everything will be OK. Oh, and another problem . . .

5) A Moroccan bodybuilder who I have never met before is coming to stay in my house.

Saturday 8.7.89

4.38 p.m.

GOT MY PHOTOS DEVELOPED FROM the parties. All great and everything. None of me – YES! YES! YES!! Though apparently there is a video of one party with me in jeans and everyone else in ball dresses. Oh, bloody great – hope no one sees that. Back to the photos: Battered Sausage spitting beer at the camera, usual staged nonsense. Sweet ones of Fig and Dobber. But the most astounding thing is Haddock. He is so bloody good-looking. I mean, it takes your breath away in a way. In a dinner jacket he looks like ruddy James

Bond. What is it about men in dinner jackets?! Black
tie makes even the most geeky bloke look gorgeous,
and as for the already good-looking ones – well, it
sends them into sex-appeal overdrive, and they know it.
And then there's me in a huge ball dress that Nan
helped to finance. It was dead sweet of her to do it, but
you can't disguise a doughnut body whatever you try
to squeeze it in. Thank God there were no photos.

I wish Haddock didn't hate me. But that's something
that I have to learn to live with.

Sunday 9.7.89

10.52 a.m.

FREAKIEST THING EVER TODAY. I have discovered
a song via Dobber's mum that could have been
written for me. It's called 'At 17' by Janis Ian. The
words of the song have just blown me away. It's a bit
of '70s folk music basically, but it's phenomenal. It's
about being ugly and young and not pulling. It's about
pretending you have boyfriends when you don't. It's
about Valentine's Day when you get fuck all and how
blokes only like the perfect women.

It is just . . . brilliant. And it's how it is. Because it
is the truth. <u>The pretty girls get it all. They have
different rules.</u>

<u>IT IS MY LIFE SUMMED UP IN THREE MINUTES.</u>

Have put it on an H-J compilation tape. Unfortunately it is sandwiched between Steve 'Silk' Hurley's
'Jack Your Body' and 'White Wedding' by Billy Idol, so
it's not really flowing at the moment.

Monday 10.7.89

7.10 p.m.

MUM IS WORRIED ABOUT THIS Moroccan body-builder coming and I can see right through her tactics. Out of the blue she just comes up to my room and says in a forced cheerful voice with shark's smile, 'Have you seen the *TV Guide* this week? There's a big bit on Chris Tarrant.' She knows I have loved him ever since he did *Tiswas*, and she could not wait to tell me that he had been a teacher – 'So he must have been to university, Rachel.' It always comes down to this. All the good people have been to university, and I MUST GO because SHE would have wanted to. No one in our family has been ever before. I must make the best of all the opportunities I have been given. Unless I leap in the air and say, 'YES, YES, YES!! I will do as you say, Mother!!' I GET THE LECTURE. If I make a mess of things I will be 'stuck in a crappy council house in Stamford with no money. Do you want that? Don't work hard, then, Rach, be stuck for the rest of your life like I am, in a dead-end job. The choice is yours.' I know this speech back to front. I think she gave it to me in the womb.

Then she remembered she was actually trying to get me on her side, and said with too much enthusiasm, 'I've done sausage and bean casserole for tea,' and then she sits me down and decides to tell me more details of her marriage break-up. I didn't want this information, but here it is:

Second husband told her he was gay back in April, BY LETTER. Well, if she won't install a phone, that's what happens. She was upset, but had 'suspected it for a while'. They will remain friends. Adnan and her are just 'close friends' – he is coming over for a study visit. He is a local celebrity in Casablanca, opens restaurants and gets stopped for his autograph apparently. He is six foot tall, and eats six meals a day – including whole chickens stewed in turmeric. He is a Capricorn. He trains every day. Now, Mort is my best friend on earth, but I don't know her as well as Mum knows Adnan! Then I started to ask some questions like 'How long will he be staying for?' and 'Is he married?' But THEN she decided that there were some burning broad beans downstairs that she had to save. There's always something burning when things get too in-depth.

I can't cope with being this lonely. Everywhere, couples. Outside, but please not inside too. I know it's selfish, but . . . there's no one just for me.

Listening to more Janis Ian. There's a song called 'Tea and Sympathy' about her setting fire to her house and throwing her life away just because there is nothing left and no one left to give a stuff about. Every time I am down Mum says, 'Have a cup of tea,' rather than face the problem or give me a cuddle. 'Tea, No Sympathy' would be my version. But my house won't burn down. I check the plug sockets and the iron too often for that to ever happen.

I take the piss but it kills inside.

Tuesday 11.7.89

6.22 p.m.

IT'S BEEN SO BLOODY HOT. This sounds like it's great, but it's bad news all round for me.

First of all – if I start sweating I feel 50 times more self-conscious than other people because I know people are expecting me to sweat more because of my size. Then there's the clothes issue. I still have to wear big T-shirts and long trousers because of my fat arms, fat gut and fat knees. Meanwhile, everyone else in the world is in bikini tops and crop tops and little bits of bloody fabric that make pretty girls look even bloody better than normal.

So – BRING ON AUTUMN – BRING ON THE RAIN – BRING ON EVERYONE WEARING 27 LAYERS AND EVERYONE EATING BIG STEWS AND PUDDINGS!

I hate summer. I hate the heat. I hate being left out. AND I HATE ME SOMETIMES.

And there is bloody ice cream everywhere. Nearly ate a whole tub of Neapolitan today. Then Mum went mental because I had left the tub out and the ants that are coming out by the gas fire were having an orgy all over it. She has refused point blank to do anything about them for ages. Don't worry, Mum, I am sure when Adnan gets here he will crush each one individually with just one look of his bodybuilder eyes. Pathetic.

189

Wednesday 12.7.89

7.02 p.m.

THIS MORNING MUM NAGGED ME from when I got up to around 12.25 p.m. when I finally said, 'OK – I WILL GO TO THE BUGGERING JOB CENTRE AND LOOK FOR A HOLIDAY JOB.'

That was approximately 45 minutes of pure earache and bile. Same old arguments: 'You don't contribute . . . You just laze around the house . . . And could you get some stuff to kill the ants from Wilko's, please?' Went down the Job Centre and checked that I am not eligible for any benefits. I am not. Then experienced the most depressing 30 minutes of my life so far, watching the casualties of Thatcher and the recession. Men of 50 that will never work again being forced to sit in interviews and then 'have a look round for something that might suit'. BUT THERE IS NOTHING. Nothing but ringing people up, trying to sell double-glazing, and lorry-driving and trainee hairdressing.

Went down the Meadows straight afterwards and tried to write a song called 'Flat in a Flat Cap' about unemployment for the over-50s.

On the shelf
Frozen foods and you
Best before date your packaging is used.

Feeling flat in a flat cap
The good days have gone bad
You were taken in by their promises
And now you have been had.

If I could find someone to write music, I could bloody make it. I know I could.

Had a 99. Came home.

Got Mum's ant spray. It's called Doom. Sums everything up.

Thursday 13.7.89

6.05 p.m.

THOUGHT I WAS GOING TO die this afternoon. Mum used the Doom spray on the ants that live in the hearth. It did kill the ants almost instantly. Unfortunately then she put the fire on so she could get a light for the oven AND ALL OF THE HEARTH TILING WENT IN FLAMES LIKE A CHRISTMAS PUDDING. I SHAT MYSELF.

It was my nightmare come true. Mum started stamping on it, and then she rushed off and got a tea towel and got rid of all the weird flames. Then she just turned round really calmly and said, 'Well, Rach . . . that's got rid of them!' At times like that I just feel such a surge of 'like' towards her – she is witty, and just gets on with things. Why can't she be like that all the time?

Party at Fig's house tonight, near Bourne. His parents are away and everyone is going – including Dobber, Battered Sausage and Haddock. I am dreading seeing Haddock because every time he clocks me now he looks at me like I am shit. And to him, the truth is I am. After what I did.

Friday 14.7.89

2.12 p.m.

ONLY JUST GOT HOME. I am knackered, but I want to get all this down before I forget. Lots happened at Fig's party last night. For a start, Fig's house is huge but looks like it hasn't been decorated since about 1976, which explains Fig's obsession with Showaddywaddy and Bruce Forsyth. Battered Sausage was in a right state – drunk as a skunk – and locked himself in Fig's parents' room with a girl from Rutland Sixth Form College and a plate of oven chips. Some of the tossers from the boys' school started to shave off the eyebrows of a boy that was so paralytic that he went unconscious. They think they are hilarious. They are not.

I spent most of the night with Dobber having a right laugh in the kitchen, until she went to bed with Fig at about 3 a.m. I tried to ignore the fact that the rest of the world was either snogging, flirting or shagging, and perched myself by the fridge (my usual spot). I chatted to loads of people while organising and making toast, and I made sure I put extra butter on the thin girls' bread – HAH!!!

About 4.30 a.m. I was going to go and sit in the back garden on the swing chair (because most people had crashed out), when Haddock stumbled into the kitchen. His girlfriend is on holiday so he was on his own. He stopped dead when he saw me and tried to make a retreat – and then realised it was too late. I

192

thought, 'Right – he is pissed, so now is my chance.' He would not look me in the eye. He did not even say hello, he just went to make himself a cup of coffee, so I said, 'Look, Haddock – can we have a chat?' He said, 'Nothing to say, mate.' I said, 'PLEASE?' He just stood there looking half at me, half down to the ground.

Massive conversation with Haddock went as follows:

ME: Look . . . I am so, so sorry for what I said. I didn't mean it. It was just a joke.

HAD: Not interested.

ME: Yes you are. You were really upset by it. And it was a shit thing to do. The shittest thing I think I can remember doing.

HAD: It doesn't matter. Battered Sausage should never have told anyone – especially not someone like you.

ME: It does matter. It does. I can't believe I said it. Please – I am really sorry.

HAD: Are you sorry because you are sorry, or because you are worried other people won't like you any more if you don't get on with me?

ME: I am sorry because I think I have been mean to you, and upset you, and I feel bad.

(PAUSE.)

HAD: What have I ever done to you? You are nice to everyone but me. I have never taken the piss out of you. When all the stuff was going on with Harry I tried to tell you what was happening. You took that the wrong way too.

ME: I just thought . . .

HAD: You just thought the same shit everyone thinks about me and shit.

193

ME: What?

HAD: Can't be bothered to go into it, mate. No point.

ME: I know all that. What can I do to make it better?

And then he just looked at me and went, 'Make me some toast.' So I did. He had two slices of white with apricot jam. Then he just winked at me and left. I don't know if that means we are mates or not.

Went to the garden. Sat listening to the birds with a glass of vodka and Coke. This was only spoilt by Battered Sausage yelling at the top of his voice, 'I haven't got another one.' No idea what this means but he was wetting himself one minute later so it couldn't have been serious.

Fig's mum and dad have concrete mushrooms in their garden. Don't know why.

Feel so lonely. I could just curl up and die.

7.12 p.m.

Forgot to tell you the quote of the week. FIG was looking at my 'Legend in My Own Lifetime' badge and he said, 'And you make a lovely slice of toast.' I know it's easy to warm bread, but it's still lovely to get a compliment about your cooking.

Saturday 15.7.89

11.51 p.m.

NOBODY WAS OUT TONIGHT SO I stayed in – everybody was either working or knackered. Rang up Mort. She had a good time in Egypt, but somebody offered her

dad 15 camels for her. Apparently, Arabs like young
women with blonde hair. Mum also says Arabs love older,
fat women of Mum's age – as being big is traditionally a
sign of wealth. Trust me to live in a country where the
men prefer their women to be like matchsticks.

Told Mort about everything that had been going on
and asked if she thought Haddock had forgiven me. She
said, 'Yes, but men actually can't say that they have, as
they can't show their feelings.' She said Haddock
sounded like he had 'more to him than a lot of boys,
underneath it all'. She also agreed with me that he does
look a bit like Bruce Willis in *Moonlighting*. Sort of
stocky, with killer eyes.

Wish I could catch some decent zzzzzzzzzzzzzzzs. You
would think sitting through Bob Holness and his *Champion Blockbusters* and the sodding film *The Odessa File*
would send me off to sleep, but it hasn't.

Sunday 16.7.89

4 p.m. (in the second Meadows)
MIND HAS BEEN ALL OVER the shop today. I
have days like this. Fields make it better.

Sanctuary above sanctuaries . . . I think that the
second Meadows is it. There's a gorgeous hum of the
A1 here, but it's still quiet.

I'm so NUMB. I just don't care, it seems – but I must
do. This is all going to sound totally incoherent. I'm
that bunged up, but totally empty. I think my worries
about who I am have reached a head. I mean – who is
Rae Earl? I think I know myself, but then other people

195

say things. Mum says I am selfish and arrogant, but her reasons for saying that are essentially selfish ones to do with our relationship. So it's difficult to judge. Haddock hates me, but then again he incorrectly thinks that I hate him. Battered Sausage made a sarcy comment about my three-day relationship, and EVEN bloody Phoebe Brown (square and quite plain really) is going out with someone, and then had the audacity to make yet another comment about my bloody three-day relationship. She likes heavy metal – but even she's pulled!

I suppose the Madonna line 'No one knows you better than you know yourself' holds true. And she knows better than most, so bollocks to all of them. You know the good people of Stamford would like you to think that the Meadows is for family days out, picnics, dog walking, water jousting and other such middle-class bollocks. It is; but like most things here, it has a flipside. It's also home to underage drinkers, people shagging, and over there a bloke is lighting a marijuana joint the size of a drainpipe. If I wasn't so scared I would ask for a puff of it – it might cheer me up. Plus the fact I've heard that hash makes you hungry . . . I don't need more appetite.

Monday 17.7.89

6 p.m.

DOWN THE MEADOWS AGAIN. LIVING down here at the moment.

I think I'm like Ruby Wax – I scare people off. Is she married? I hope so.

I'm too over . . .

A BLOODY WOLF JUST CAME AND SNIFFED ME.
THAT'S A HAZARD OF FIELDS.

. . . powering but I can't seem to help myself. You
see, I don't know if it's just Stamford and my age. I
love being with people and I hate being disliked. I love
making people laugh. It's a mass thing . . . but I want
a special kind of relationship with one person too. I
just can't seem to have both.

Being so fat is driving me insane.

Being at home with Mum is driving me spare.

She calls me 'self-centred' all the time. Do you think
I am self-centred, Diary? I think this may be the
problem – YOU, Diary! I'm that took up with you and
what I feel that I completely forget about the feelings
of other people.

It's so safe here I could stay here for ever. No sounds
– except the old church bell, water sounds and the birds
and the bees (no innuendo meant). It makes you think, it
puts you in touch with what is under all this fat.

A dog owner has just informed me that 'lying down,
non-moving people' – i.e. me – are fair game for his
dogs to piddle on. Typical Stamford Tory.

I'm sure if I got off with someone I would feel better.
I want to feel like a woman. I hate being so inexperi-
enced with men. It's appalling. If I could just find one!
Just one . . . who could prove to me I'm bloody normal
and not a completely overpowering, fat freak.

The pub opens in ten minutes. At the end of the day,
a half of Samuel Smiths cider and a packet of nuts can
always make you feel better.

Tuesday 18.7.89

8.40 p.m.

LISTENING TO SOUL II SOUL in my bedroom. The woman who fronts Soul II Soul is quite big and she is a pop star and still pulling so there must be some hope. And that Jazzie B bloke has got a potbelly and I bet women drop at his feet now he is in the Top 10. Mind you, it's different for blokes. Women are fighting for equality in the workplace, but why don't they fight where it really matters?

I WANT TO SEE A REALLY UGLY, FUNNY BIRD GOING OUT WITH THE ATTRACTIVE BLOKE OF HER CHOICE, WITH HIM ENDING UP ADORING HER.

Now <u>THAT</u> would be equality!

Wednesday 19.7.89

10.25 p.m.

SOMETHING ODD AND EXCITING HAPPENED tonight. Me and Dobber were walking in Red Lion Square after what was quite a normal Wednesday night in the pub, and this bloke in a car screeched up behind us and said, 'Do you know where the RAVE is?' We were like, 'Err . . . no.' Then another car turned up and asked us exactly the same question, which is amazing because that surely means that there are illegal raves going on in LINCOLNSHIRE!

We have GOT to find one. I've never even seen any

real drugs up close. I am very chuffed indeed that I look like the sort of person that would be into rave.

Thursday 20.7.89

Late

TOLD MUM TONIGHT I HAD been asked where a rave was. She went mad – I haven't even done anything yet! She said, 'You keep away from those places, Rachel – DRUGS!' I said, 'I can't afford to buy a packet of cigarettes, let alone some drugs.' She went, 'SO YOU SMOKE, DO YOU?' I don't, by the way, because I could never master inhaling. But she now totally believes that I do. She said, 'You can get sucked into the lifestyle, and before you know it you will be on heroin.'

I would just like to point out to you that this over-reaction comes from me just saying IN PASSING that someone had asked me where a rave was going to be held. I knew she was wound up, so I said to her, 'Don't suppose you know where these raves are being held?' She said, 'Don't push it, Rachel,' and then, 'You need to get a job, my lady,' like I am 12. I don't do anything wrong and I get in trouble. She is the thought police.

Friday 21.7.89

11.44 p.m.

JUST GOT IN FROM THE pub. Mum was practically waiting by the door. She said, 'Have you been to a rave?' I said, 'Of course not! They don't end until five in the morning usually.' She said, 'Let me look into your eyes,' (I have had one pint of cider) and then just walked off.

What I did find out tonight is that the rave scene in and around Stamford is on, and it's happening now. I think the first one was about a year ago (when I was going through the breakdown – that's probably why I had never heard about it), and there have been a few since then. According to people in the know, another one is imminent. Dobber and me have agreed: we HAVE to go. Even if we have to make friends with people we don't like to get there.

Nothing else happened tonight, except for a weird conversation with Haddock's girlfriend – who told me that Haddock had mentioned to her that he needs to speak to me. If this is a good or a bad thing, I don't know. Perhaps my toast made him sick or something? He is out tomorrow night, so we will find out.

Saturday 22.7.89

4.50 p.m.

THE RUMOUR GOING ROUND IS that the raves are being held in a field run by a local farmer. Apparently, it's a sideline that he does! You don't know where they are until the night, and then word spreads and you just turn up and dance. We are keeping our ears to the ground and hoping. Getting there may be a problem, but we can cadge a lift or just walk. I won't do any drugs because knowing my luck I'll have a massive allergic reaction. I'll just stick to 20.20 and vodka. Apparently, there is one next Saturday, and I am going.

Going to the Vaults tonight. Hopefully I will find out more. RAVE ON, '89 – KEEP THIS FREQUENCY CLEAR!!

Sunday 23.7.89

2.15 p.m.

LAST NIGHT WAS PRETTY EVENTFUL. In fact, that is a major understatement. Great night in the Vaults pub garden. Battered Sausage was really pissed. I walked, no . . . basically *carried* him home. In the chippy he ran off with the money before we could pay. All these yobs were getting really pissed off and they yelled at me, 'Fucking twat,' and 'Bloody fat cow,' etc. So I can't raise my head in Des's Super Chip for a long time.

But that didn't matter too much, because . . .

HADDOCK!

OH. MY. GOD.

Just everything changed last night. Firstly he was chasing me round the beer garden of the Vaults with a drink he had bought me, and I thought, 'Eh up!' Then for a laugh he kept saying all these crap chat-up lines, like 'Is your dad a thief? Well, who nicked the stars and put them in your eyes?' And then he followed me into the girls' bogs and we had – well – it was like this mass chat. It was unbelievable. We must have been talking for about an hour. I've never talked to a man like that before. At one stage, Battered Sausage came up pissed, and Haddock said to him, 'I want to talk to Rae. I will buy you a drink if you go away'!! And this is the thing – he is not a rugger-bugger twat. He is such an amazing, wonderful person. So sweet.

How could I have got everything so wrong?

He's a supernatural epic. I'm trying to remember every-thing he said. He said lots of people thought I was just a loud bitch, but when he got to know me he realised what a lovely person I was – and that's why he was so gutted when I said what I said . . . And how I wasn't ugly, just a bit plump. He was telling me all about his life. His family life. Being sent to boarding school. He's not rich – his dad was in the Forces and they paid. How he felt about his girlfriend, how he felt about himself – he is very down on himself. It was just bizarre, and wonderful.

How could I have got it so wrong? I keep asking myself. What else have I got wrong in my life?

We talked for ages. How can anyone be that good-looking and that nice? He must have a massive bad side somewhere – but I can't see it. Oh God.

ODE TO HADDOCK

O Haddock
You are gorgeous
And you are gorgeous inside as well.
O folly
I've got a crush
Only your girlfriend is marv
She is my friend and she is brill
Sometimes I wish I wasn't so loud and chubby
Then you'd be my lover, and then my hubby!

I got home last night and I now can't sleep. Played the Lotus Eaters' 'The First Picture of You' again and again. Playing it now. I think . . . for the first proper time ever . . . I almost don't want to write it . . . I think I truly love a man. I KNOW I have written it before, but honestly – I have had trouble eating today. I know it sounds pathetic, but he is just so perfect inside and out. When he went to give me a hug goodbye, I felt dizzy.

Can't stop thinking about him. Read this diary back. Feel like an idiot. I am always saying people don't get me and just think I am fat and loud, but I have done exactly the same thing to somebody else.

Can't believe how similar we are, too. He feels bad about himself. So do I. We talked about how difficult it is being in a relationship. I told him I wouldn't know. He said that I will one day. Then he said, 'I wonder if an arranged marriage wouldn't be better?' I said, 'I have so often thought that.' Then he said for a joke, 'We should have one, Rae. Me and you.'

I laughed and punched him, but . . . oh my God!

Raves went out the window last night. Don't care.

Haddock doesn't like the idea of a rave. He likes dancing, though. I've seen him.
Oh God.

His girlfriend is lovely.

WHY AM I FAT?

Monday 24.7.89

11.34 p.m.
I'LL GIVE YOU AN EXAMPLE of how me and my mum compete. I MENTIONED HADDOCK'S NAME tonight, and she said, 'Oh, I remember him!' Turns out when Mum was ironing shirts at the boys' school,

203

Haddock was a boarder. 'Lovely sweet boy,' she said, 'even then!'

So she has helped care for Haddock, and has probably seen him naked and all sorts. She always has to have one up on me.

Tuesday 25.7.89

8.36 p.m.

I'M ON A COMPLETE HIGH because I am in love. It's tragic.

Asked Mum for some money today for clothes. I need some new ones – can't be a scruff for ever. She said, 'Rachel, I have got none. Why don't you ask your father? He hasn't paid maintenance since 1982. He said he had sent it for six months and claimed he had been putting it in the only postbox in Britain that was never collected from.' I know this story. I know she is angry, but why does she have to rub it in? I can't go and ask my dad for clothes money – I only seem to ring him when I want something, it's embarrassing.

There's nothing for it. I am going to get a job. It's drastic, but there's no other choice. I even tried to get the pay and display machine in the car park by the police station to pay up by repeatedly pressing the 'return change' button. Nothing happened. That was a sign. Battered Sausage said he might be able to get me a job at the hotel where he is a waiter.

Just want to look a bit nicer, that's all.

Wednesday 26.7.89

4.55 p.m.

I'VE GOT A JOB AT the hotel washing up. Battered Sausage wangled it for me – £2 an hour.

Had to go there today – Battered Sausage said, 'Whatever you do, don't look at the chef who is interviewing you – as his bottom is in two parts.' I did look – and it's true! It looks like he has got four buttocks! My duties are to wash up the plates and the pans as they come in and to assist the chefs 'as they ask'. I was trained on the washing-up machine by an old bloke called Les, who said, 'Whatever you do, have a system. If you have a system, you will be all right.' It doesn't look too complicated, but honestly I wasn't paying much attention as the four-buttocked chef leant over to get something and I could not stop looking. He must have had an accident or something. It looks like someone must have cut his bum in half with a cheese wire. Perhaps it was a catering-school prank gone horribly wrong!

I start on Sunday. Bloody dreading it. This will be my first proper job, and don't get me wrong – the money is good, but I'd rather be in the pub.

With Haddock.

Thursday 27.7.89

3.20 p.m.

WENT TO FIG'S LAST NIGHT. Battered Sausage and Fig ended up watching this porn film called *Magnificent Obsessions*. It was appalling, it really was. It involved washing machines, bananas, really fit women and average blokes with bad beards. They reckoned they were watching it for a laugh; but Battered Sausage went very quiet, and Fig had to go for a walk round the block. So I think it created some kind of reaction.

Saw Haddock's girlfriend in the pub earlier. According to her, Haddock has bought me a present. With a laugh, she added that she is 'getting suspicious of us two!' I wish she had something to be suspicious about. I wish I was a threat. But I'm not – I'm fat, and safe.

Like a human bouncy castle.

Friday 28.7.89

11.25 p.m.

PUB WAS A BIT BORING tonight. Haddock wasn't out, but his girlfriend was. Weirdly, we are becoming really quite good friends.

I know what you are thinking, Diary. You fancy him, Rae. You love him. You bitch. How can you be friends with her? Well, the fact is, however much I want it nothing will, and can ever, happen. This is one of the best-looking blokes in the boys' school, and I am just Big With a Big Gob Rae. I am not a threat, and these are just things I think and tell you, Diary.

But given half a chance, I would. I would. I would. I know it's bad, but I would.

The big rave is on TOMORROW. The bloke who works in the Baker's Oven bakery came up to us – clearly off his tits – and said, 'Rave. Tomorrow. Meet outside the Lincolnshire Poacher. Get instructions at ten.' I have to go to at least one rave. Just to give it a chance. I can always come home if I don't like it.

Listening to S-Express and D-Mob to get in the mood for it. Think I am going to wear just a sweatshirt and jeans with my raspberry Converse All Stars. I don't know what people wear to raves, really.

Haddock out tomorrow. I can't see him going to a rave. Unfortunately. He is just not a 'put your hands in the air' type.

Saturday 29.7.89

AFTER THE PUB (DON'T CARE about time – daren't look – alarm is set for 7 a.m. for work)

Dobber and me went down the Vaults at about 7 p.m. There were loads of people out tonight, ready for the rave. They were not wearing sweatshirts. They had vests, whistles, and some of the girls had hotpants. I am not a lesbian but they had figures that were just unbelievable – legs just perfectly smooth, stomachs like ironing boards. I can't compete.

Haddock came in around 8.30 p.m. I swear to you,

my heart just leapt ten foot in the air. He was wearing his old school rugby shirt and a pair of ripped jeans, but he looked so, so horny.

I was acting like I hadn't seen him, then he came over to me and went down on one knee and said, 'Rae, will you marry me?' I said in an affectionate way, 'Fuck off, you big twat!' but inside I was nearly sick. He obviously has no idea. I'm hiding it well. He then gave me a joke engagement ring. He did it for a laugh, because we were talking about having an arranged marriage. We had a quick chat, then he said, 'Are you going to this rave?' I said yes. And he said, 'Oh, don't bother, stay here and have a laugh with me and Battered Sausage.' I said, 'I have got to go, mate – I have promised Dobber.' I might be reading too much into this, but he looked quite disappointed.

Anyway, we all traipsed up to the Lincolnshire Poacher before ten, and then the bloke from the Baker's Oven ran up and shouted, 'The pigs have got wind of the rave. It's on next Saturday instead. Same time.' So we all went back to the Vaults – where Haddock, according to Battered Sausage, was in the corner having an in-depth chat with his girlfriend. This means a row. She was crying. He was stroking her shoulder. I couldn't look.

The ring Haddock gave me has started to rust already, but I don't care. We can all dream.
I am well in love. Shame he isn't.

I'm dreading work.

ODE TO HADDOCK (PART 2)

O Haddock, O Haddock, Arian Gorge stuff,
The greatest male ever born.
You possess a gorgeous personality,
And your middle name is Horn.

Sunday 30.7.89

10.50 p.m.

WORK WAS A BLOODY, BLOODY nightmare.
Got there about 9 a.m. for a nine-hour shift. I could cope with the breakfast stuff, as there was just loads of eggs. But then Sunday lunch started.

It was horrendous – I saw the same pot about 15 times. People kept having things with bloody gratin. When I eat in posh restaurants, I will never have gratin – because it solders itself to the dish and tortures the washer-upper. At one stage there was a real backlog, and the chefs were shouting for pans, and I was scrubbing and scrubbing but stuff wasn't coming off. The system I devised obviously wasn't working. Les, the old washer-upper, had to come from the other kitchen and bail me out. He has now lent me his system and it works a lot better. You are not even allowed a radio. I mean, what sort of place is this?

Got through it by thinking about Haddock. A thousand different scenarios, usually involving me losing five stone and we end up having it off. Unfortunately thinking about Haddock didn't stop a lecherous middle-

209

aged chef grabbing me and saying, 'I love them when they are cuddly.' Why do middle-aged men like me? And not gorgeous, young, nubile rugby players?

Back there on Tuesday. Dreading it already. This is no way to live.

Monday 31.7.89

10.10 p.m.
SPENT ALL MORNING IN BED aching all over. Mum was gloating: 'This is what proper work is like, Rach. If you go to university you won't have to do this crap work for the rest of your life.' Blah. Blah. Blah.

And that's not the only thing. At the pub tonight a new torture started. There is a rave song out at the moment called 'Voodoo Ray' by somebody called a Guy Called Gerald, and everyone seems to think it's hilarious to sing this song at me and make death-ray wiggling hands. It's not even spelt right. Some people are even calling me Voodoo Ray. This is in addition to Raymond, Raemondo, Rayfonce, etc., etc. My name is RAE, thank you. It's people trying to make me even more masculine than I already am.

Tuesday 1.8.89

11.40 p.m.
WORK IS A PIG, IT really, really is. Volunteered for a late shift. No money in the world was worth what I just went through.

People at night seem to eat more stuff based on cheese

210

and crumbles. Apple crumbles stick like tar to bowls. Came to fear lasagne dishes – they were just hell. I walked home with greasy hair smelling of kitchen, and who did I walk straight into? Haddock. I looked like a really fat hamster who had fallen down a drain. He was lovely, but it was pity. Went home and thought that if I can just be thin, I will let the house burn down.

They don't need me now till the 12th. Thank God. I honestly don't know if £16 a day is worth this hell.

Wednesday 2.8.90

Late

HADDOCK, I ADORE YOU.
It's so sexual. He just touches me and I get seriously soppy. Tonight he kept hugging, cuddling and kissing me in a jokey way. We had such a laugh. I'm so in love. I KNOW if I was thin and pretty he'd fancy me – it's so annoying. He's so horny, CARING and funny. I WISH I was going out with him. Oh, I envy his girlfriend so much – I wish I was her. I really do. I reckon he is the only man on earth I could do all the business with. But a) he doesn't fancy me, and b) he has got his girlfriend anyway.

But I have made a pledge and I intend to honour it: in a few years I am seriously after Haddock, and I mean it. I intend to do it with that man.

The lads all have their little roles:

BATTERED SAUSAGE – like my husband, minus
    the sex.
FIG – my friend.

211

HADDOCK – just the best example of man you will ever see. Stocky, but magnificent.

I'm going to write him a letter he will never see. It makes me feel better.

Dearest Haddock,

As your arranged 'intended', I feel I have a moral obligation to say the following in your direction. But I will make absolutely sure that if I do give this to you, I will never see you again – as embarrassment of the highest degree would still prevail, even after a lengthy period apart.

This letter's alternative fate is between the pages of my diary, as an example of the emotions dodgy hormones can produce. But I hope there comes a time when I can give it to you. It may simply serve as an ego boost, but I hope it goes a bit deeper than that.

I know we didn't get on to start with. You always seemed grumpy. This is where I got the impression that you did not like me. Well, it would figure, wouldn't it?

I never hated you, though – quite the opposite (careful!). But I did not really know you. I simply knew you as 'Haddock', slice of all right if ever there was one. Sorry about that, dearest, but I must admit that rugged looks are a major factor in my adoration.

No – I was only a sod to you because I often am to people I think are a bit marvellous (r.e. my continual arguments/bantering/all-out war with Battered Sausage). It's my personal defence system, but we won't get into my mental condition now.

Basically, you are extremely special, I totally mean that. I tell you what, Haddock, I only really clicked on to what you were about the other Saturday night when we were talking about stuff, and you bought Battered Sausage a drink so he would go away. NO ONE has EVER done that for me – even the child psychiatrists looked bored when I told them about my problems. I wish that you hadn't done that in a way. Because being in 'lurve' with you in only a purely 'physical' sense, I then realised what a bloody epic you are inside as well. So it completed the overall picture of you, as it were.

OK – you won't appreciate the next bit, but I don't give a shit, baby! I say what I feel. You suffer from a classic case of under-confidence. Luckily you have been able to shield this with your rugger-bugger image. Look at yourself in a mirror, Haddock. You are majorly handsome. URGH! This does sound creepy and gross, but never mind. To get any kind of praise from me in spoken word, let alone in letter form, is a major achievement. You must be a pretty marv bloke.

For God's sake, Haddock, you are not perfect but you are an epic. I envy you, I really do. Being humble is one thing but you're ridiculous. ARGGHHHH! YOU MAKE ME FUME! DO SOME-THING ABOUT IT, HADDOCK!

Well, I think this will end up in my diary for a very, very long time anyway. I tell you what, though – I wish you had seriously given me that engagement ring.

May you flourish in your twenties wherever you are . . .

Rae xxxxx

PS Did you know one of my infamous cocktails is called a Haddock, because it's got a sound head and a firm body?!

Weird thoughts are bad tonight. They are saying that unless I do all the things I need to do, Haddock and his girlfriend will find out what I feel about him. It's loopy but it's how I feel. Can't stop it.

Thursday 3.8.89

11.50 p.m.

ANOTHER NIGHT OF FEELING LIKE the biggest Judas on earth, as I spent the evening with Haddock's lovely girlfriend and she tells me about their relationship, and, oh, she is so sweet but all the time she is giving me Haddock info and titbits, and the evil part of my brain is thinking, 'Remember all this, what he likes and doesn't like – because one day all this may be useful.'

He likes Abba, on the quiet. Oh, come on now – this is all too similar and coincidental! This comes barely a week after I borrow Dobber's old *Top of the Pops* album, just so I could listen to 'Fernando'.

Then I get home, feel racked with guilt, and eat half a packet of Tesco bourbon creams.

Some abuse down the pub tonight. The worst one: I was eating some nuts and a bloke who doesn't even deserve a mention here said, 'Haven't you had enough to eat?' Much to the hilarity of his mates. That's on top of their nickname for me – Slug. I always manage some biting, witty comeback, but when I'm sat here in bed and my belly is rising up and down like a big throbbing K2 of a gut mountain, I could just pull this duvet over my head and hibernate until I lose all the weight.

Friday 4.8.89

11.35 p.m.

PISSED OFF.

Quite a boring Friday night down the pub. Battered Sausage was off his face and decided it would be hilarious to have a piss in the pub garden and spin round as he pissed. You have never heard so many grown men scream as they got splattered in Battered Sausage wee. Because he is big with a shaved head, no one went to punch him. Apart from that, nothing happened tonight. BUT . . . at the end Haddock said, 'I'll walk home with you if you like – it's a bit late,' and I said, 'Yeah, you can do.' OH MY GOD!

Anyway, we chatted about music and stuff and I was feeling like YES!!! I LOVE THIS MAN! Then, out of the blue, on Mountbatten Avenue, he said, 'Do you know what, Rae? You are like a big sister to me.'

Like a sister.

This is what good-looking blokes say to fat girls to make them feel loved but to put them off sexually. It's like saying, 'I love you but not in the way you want.'

I said, 'Well, that's good – because you are like a brother to me.' I said it with a smile but inside I was just dead.

215

Somebody has shit-stirred. Battered Sausage suspect number one. Why would Haddock say that otherwise?

I can't think about it. Just end up crying and hitting everything in sight.

Rave tomorrow. Just going to think about that.

Saturday 5.8.89

7.12 a.m.

WOKE UP, FELT GOOD FOR five seconds, then remembered last night. Like a sister. I don't want to be your sister, Haddock. I want to be your everything. I want to be the girl you meet down the pub. I want to be the girl you go on holiday with. I want to be the girl you do senseless. Not the girl you bicker with and have play-fights with. Not the girl you see as one of the lads. And that's it now because once they see you that way you can never change it.

Mum is shouting up to me. Do I want a bacon sarnie? Yes, I do. I want 20 of them with butter and sauce and everything.

Glad I am going to the rave tonight. Don't want to see anyone. Just want loud 'make my nose bleed' dance music.

Sunday 6.8.89

2.23 p.m. (POST-RAVE)

I DON'T KNOW WHERE TO START.
Last night was one of the weirdest nights of my life. And remember – I have already been in a psychiatric ward.

Dobber had her mum's car (her mum is in Spain and doesn't know we borrowed it), and parked it outside the Lincolnshire Poacher at ten. About 20 minutes later this Morris Minor screams past us, and someone in the passenger seat shouts, 'Go to the Marsh Harrier!' We couldn't believe it because the Marsh Harrier is what we call a 'grave-dodger's' pub – because it's just full of blokes over 70. Anyway, a load of us ended up there. The Marsh Harrier locals were not happy about this – they thought they were going to get mass-mugged. We found out later the 'organisers' had picked the Marsh Harrier because 'The pigs don't pick on old people's pubs.' Then a bloke rushed in and said, 'Head towards Ryhall!' So we did, and there was nothing but fields of donkeys. We thought, 'Typical,' and were about to give up when a load of cars screamed past us the other way. Dobber said, 'Let's just see where they are going,' so we followed them – with 'Voodoo Ray' playing full blast as it was the most rave thing on Dobber's tapes. (Dobber wanted 'Got To Be Certain' by Kylie Minogue but I pointed out ravers hate chart dance.) Eventually we ended up somewhere near Uffington, and then we heard it! Just REALLY loud dance music.

We parked up on a verge, and as we got nearer we could see people going totally mental. The bloke from the Baker's Oven was wearing his actual baker's hairnet and blowing a whistle! The music was fast – we were counting the bpm and we lost count it was that fast. I didn't know any of the songs except 'We Call It ACIEEDDDD' by D-Mob, and during that some people sat down in protest saying it was 'chart'. Everyone seemed to be chewing all the time, and people kept coming up to you – touching you – asking if you were

217

OK. It was weird. There were blokes going round asking if you would like 'some'. Whatever some was, it was £30! Me and Dobber both turned that down.

After a couple of hours of mainly watching, we left. Good job too because we saw a cop car heading towards the field. Dobber and me went back to hers for some toast, and then I crashed on her sofa.

We both agreed it was a bit of a let-down.

It was just all odd. I didn't feel part of it. It was like being invited to someone else's party – just to watch.

I did get touched a lot, though, by fairly nice-looking men that actually seemed quite interested, so it might be worth going again.

But Haddock would have hated tonight.

Monday 7.8.89

5.14 p.m.

HA!! MUM JUST SAID TO me, 'The lady in Woolworths told me there was a rave on Saturday night near Uffington. Good job you didn't go – there were DRUG arrests.' I said, 'Oh, were there?' I have had to come upstairs and jump around! It's brilliant to get one over on her, especially when – YOU MUST BE BLIND, WOMAN – there are grass stains all over my jeans!

Just getting ready to go out again. Fig is having another party. Dobber is driving over, and we are staying the night.

Haddock will be there.

No, nothing will happen. His girlfriend is there – and even if she wasn't, nothing would happen.

Tuesday 8.8.89

12.50 p.m.
FIG'S PARTY WAS FULL OF pot-smoking hippies.
Had a brilliant chat with Dobber, and we are going
to Alton Towers on Friday!! Haddock and girlfriend
went to bed at 11 p.m. and didn't emerge till 8.30 a.m.
I was absolutely racked with jealousy – I felt GREEN.
Ended up raiding the freezer in annoyance – discovered
Fig had a Screwball ice cream, nicked that, and chewed
the gum at the bottom of it pissily all night. When
Haddock finally appeared, he pinched the back of my
neck and said, 'Do you want a coffee, then?' He made
me a coffee. It was lovely.
    The coffee, I mean. But when Haddock pinched my
neck . . . it was beyond lovely.
    Battered Sausage is constantly pissed off at the
moment. I had a chat with him, and he divided the
female sex into two categories: bitches and slags. I'm a
bitch because I am (quote) 'too good-natured to be a
slag'. I think it's only his confusion over a certain ex-
girlfriend (who I thought was as innocent as the new
day, but actually turned out to be RAMPANT with other
men while she was seeing him!). HA!!!
    Isn't it good to know that men hurt too?

Wednesday 9.8.89

11.19 p.m.

NOT THE BEST OF NIGHTS. Haddock horrible to me tonight. There was a load of lads out, and he just acted like he didn't know me. He barely said two words to me, and just shoved one eyebrow up when we were at the bar and said, 'All right, Rae?' When men get with other men they change completely. It's pathetic.

I imagine he's trying to make me hate him, but there really is no need. I'm sure in the end I will learn to love him as just a friend. In fact I think that is happening already.

Thursday 10.8.89

12.27 a.m.

CAN'T SLEEP. THAT LAST ENTRY was total lies. I still fancy the hell out of him. Like if he asked me out tomorrow I wouldn't say YES??!! He can never be just a friend. If there is such a thing as a friend anyway. When it comes down to it, we are all on our own. Just me. And the cat. And even she goes for me sometimes, and moults on my duvet.

There is so much wrong with me. I've created an absolute monster, but there is a part of me that always wants the laughs and wants the attention. How do I balance that with the need for dignity and respect? I must start trying.

11.57 p.m.

What a top night down the Vaults with everyone. Got a
bit tipsy and ended up falling
down a pothole. Nearly wet myself – brilliant!

Friday 11.8.89

Late

HAD A GREAT DAY AT Alton Towers with Dobber.
It was such a laugh, but there were a few dodgy
moments. Dobber only passed her driving test in
February, and all of a sudden on the way there she
went pale and started saying, 'Oh my God, Rae, oh my
God. It's a motorway, Rae, it's a motorway.' Turns out
she has never done three lanes before. Anyway, we
stayed all the way there in the left-hand lane and she
coped with it absolutely fine.

When we got to Alton Towers it was packed, but
brilliant. But even there I felt like a big lump. On the
Corkscrew roller-coaster, the safety bar rested on my
belly. It was at least three inches above Dobber's. If we
had been sharing it, she would have fallen out because
of me. On the log flume you have to ride with people
you don't know, and you could see people looking at
me, thinking, 'I hope we don't have to get on with her.'
THE FACT IS – EVERYTHING WOULD BE BETTER IF
I WAS THIN.

Work tomorrow. Early shift. 6 a.m. till 2 p.m. Feel
sick with the thought of it.

Saturday 12.8.89

3.40 p.m.

THAT'S IT. I AM GIVING UP WORK. IT'S NOT WORTH IT.

Did the early shift. The chef with four buttocks was on duty, and he said, 'As well as washing up we would like you to do some preparatory work.' This meant going to the other side of the kitchen, taking bits of seafood, dipping them in egg and covering them in breadcrumbs. It was like handling snot.

I could see the pans piling up, and the other chef was getting really pissed off. The floor of the kitchen looked like a water main had burst, and I didn't have time to mop it. The chef with four buttocks just said, 'Pass the mop to me,' which meant he had to bend over – and expose that weird backside. I got the giggles, and he shouted, 'THIS IS NOT FUNNY! We are running a hotel business here!' Teachers have not spoken to me as badly as he did. I welled up, and he said, 'Go to the toilet and pull yourself together.' I looked at my watch – it was only 10 a.m. I had another FOUR hours to go! Managed to get through it – and there was only a little bit of mess at the end. No one said goodbye to me. It's shit, and I am not working there any more. Don't care what Mum says.

Fig is having another party at his house tonight. Haddock isn't there – he is working. I am almost pleased about this. It means I don't have to see him in

222

the morning after he has been shagging someone else
all night. With his hair all over the place looking
scruffy in a big shirt. BLOODY HELL, I FANCY HIM SO
MUCH IF HE SAID WASH UP LASAGNE DISHES NON-
STOP FOR TWO WEEKS I WOULD.

Sunday 13.8.89

12.50 p.m.

FIG'S PARTY WAS RATHER INTERESTING. Spent
most of it on the gravel outside his dad's study
downing a bottle of Smirnoff with a girl from the year
above called Emma.

At one stage everyone was in Fig's back garden
pissed, dancing to Echo and the Bunnymen. That is
until Fig's next-door neighbour complained and threatened to tell his mum and dad. He shit himself and
imposed a total music ban.

By the end of the night, the usual. The ocean of
snogs, and me leading the ugly ones in the kitchen –
getting not a quick fix of sex, but a quick fix of toast.

COME WITH ME

Come with me to the end of the party
With the lonely ones.
Join me
With some toasted bread and a bottle of
Something bad.
Right now we are in the swing-top bin of life
Not fit to be lover or a wife.

But some day things will be different
You will see,
Things will rise in the love oven for you and me.
But right now – let's commiserate and avoid a fight,
And drown our sorrows with vodka and Marmite.

Monday 14.8.89

11.10 a.m.
SOMETHING SO BRILLIANT JUST HAPPENED. It's just a joke, but it's the best thing that has ever come through a letterbox in the history of time.

Haddock has sent me a gorgeous postcard, carrying on our arranged-marriage protracted joke. It's a postcard of the church where he says we are going to get married if we can manage 'to get our pissed selves out of the pub'.

Have already put it on the bookcase by my bed. Have wished on dandelion clocks, sneezes, black cats, cracks in the path, magpies and bloody everything that one day it becomes a reality. But frankly there is more chance of me getting off with the Pope.

Have 'Pure' by the Lightning Seeds on loud. It's by a speccy Scouse geek, but it's beautiful – about being in love and how it makes everything seem better. It's so true. Even Mrs Bark's privet bush has got a brightness that it's never had before, and it's nothing to do with summer. The rest of the song is just poetry. Fuck John Donne at school, THIS is what's happening.

One day I <u>will</u> get off with Haddock, and I will write at least one great pop song. I swear it.

Tuesday 15.8.89

4.30 p.m.

JUST BEEN TO GIVE UP the job. Had to see the chef with the four buttocks. I told him I've got an ongoing back problem. He made some crack about how he could see that my spine was under pressure. He means fat. Yes, well, at least I've only got ONE fat arse, you wanker – you've got four!

I didn't say that to him, by the way. I just said, 'Thanks very much,' and left.

Mum will go mental but I don't care. She won't chuck me out – because if I do get to university, she will be able to boast about it for the next 20 years.

Wednesday 16.8.89

8.03 a.m.

MOTHER IN A RIGHT STONK. Oh, get over it, woman . . . So I gave up my job?! If you'd had to see the same pot 20 TIMES in one night, you might think differently too. There are only so many fantasies I can dream up to get me through it. Anyway, I had to go or I'm sure I would have got the push. Battered Sausage, who has been a waiter there all summer, told me some rogue prawns in hollandaise sauce were found blocking up the sink. HA!

Lack of man syndrome is settling in again. I am relieving

225

the . . . err . . . 'tension' . . . with the help of pillows, but it's hardly the same as the real thing, I suppose.

A-level results for the year above tomorrow (aka Haddock, Battered Sausage and Fig). An all-day session at the Vaults is planned. I haven't been paid yet, so the question is, can I nurse a soda and blackcurrant for eight hours?

Thursday 17.8.89

11.55 p.m.

LOADS OF PEOPLE BOUGHT ME drinks today so everything was fine. Even tight-arse Battered Sausage forked out – crucially BEFORE he got his results.

RESULTS

Fig got CCD and seemed pretty pleased with himself. Battered Sausage got UDD!

Battered Sausage made out he didn't care for the first couple of hours, saying, 'I don't care. I got a U – what a battered flange!!' etc. But then he got really pissed and disappeared down the Meadows, where according to sources he ended up crying, swearing and kicking the bridge repeatedly. Some girls were worried about him – but us seasoned Battered Sausage-watchers know violent outbursts and foul language are normal behaviour to a pissed Battered Sausage. Especially one that has so royally fucked up his A levels.

Haddock got the best A-level grades out of all the lads: BCD. Yet he still wants to go into the army!

Sometimes I just want to . . . Oh, I don't know. Listen to this speech: 'I'm very happy with my girlfriend. We have a laugh – she's classic – I love her, etc.'

When I see how happy he is, perhaps I should be all selfless? And say that his are real emotions – and if I really care for him, I should be happy if he is happy. It should be like the old bird thing – if you love somebody, set them free.

Horse crap! Because the more I find out about him, the more I like . . . I mean, I just ACHE for him. He told me last night he was jealous of Battered Sausage at first because Battered Sausage knew me and it was like I was ignoring him. And he makes me laugh so much! His Phyllis Pearce from *Coronation Street* impression is fantastic.

If he went into the army and we had a war, I swear I would assassinate Mrs Thatcher.

Friday 18.8.89

7.12 p.m.

EVERYONE TOO HUNG OVER. No one out.
Mum has cleared the spare bedroom for Adnan coming to stay. All my brother's posters of motorbikes and AC/DC have come down. Even his ceiling poster of a pork pie (which he put there when we first moved in 11 years ago so he could dream about pies) has come down. Yes, he has left home – but it's still a cheek. The jet-black walls have been painted, and she has even managed to get specially slaughtered meat in, as Adnan is a Muslim. This meant a SPECIAL visit to Leicester.

Notice the lengths she is going to to please this man? This is not just another houseguest. In fact – we never have houseguests!

Oh, bloody hell. Can you imagine the talk around town, and the questions and the gossip?

There is only one thing to do in a situation like this. Put on 'Oliver's Army' by Elvis Costello full blast and sing it word for bloody word. Yes, Mum, I know you can't hear your programme properly . . . Live with it, because Costello is more bloody important than *Wish You Were Here . . . ?* or whatever holiday programme you are currently watching. And, no, I don't fancy Mexico. Why are you asking me? Will the DHSS pay for that too?

Saturday 19.8.89

11.50 p.m.

JIBBED TONIGHT AT THE PUB. Just feel so flat about everything. Oh, and then Haddock . . .

Haddock is such a gorgeous bloke it's phenomenal. He is so caring, and his girlfriend is so classic. Don't get me wrong, nothing is ever going to happen, but sometimes I can see her getting jealous just because I have his time and attention, and it gets uncomfortable. He was lovely tonight. Lent me his Barber jacket thing because I was cold. Oh, I fancy the shit out of him. But he's hardly seeing the best of me – depressive, nuts, with a gravy stain down my hooded top – WHICH I DIDN'T HAVE TIME TO WASH BECAUSE MUM WAS WASHING ADNAN'S SHEETS . . . He isn't even here yet and he is getting on my nerves.

Sunday 20.8.89

9.14 p.m.

RADIO 1 ARE A BUNCH of hypocrites. They banned Frankie Goes to Hollywood's 'Relax', YET nobody seems to have noticed (or have they conveniently forgotten?) that the LIL' LOUIS song 'French Kiss' has a woman having a full-blown orgasm on it. And let me tell you – if you are sitting there listening to the charts with your mum, it is bloody, bloody embarrassing. Mum was embarrassed too, as she started telling me about something irrelevant from her Woman magazine to cover up the noise! It's such a full-on coming session you can't even dance to it.

Adnan arrives tomorrow. Great.

Monday 21.8.89

10.10 p.m.

WELL . . . ADNAN – MUM'S NEW Moroccan 'friend' – is here.

Bloody great enormous mountain of man. About six foot three, and that wide. Can't speak a word of English, but I am managing to communicate with my GCSE French. Unfortunately that is a bit limited, so at the moment our conversations are mainly about fish, clothing, going to the zoo and the weather – those are the only bits of vocabulary I really remember. He seems

229

nice enough. Terrible teeth, though. Mum reckons he is 'just a friend'. Oh yeah – and I'm Madonna.

Keep looking at Haddock's jacket. It sounds ridiculous because it's just a wax jacket, but it's a thing of beauty. It's the way it just hangs off the chair. All droopy and male and smelling of aftershave.

Tuesday 22.8.89

LOADS OF MY FRIENDS ARE passing their driving tests and getting cars. I'm still on my Raleigh Shopper with a bloody basket on the front. No wonder no bloke is interested.

Mum and Adnan are NOT just good friends. I'm not stupid. I heard her go to his room at 2 a.m. this morning. Then I put the radio on. Full blast. Don't want to hear anything. She leaps from one relationship to another. No matter that they have to talk in sign language. No matter that she has only known him about five minutes. No matter that he eats in a day even more than me (and he's still in shape – git!). No matter all of that. I guarantee they will get married. Today he ate an entire Battenberg cake like I'd eat a Mars bar.

Wednesday 23.8.89

7.25 p.m.

SAT IN A FIELD LISTENING to Enya. Proper field music. It's times like this when everything that troubles me is here in my head. Sometimes I feel I am bad, rotten, dreadful. And the thoughts spiral out of control and I can't stop them. And all the questions:

> Who made us?
> How does He judge us?
> Who made the rules now?
> Will I ever lose my virginity?

'Evening Falls' by Enya – bloody appropriate.

It's so bloody gorgeous out here. What is life? We do not know. They tell us we must do our best here and worry some other time about what is coming in the next life, but my brain says I control everything. The sun is gorgeous – you can't hide from it. Can't stop the need to do some things time and time again, and feeling if I don't do this, terrible stuff will happen. You know this, I have told you before. I don't want to write it but it's there in my head. And I can't share this with anyone else because I KNOW no one else feels this way. It's just mad.

Fat and mad – who wants that?

'Waterloo' by Abba at the end of the tape slightly buggers up contemplative mood.

Thursday 24.8.89

9.15 p.m.

GOT HOME TONIGHT TO HEAR grunting from the back garden. Adnan had filled up two buckets with mud and was using them to weight-train! I said hello to him but he was in a world of his own. Mum says he is worried about losing 'definition' and 'muscle mass'.

Am I living in this house? Is this all happening? Now she is talking about getting an aviary because they both like budgies. And she wonders why I live in my bedroom listening to music and eating Maltesers!

Adnan sings everything with an Arabic wail. Today I had Madonna on full blast and he started singing 'Material Girl' like it was a prayer. This shouldn't be my life. This is Edinburgh Road, Stamford, Lincolnshire. I want normal. I want oven chips and roast dinners – not bloody tajines and fucking couscous.

11.20 p.m.
Adnan just tried to iron for the first time in his life, and left the iron on!! I check every plug in this house at least 20 times before I go out. It's my worst fear come true. This is a nightmare.

I wish Haddock would come and save me. Preferably on a white horse, but frankly on bloody foot would do today.

Friday 25.8.89

Late

DIDN'T GO OUT. CAN'T STAND no more questions. To get away from Adnan's 'definition' problems (HELLO, SOMEONE! I AM ABOUT TO DO MY A LEVELS . . . THAT IS A REAL PROBLEM!), I went to the market this morning. Everywhere there seemed to be whispers, and I wasn't being paranoid. I know this because eventually I was cornered into endless false stops. You know 'false stops' – people who only vaguely know me pretending they were interested in me when they were just on a mission to extract as much juicy information from me as possible.

For example: this conversation took place near Needle-crafts the sewing shop with a woman who used to live near us. A woman who has got so much dirt on her it's unbelievable. She shagged the gardener for years!! That didn't stop her from trying to get my dirt, though:

MRS BEEN HAVING AN AFFAIR FOR YEARS:
Hello, Rachel!
ME: Hello, Mrs Been Having an Affair for Years
With the Handyman Who You Claim Is Just Coming
to Tie Up Your Tomatoes in Your Greenhouse.
MRS BEEN HAVING AN AFFAIR FOR YEARS: How
are the A levels coming on?
ME: OK . . . Well, actually I'm struggling a bit. I'm
finding histo—
MRS BEEN HAVING AN AFFAIR FOR YEARS
(interrupting): How's your mum?
ME (having just clicked on): Fine.
MRS BEEN HAVING AN AFFAIR FOR YEARS: Who
is that young black man staying with you at the
moment?
ME: Adnan.
MRS BEEN HAVING AN AFFAIR FOR YEARS: Oh?
Where's he from?
ME: Morocco.
MRS BEEN HAVING AN AFFAIR FOR YEARS: How
long is he here for?
ME: I don't know.
MRS BEEN HAVING AN AFFAIR FOR YEARS:
What's he doing here?

ME: Don't know. Got to go – I'm meeting someone.

And that's how it continued. Eventually I couldn't face it any more. I used all the old shortcuts and passages to get home. I even went through someone's hedge off New Cross Road. I made a big hole in someone's hedge. Sorry, someone, but your hollyhocks were the least of my worries.

Listening to 'Rat Trap' by the Boomtown Rats. And this place is a rat trap. I know people say Bob Geldof is a do-gooder who needs to comb his hair, but he knew what it was like to be stuck in a small town where you can't breathe without it being reported, and it's a bloody great song.

Going down the pub tomorrow night. Pray Haddock will be out. I will pretend I have forgotten his jacket. Don't want to give it back just yet. When it's here it's like he's here. Bloody hell, if anyone ever saw this . . . Everyone thinks I am super-confident, funny Rae – and I am just such a total, total mess. I am even pleased about having someone's jacket. Pathetic!!

It's not just someone, though, is it?

Saturday 26.8.89

Nearly midnight

IT WAS ALL GOING SO well tonight. Battered Sausage picked me up in Clarence the Cortina at about 7.30. He knew I was a bit flat and tried to cheer me up by saying, 'Don't worry about it, Battered

234

Flange. If your mum wants to get her oats, then fair play.' I think this was meant to make me feel better. It didn't, but I appreciate what he was trying to do. We met Dobber down the Vaults and we were just having a brilliant game of Captain Birdseye the drinking game, when SHE walked in . . .

BETHANY IS BACK.

From Inter-Railing. Tanned to bits, wearing a short skirt and a neckscarf. She looked shit. No she didn't – she looked amazing. I could be sick with it. She pretended she hadn't seen me for ages. She had. She then sauntered over and sat on Battered Sausage's knee immediately. She purred a 'Hi all!' and then goes, 'Rae, do you want to meet for coffee tomorrow?' I was thinking I'd rather pickle my own eyes, but my mouth said, 'Yes!' in a totally fake enthusiastic voice. Bitch. Bitch. Bitch.

Just then Haddock came in after yet another argument with his girlfriend and – HA, HA, HA! – ignored Bethany completely, despite her wriggling on Battered Sausage's knee like a really wet snake or something. A snake with her skirt riding up higher and higher.

Eventually she went, after telling us about Dieter – her new Swiss boyfriend, who is six feet tall and plays the drums.

I am going to hate tomorrow. Why am I going?

After she had gone, I felt shit. Battered Sausage didn't notice I was narked off, but Dobber and Haddock did. Dobber bought me another snakebite and black, and Haddock . . . well, we had a chat while Dobber was at the bar and Battered Sausage was having a piss. (Why is it I can remember everything that Haddock says? It burns itself on my brain.)

HAD: What's up with you?

ME: I'm a bit flat . . . Nothing really.

HAD: Come on, tell me.

ME: No. It's nothing.

HAD: Tell me.

ME: OK. My mum has moved a Moroccan body-builder in. I'm sick of . . . Oh, forget it.

(I can't tell him everything. He can see half my problems – and the ones he can't see I don't want him to know about.)

HAD: But you are a really good dancer, you make me laugh, and in pop quizzes you are unbeatable. Where's my jacket?

ME: Sorry – I forgot it.

HAD: Don't worry. Just look after it for me.

Then Battered Sausage came back and they started talking about rugby and tits.

I won't let that jacket out of my sight. I'm looking at it now.

Might wear it to meet Bethany. It can be like my armour. Dreading tomorrow.

Sunday 27.8.89

10.19 p.m.

JUST THE FACTS, BECAUSE I am too pissed off to write in full:

1) Bethany had the greatest time ever Inter-Railing. (Of course she did.)

2) Dieter 'goes like a train', and his dad owns a plastics factory.
3) 'Don't Wanna Lose You' by Gloria Estefan is their song. (Spare us.)
4) She lost nine pounds abroad. (Bitch features.)
5) She can't understand why I haven't lost weight.
6) Obviously we are not, according to her, close friends any more, but have to be mature and civil to each other at school. She realised while she was away that the 'disintegration of our friendship' was because of my insecurity about her 'duckling to swan' transformation. Her mum agrees.

Haddock's coat felt lovely on the way home. And 'You're History' by Shakespeare's Sister came on the radio. That was telling me something.

Monday 28.8.89

9.14 p.m.
SOMETHING PISS FUNNY AND WEIRD happened today. I was just listening to Hereward Radio and they had an astrologer on called Wyn Baines who was saying to call in if you want your fortune done – SO I DID – and I GOT ON!! And what she said was so true, it was painful:

I am a Sagittarius with a Scorpio moon. This means I probably have a dominant mother, and I am an extrovert 'hiding some more complex secrets'. My perfect partners are Geminis, Librans, and Arians were perfect. Haddock is an Aries. Enough said.

She also said there was lots she could tell me but not on-air. I hung on after they had said goodbye to me, but she didn't come back and I eventually got cut off. Perhaps it was really dark stuff? Perhaps I'm a potential murderer or something. Hope not.

Anyway, Mum was really impressed, and said I sounded very natural and confident. Praise from her is a bloody miracle.

I've always known there was something mad between me and Haddock, but I didn't actually realise it was cosmic.

11.52 p.m.
Just remembered I think Bethany is an Aries and I don't get on with her. Either she has got a strong moon sign or astrology is bollocks.

Tuesday 29.8.89

So late (Adnan is snoring like a cement-mixer)
ON THE BACK OF YESTERDAY'S astrology, got Mum's second husband's Tarot cards out. I used to play with them loads; but ever since one of the twat child psychiatrists decided to end one of our sessions by asking me to pick four cards from her Tarot pack, I have gone right off them. I mean of course I picked Death just to shit her up. (Besides, it looks cool – a skeleton on a horse.) I wish I hadn't. That meant more sessions talking about . . . the stuff that happened.

Anyway, I did a spread today and it was basically crap except for the King of Cups card, in a place which meant 'a significant person or event in your life'. Now listen to this description from the book: 'A good-humoured man with a calm exterior who is difficult to work out and may be emotionally complex.'

IT IS HADDOCK – AND IT IS FREAKING ME OUT NOW.

Everything is pointing towards it – it is scary. I have to lose weight. The fat is the only thing that could stop the planets and Fate and everything else.

Wednesday 30.8.89

2.12 p.m.
THE INSANITY CONTINUES. ADNAN IS currently building an aviary for Mum in the back garden. He is singing in Arabic style to everything on the radio. So far today I have heard the wailing Arabic versions of 'Nights in White Satin' by the Moody Blues, 'Never Gonna Give You Up' by Rick Astley and 'Blame It on the Boogie' by Big Fun.

Meanwhile, Mum keeps playing 'Swing the Mood' by Jive sodding talentless Bunny, and 'The Glenn Miller Medley' on the B-side. It is HELL.

And if she asks Adnan one more time (in really annoying pigeon English/French) if 'Addy would like *le poisson* and *pomme de terre*', I will go loopy. Sick of living in love land. I am going to the pub tonight to get slaughtered, and then I am coming home to let all the budgies free.

239

Wednesday – no, now it's Thursday 31.8.89

12.20 a.m.

MUM IN STONK. I HAVE BEEN VERY DRUNKS.

4.13 p.m.

Plastered last night. Just about managed to get home but was sick in a yew tree.

Turns out that me and a certain person have a lot more in common than I thought.

But it's bad. And to see it – to catch them doing the thing that I do – oh, it's like looking at a really good-looking mirror image.

This person hates everything inside like I do. I find this impossible to get my head round. I mean . . . they are everything that I would be happy with. But that thing I do . . . ? They do too. I am covered in bruises. And so are they.

I hit myself. Because I hate what I am. But why this person does it, I will never know.

No one is what you expect behind closed doors. And some brilliant people are eaten up by some terrible things.

In an awful way I feel better. Because I thought it was just me.

Shocked, though. Shocked. And want to make it better but I can't. I can't sort this head out, let alone anyone else's.

No budgies to let free, by the way.

Going out again. Can't stay here with Jive Bunny, pigeon English and talk of bulk-loads of Trill.

Friday 1.9.89

10.25 p.m.

LAST NIGHT I WAS MAJORLY bricking myself for about five minutes as Haddock and girlfriend ignored me. I thought, 'Oh shit no – they know about what I feel.' As I found out, it was just another row they were having. This information came from Dobber (who I deliberately went out of the pub to find in order to ease mind-paranoia situation). Came back to find Haddock and girlfriend making up. Ignored them. But then as I left, Haddock caught up with me, and our conversation went as follows:

HAD: Hello. How have you been?
ME: Fine! (Oh yes, really, sure. Still, never mind, standard answer.) Have you been crying, Haddock?
HAD: No.
(He had been. I am telling you – his eyes were red.)
ME: I wish you two would stop bloody arguing.
HAD: Can't help it. It's in my blood.
ME: Well, I wish you'd stop it.
(Bloody massive pause. I always get these with him and he looks at me straight in the eye – very unsettling.)
ME: Sorry if my card offended you. (I'd sent him a card about having his jacket and my intention to

241

nick it off him for ever because it suited me better than him.)

HAD: Oh no – it didn't offend me. I just sat there looking at it watching a Bing Crosby film and getting depressed and thinking I might get pneumonia this winter because my jacket has been nicked by a little Rae Earl.

ME: Piss off. (Affectionate shin kick.) Wear a thermal vest.

Saturday 2.9.89

8.24 a.m.

HAVE JUST WOKEN UP. BIRO is all over my duvet, but will carry on from last night:

HAD: So you're walking home on your own?

ME: OF COURSE! (Was I supposed to hint at him walking me home?)

HAD: I'm off to meet my mum.

ME: Oh, he's 18 and he is still a mummy's boy! (H and R play-fight breaks out.)

HAD: Anyway – bye, Rae.

ME: Bye, Haddock.

HAD: (A few incomprehensible comments.)

ME: What??

HAD: (More incomprehensible comments.)

Oh, me and Haddock are just too bloody alike. I do share his nasty hang-ups, but here's the key difference – I MEAN, JUST LOOK AT HIM. It cannot be denied

242

that he is just bloody horny. Yet he can't see it. I mean, a lot of people think he's a right cold bastard. I mean, I did at first, but underneath it is the most strong, sentimental, gentle, very funny bloke on the planet – and I can't believe he hides it.

You know, I get to see a side of him that hardly anybody else in this world does.

I really want to talk to him but it's virtually impossible, as a) always with girlfriend, b) his piss-take personal barrier to deep chat of any sort is very effective, and c) I know whatever he tells me will make me like him more. He could tell me he likes train-spotting and I wouldn't give a shit.

I don't know. I just reckon I could really help him. Oh, Rae, stop being a patronising bitch. He's not hopeless or pitiful. It's you who is the one that is not getting it, not him! Excuse me – I'm in love, and it sends you funny.

Give it five years and pray he's single!!!

7.30 p.m.
Thank God for Mort. Just rang her. Can tell her anything and everything and I know she won't tell a soul, but will say something just naturally that makes me feel better. She agrees Mum's aviary is a step too far. Her mum has a budgie called Juliet that lives in a white cage in her dining room. Her partner, Romeo, died after Mort's terrier-cross, Poppy, gave him a heart attack. It shows that we are all left alone in the end – even budgies.

Sunday 3.9.89

9.15 p.m.

JIVE BUNNY IS STILL BLOODY in the top 5. Mum celebrated by putting on the Glenn Miller B-side full blast. She reckons it is the best song of the last decade. Take no notice – this is the woman who thought nobody would use instruments after the Flying Pickets did the acoustic version of Yazoo's 'Only You'. That was shit too.

Well, it's all over – the summer of '89. It's gone, and what a summer!

I've gotten to know Fig really well, and Dobber has become a top friend. I know it's hard work next year, but this summer has been brilliant.

And only Fig is leaving, Battered Sausage is retaking, and HADDOCK IS HAVING A YEAR OFF.

YES!!! There is time. There is time to make a change in me. To become the swan that shocks. To reinvent Rae Earl. To stick two fingers up to all the piss-takers, the doubters, the bitches and the patronisers.

Watching a programme on the Nazis. It's so bloody awful. How can one human do that to another? BASTARDS. This is the problem I have with the A-level history we do: who gives a stuff about what happened three centuries ago when this happened less than 50 years ago? THIS is what we should be learning, not some crap about Anne Boleyn and her six fingers! It's not even that rare – it happens every day in the Fens!

Tomorrow I have to go to the school shop to get a new uniform. Mum is insisting on coming, even though I am 18 in three and a half months' time and can choose my own clothes, thank you very much. It will be a chance for her to say, 'Ohhh . . . you have put on a bit since last year, Rachel,' and I have. I'll be up a skirt size. They'll have to go to the special drawer and say stuff like, 'We *might* have one in stock,' etc.

Monday 4.9.89

11 p.m.

TELL ME THIS: I HAVE been wearing a red tie of some description since September 1977. So why does Mum STILL make me try it on to see if it fits? IT'S A TIE!! I have got a few chins, but not that many.

I had gone up a skirt size. But I am telling you now – this year I am going the other way. And you know why I am doing it, and FOR WHO I am doing it. Just listening to the 12-inch of 'Breakout' by Swing Out Sister. That's how I feel right now. Like in the video for the song where the lanky girl with the dodgy bob comes out on the catwalk in an electric-blue dress and shocks everyone – THAT WILL BE ME!!

Well, back to our fine establishment tomorrow. Can't say I'm upset. This holiday has had its fair share of ups and downs, but the fact remains that being at home has been a complete downer. Felt angry and aggressive all today. Irrational thoughts all over the place. Cure would be a bloke – take two times a day.

Tuesday 5.9.89

6.14 p.m.

BACK AT SCHOOL. USUAL 'ON the pain of death'
speech by Miss Byron. Uniform check, etc., etc.
Seemed really weird sitting on the stage where the
upper sixth have always sat, and then going to the top
common room. Good to be back, though. But crapping
myself that this is the very last year at school. The
thought of A-level results and university just makes me
want to vom everywhere. Think I might apply to do
American studies; don't think it qualifies you to do
anything, but you get a year in America free – so it's
worth doing it for that.

Wednesday 6.9.89

8.54 p.m.

HYSTERICALLY FUNNY TODAY AT SCHOO1
because someone bought a copy of *Lace* into the
common room. I didn't read it, but apparently on page
200 and something, a male character uses a goldfish
and sticks it up a woman's thing as a love aid. URGH!!
I don't remember that being in the mini-series!! Everybody was passing it round and reading it, and
according to Jasmine apparently Jackie Collins is even
worse. In one of her books women do it in front of
men for their pleasure because blokes get turned on by

246

lesbians. But only by pretty lesbians, not butch ones. The more I hear about men, the less I understand them.

Five girls lost their virginity over the summer holidays, and one lost her blowjob virginity in a kitchen in St Bart's. Bethany was going on about Dieter, who is meant to be visiting her in a few weeks. Thank God the bell went before they got round to asking me what I did all summer.

Thursday 7.9.89

Late

WAS FORCED TODAY TO GO into Woolies and buy 'Ride on Time' by Black Box. It is possibly the finest example of Italian house music you will ever hear. Typically skinny giraffe of a lead girl singer, but never mind. Came home, stuck it on, and bopped till Mum got home. Unfortunately did a spin and made the record jump, and now there is a bloody great scratch in it. Never mind. Now it just sounds like a remix.

Friday 8.9.89

9.02 p.m.

THE TROUBLE WITH STAYING ON for sixth form at school is you are still treated like a kid. Today was chips day like any other Friday, unfortunately it was also the day that Miss Tennyson decided to go on some sort of nutritional crusade. I am 17 years old, but today I was told I couldn't just have a plate of chips – I had to have peas too.

HELLO????!!!

What's worse, Miss Tennyson then stood by the conveyor belt where you put your empty trays and checked you had had 'at least a mouthful'. I can get married and I will soon be able to vote and fight in wars – YET I HAVE TO PROVE I AM EATING VEGETABLES!! On top of that, a lecture to those of us who skived off games (including obviously me) saying that exercise was an important part of life. Yes, love, but so is sex – and I'm not getting any of that either!

Saturday 9.9.89 (actually it's Sunday morning but it's all about Saturday night)

AND WHAT A NIGHT. I can get through this A-level year if every Saturday is like this.

First of all, me and Dobber went down the pub and met all the lads there. Then a load of us (INCLUDING HADDOCK and his girlfriend) went up Oliver's night-club. It was brilliant!! I was just dancing all night, and THEN 'Pump Up the Jam' by Technotronic came on. Haddock started bopping like nothing you have ever seen. It says everything about a man who is hard as nails on the rugby field but is almost of a professional standard when it comes to dancing.

When the Motown bit came on, I was just having a drink with Mort – when Haddock DRAGGED me to dance with him to 'Jimmy Mack' by Martha Reeves and the Vandellas. It was brilliant – but I couldn't look him in the eye. If I hadn't have been pissed I wouldn't have been able to do it at all. When I sat back down, Battered Sausage

said, 'Big Razza, I'll give you this – and I've said it before
– you are a big bird, but you can move.' Haddock just
winked at me and said, 'I've got a new name for you –
Funky Chick.' He called me it all night. I was acting cool,
but inside I could have cried with total joy.

We then all lined up for the dance to 'Can You Feel
It?' by the Jacksons, and all went mad for the Northern
Soul bit – especially for 'Nine Times Out of Ten' by
Muriel Day. Battered Sausage tried to do proper
Northern Soul dancing by doing a one-handed somer-
sault flip thing. Unfortunately he kicked a bloke in the
ribs, and got thrown out by a bouncer. It was nearly
closing time anyway. At the end, Haddock said, 'Funky
Chick, see you for another shimmy next week.'

Knackered – but had to write it all down because I
feel like Cinderella . . . It was bloody magic tonight.

By the way, Haddock's girlfriend doesn't get narked
when he dances with me because she knows we are just
mates. Nothing will happen. She can SEE with her own
eyes nothing will happen.

Wish I could freeze time tonight. Except for the
tinnitus in my ears, and playing Jive Bunny once,
everything was perfect tonight.

And I think I woke up Adnan when I came in. HA!!!

Sunday 10.9.89

7.12 p.m.
SUNDAYS IN LINCOLNSHIRE FEEL LIKE the whole
world is ending. Nothing is open, except for the corner
shop for the papers. Once you have trailed through the

News of the World and watched the *EastEnders* omnibus, you are reduced to sitting on the sofa trying to find inspiration on *Songs of Praise*, wondering when it will all end.

And all the time there is shed-loads of work to do: bloody American politics essay on the role of the vice president (which I still don't understand), and history and English. Today is the day when not having a boyfriend seems even more painful, and thoughts turn to houses where <u>he</u> is – where they talk about schoolwork and stuff on her bed and . . . Torture.

It's even getting too cold to sit in fields. End up having a fry-up, then roast, then tea, and hoping. Don't even know what I hope.

Morrissey understands all this shit. I reckon he was in Stamford when he wrote 'Every Day Is Like Sunday'.

He wills Armageddon to come in that song. Even though nuclear war shits me up like nothing else on this earth, nobody would miss Lincolnshire if it blew up. Except people who like turnips and swede.

At least 'Ride on Time' by Black Box is number one. This could be the start of a new dance revolution.

Monday 11.9.89

6.16 p.m.

CAME HOME FROM SCHOOL TO find Mum and Adnan in the back garden about to release the budgies into the aviary. I hate caged birds. I hate to see them restricted and fluttering their wings and banging their heads on the ceiling wire as they try desperately to get out. Mum and Adnan watched as they all fluttered in and sat on their perches squawking. Mum said, 'Don't they look happy?' I said, 'No – they look like prisoners all having a panic. And what if they don't like each other? They all have to pile in and pretend they have to get on.' Mum said, 'Lots of us have to do that, Rachel.' Yes, dear. I know what you mean – you don't need to tell me that.

If I had the nerve I would let them all go, but I don't yet. Mum would go loony, and the odd bit of money she does give me – well, even that would run to nothing. I would pay for what I know is right by being even poorer than I am.

Listening to 'Mandela Day' by Simple Minds. Can't believe he is still in prison after more than 25 years just for saying black people are worth the same as white people. There are people in prison for all sorts of shit reasons. It's not fair to cage things up. Whoever – or whatever – they are.

Bloody hell – 'Belfast Child' is a great record too. Simple Minds are bloody brilliant, but they are at their best when they are moaning about something.

Tuesday 12.9.89

9.10 p.m.
I HAVE CALLED THE BUDGIES AFTER living or dead prisoners of conscience, because they are all prisoners being held against their will.

Mandela (the blue fat one) – bad eye, but the
budgie with the most personality.

Biko (or Beako – get it?) – green one that has a
   madly coloured bit above his beak. Hope it isn't
   a disease or something.
Solzhenitsyn (Alex for short) – yes, I know
   Solzhenitsyn isn't in prison any more, but he
   was still fucked over by Russia.

The other six all look the same so it's impossible to
name them. I went out to see them tonight. They are
already terrorised by Dave the local tomcat, who is
trying to turn them into a snack. These birds are being
mentally tortured. White the cat keeps well away from
the aviary too. I think even she has been brainwashed
by Mum into not going anywhere near it.
   It can't be right to have wings and not be able to use them.

BIRD IN A CAGE

> Tethered up by wire
> While felines prowl and lurk
> Imprisoned by the human
> Upon the wooden perch
> Flutter for the amusement
> Add a dash of sing
> A bird inside a prison
> This is a special wing
> But me and you are similar
> We are prisoners, you see,
> Of convention, of expectation
> But you have nicer feathers
> Than me.

Quite pleased with that!

Wednesday 13.9.89

7.32 p.m.

HEARING MUM SHOUT, 'ADDY, GET me cuttlefish *siv vous plias*,' has pushed me over the edge. I am releasing the budgies – because some principles are worth more than money. They should at least have one crack at freedom. They should at least get one chance to be a real bird. I'll do it tomorrow before I go to school, and then leg it before Mum realises what I have done. I know it's a risk, but it has to be worth more than a bit of money to buy a pint of snakey B. I'll sit down the pub with a pint of tap water if I get to see Haddock.

Thursday 14.9.89

10.15 a.m. (in study room 4 at school!!)

THE BUDGIES ARE FREE!! I did it at around eight this morning. I just left the aviary door open. They didn't seem that keen at first, but then Solzhenitsyn made a run for it and they all followed. Then I made a run for it. Mum said, 'You're in a hurry this morning.' She will go mad when she realises what I have done – but it will be worth it.

9.45 p.m.

Got home tonight. At first Mum said nothing. Adnan was watching *Rocky III* on video. I went upstairs, and then I heard her coming. She was stomping so I knew I was in the shit – big time. She then just went on and on:

MUM: Why did you let the budgies out?
ME: Because it's not fair and they were miserable as sin. They have wings – they should fly.
MUM: They are bred for captivity. They won't last the night. Other birds will kill them. They are brightly coloured, cats will have them too. You have murdered them!!
ME: Better to live one day as a tiger than a lifetime as a sheep. (I was proud of this – it's an old Chinese proverb I read once.)
MUM: Stop talking claptrap, Rachel. It's better to be in a cage than ripped to shreds. You are paying for some new budgies – and if you do it again I am binning everything you care about. Books, Smurfs, everything.

Now that is just shit. I don't play with my Smurfs any more, but it took years to build up that collection, and I will probably be able to retire from selling it in a few years' time. So I suggested she think about what she is doing.

Then she slammed the door. I daren't ask her what is for tea.

All shit. But at least the birds are free.

Friday 15.9.89

7.35 p.m.

MUM FOUND HALF OF WHAT we think was Mandela dead in the garden this morning. She just said, 'Probably a sparrow hawk had him. He would have been frightened to death. And probably eaten alive.'

Perhaps it might have been the wrong thing to do, but at least Mandela had a few hours of freedom – unlike his namesake. I bet the others are thriving . . . And if they are not . . . ? Well, at least they are not stuck here like me.

Nobody is going down the pub tonight. Everyone is writing essays, and Haddock is on the night shift. The thought of him in an overall stacking shelves . . . even that is a lovely thought.

Listening to Sydney Youngblood 'If Only I Could'. I tried to make this world a better place – like he suggests – and I got shafted for it.

Saturday 16.9.89

6.45 p.m.-ish

SEEMS LIKE THE WEEKEND ACTIVITIES have dropped off a bit. Unless I am being left out of things. Could be complete paranoia but it is possible. Perhaps everyone has realised that I'm just rotten underneath all of this, and secretly I plot to nick people's boyfriends once I am thin.

I've run out of batteries in my personal stereo and can't afford to buy any more. I put the old ones on the fire to try to breathe some life into them, but no joy. Obviously can't ask Mum for any money, after the budgie affair. She is getting some new budgies next week to keep her company after Adnan has gone. More prisoners, but this time I cannot form an emotional attachment to them. There will be no names, and I am going to refuse to even feed them.

Sunday 17.9.89

9.14 p.m.

WENT TO SEE NAN TODAY and took her some dinner. I know I'm too old really to enjoy belting down Drift Road hill on my bike, but secretly I still love it. Nan admitted she doesn't like caged budgies either, and no one had them in the war so why should people want them now? I don't think she is keen on Mum being with Adnan, but she won't say anything as she is kind of dependent on Mum to look after her. We watched the Antiques Roadshow on video (well, Nan just listened because she is blind), and we played 'guess how much it's worth'. Nan thrashed me. Even with no eyes.

Came back. No one said hello to me. So just sat here in my bedroom listening to some old Motown albums, dreaming of eating one of my favourite recipes – white bread filled with Walkers prawn-cocktail crisps dipped in milk.

Beauty is apparently only skin deep according to the Temptations. Try moving from Detroit to Lincolnshire, mate. Things are different here. I shouldn't slag the music – it's the only thing getting me through at the moment.

Monday 18.9.89

7.36 p.m.

ADNAN IS FLYING BACK TOMORROW after four weeks of being here. Mum is packing his case as we speak. I know he will back, so I don't know why she is getting so emotional about it. And if I come home from school tomorrow and bloody 'Without You' by Nilsson is anywhere near the hi-fi, I will personally smash it to pieces. Mum is cooking him a special tajine tonight, and the smell of cooking olives is honestly making me want to boff big time.

In *Coronation Street*, Gail Tilsley has got a toy boy. That's the last thing I need to see, thank you. I know they are all the rage – my mum has got one!!

Tuesday 19.9.89

9.05 p.m.

ADNAN HAS GONE. I DIDN'T say goodbye to him before I went to school. I know that was bad of me, because actually he is an all right bloke. It's just that he just represents . . . crap things. Like Mum acting like a love-struck teenager. I do not want to

walk into the front room to see my mum kissing – it's
foul and pathetic when you are a woman of nearly 50.
Of course now he is gone, she is sitting on the sofa
looking mournful. OH, JUST GROW UP, WOMAN!!

And, no – I am not jealous of her before you say
anything – and I know she is thinking the same thing.
Yes, I would love a boyfriend. But unlike her, I am
going to be choosy.

It's Haddock or nothing.

Wednesday 20.9.89

11.23 p.m.

WHAT A BLOODY DREADFUL DAY. Will I ever
get on with my mum?

It was her birthday today. She was 47 – big deal –
it's hardly being 21, is it? I am totally skint – so I
made her a card from a bit of A4. I spent about ten
minutes on it and used felt tips – it was pretty impressive. She practically burst into bloody tears. Stomped
around for ages hardly saying anything, then started
whistling – which is always an indication something
very bad is up – and then EXPLODED. Usual pre-
rehearsed speech involving usual elements: me being
selfish, me being a 'taker', me not doing enough round
the house, etc., etc., etc. How materialistic is that? Sorry
I couldn't afford a gold watch, love – but I'm an A-
level student. The expectations put on me are totally
unrealistic. Get over it, woman! I'm the kid – ACT LIKE
THE PARENT.

MUM

Mum, you bore me,
But now you can't bear me.
Well . . .
The feeling is mutual –
And I'm bored now.

Thursday 21.9.89

Late

I HAVE TAKEN DOWN MY BRITISH Number Ones
Chart Wall Freeze 1960–87. I love it but it just
reminds me of the child psychiatrists. I made it when
they suggested that I needed something to focus on
when I was going loony. It took me ages to do – on
every page of a massive line of computer paper I wrote
down all the number ones and stuck in pictures of the
artists. For the pictures of '80s artists I just used my old
Smash Hits, for the '70s I used old *Jackie* annuals, and
for the '60s I cut up some of Mum's old album covers.
She would normally have gone ballistic – but I was so
mad at the time no one dared to say anything to me.

Funny to think that this time last year I was off it.
Funny to think I am still off it, but keeping it quiet.
Funny that one of the psychiatric nurses thought it was
important to tell me that Hermann Goering would have
lived in Burghley House in Stamford if the Nazis had
invaded Britain. Why do I remember that? Actually, I
remember everything about that place. Wish I didn't.

And that will now be on my medical records for ever. Everyone will always know I am a nutter. Behavioural problems. I'm just a bloody label . . .

A label written on a white board in a single room without a radio, in a place where everyone else was at least 20 years older than me. Can't think about it. It's anger that goes nowhere.

Friday 22.9.89

7.01 p.m.

BETTY SLATER WAS IN TEARS at school today. She has done something so unbelievably stupid. She had read in one of Daisy's Mills and Boon books of a character that sent flowers to herself just to make her husband jealous. Well, she thinks her boyfriend has been treating her like shit lately, so she did the same thing. She wrote the message: 'Betty, thank you for Wednesday night, M x' and had them sent to school. Of course it got back to her boyfriend – and in a jealous freak-out, he rang the florist to find out who sent them. Unfortunately the florist – who must be a man or a total bitch – told him. So the boyfriend has told everyone that she is a weirdo, and dumped her.

Betty is worried that she will never shag again. I said, 'Come on – look on the bright side. He is a total cock – and at least from it all you have a lovely bunch of flowers. It will all be forgotten in two weeks' time.' She said thanks and tried to hug me, but I was having none of that. Then she said, 'I used my dad's credit card to order the flowers. I will be in the shit.' I couldn't help her with that problem; but how come I can give advice and cheer up other people, but I can't do that with my own life? I don't understand it.

Saturday 23.9.89

11.45 p.m.

JUST GOT BACK FROM THE pub. Bethany turned up with DIETER!! Her mum is even allowing Dieter to stay in the same BED as Bethany. Hippy or what?! Dieter is tall and blond, like Henry from *Neighbours*, with a semi-crap curly perm. I don't fancy him.

He was hanging off Bethany like a bogie hanging from a nose. Everywhere she went *he* went. 'He is possessive,' she says. Just like that boyfriend Vroom she had ages ago. She must go for jealous types who can't bear the thought of being without her. Bitch.

She sat with me and Battered Sausage for a time, and Dieter was laughing at everything Battered Sausage said and I was getting well fucked off. Then HADDOCK came in!! He is always a bit off with people he doesn't know, so he just sat there looking fantastically pissed off with everything . . . with one eyebrow ten foot above the eye . . . twiddling his fingers round his pint. Everything he does my brain records, I can't help it. In a lull in the conversation he said, 'FUNKY CHICK(!) – come to the bar with me and help me get the drinks.' So I did, and we had a <u>very</u> interesting conversation:

HAD: You don't seem to be very good mates with Bethany any more.

ME: No, we don't really get on.

HAD: I can't stand her. She's a prick tease, and she always slagged you off behind your back, which I was never happy with.

(I NEARLY DIED WHEN HE SAID THAT! NOT THE FACT THAT SHE SLAGGED ME OFF, BUT THAT HE WAS PISSED OFF AT HER FOR SLAGGING ME OFF.)

ME: Yeah.

HAD: And she loves herself.

ME: She does a bit.

HAD: And she's not as good at shagging as she thinks she is. Apparently her love bites draw so much blood she's like a fucking vampire.

ME: Pardon?

HAD: She gave Battered Sausage one in the Vaults beer garden. It was so painful he nearly cried – he thought he might have to go to hospital. It looked like he had done ten rounds with Mike Tyson. Battered Sausage went on about it for weeks. But don't tell anyone I told you.

Then he winked at me and we went back to the table, where he kept grinning at me. When no one was watching he was gnashing his teeth trying to make me laugh. Then his girlfriend came in and he went and . . .

Oh God, I love him so much it feels like the cramp you get in the arch of your foot. It is painful.

I was left with Dieter, Bethany and Battered Sausage. At the end of the night when I went to go, Dieter went to give me a continental two-kiss goodbye. Bethany said, 'Don't do that, Dieter, she doesn't like being kissed – she's a bit of a frigid one,' then quickly said, 'Only joking.' No she wasn't. Battered Sausage found this hilarious – until I said, 'What's that on your neck. Looks like an injury. Bethany, can you see it? Do you know what it is?' There was nothing there but they both shut up. Dieter looked confused. I may be fat and frigid, but I can come up with nasty shit if I need to.

When I left, Haddock winked. Haddock makes me unfrigid with an eye.

Sunday 24.9.89

6.25 p.m.

MUM JUST CAME IN AND said, 'Where has your number one wall freeze gone? I liked that.' I said, 'I have taken it down because it reminds me of having a nervous breakdown.' Mum got angry and said, 'You have got to stop living in the past, move on from your problems, and stop harping on about your nervous breakdown!!' I said, 'THAT IS WHAT I AM TRYING TO DO.'

You can't win. I am not allowed to mention the psychiatric ward, and we all know why. She feels guilty that I went in there. Not my problem to deal with.

I have to write an essay on Caliban in *The Tempest*. He is the ugly, misunderstood, monster character. I should get a fucking A grade for this.

Monday 25.9.89

7.32 p.m.

WELL, I HAD TO PUT the A-level work first yesterday, but now it's time for a rather massive . . .

EMOTIONAL UPDATE!

Right, here we go:

Haddock

We have so much in common. I just feel there is a genuine connection there. But my 'fat cloak' means I am in the Fourth Division of women: he is a Liverpool – I am relegated. He loves his girlfriend – I love him and I am very fond of her, but they are always so wrapped up in each other and *always* going through a rough patch. I have been instructed not to talk to her about him. But when I think about it, no one comes close to the way I feel about him. He is just different to all other men I know. Oh, this is hopeless. I can't stop thinking about him. But there is no point thinking about him.

Battered Sausage

Continues to mystify me as ever. I mean, at the moment he is being pretty gorgeous to me – such a love. But how long will it last? And he has a real tendency to turn into a right wanker when he gets drunk. He hit someone the other day and they threatened to get the coppers on him. He got out of it with a smooth apology; but how can someone who is capable of being so caring, funny and generally extremely lovable be such an utterly despicable bastard in the same breath? I mean – which one is he really?

I am too fat. I need to lose weight. I have potential, but it is wrapped under mounds and mounds of lard. Loads of people say I have nice hair and a nice face, but what use is that when I look like the bloody Marsh-mallow Man out of *Ghostbusters*?

Really looking forward to the party on Saturday. My dress is sorted. Hanging up there, it looks huge – ginor-mous black velvet bodice and silk purple skirt. And then I think, 'It's my body that fits in that – that's my shape.' That fits to every roll of fat I have, and I hate me – I hate me.

But even seeing that does not stop me coming home and eating a Walnut Whip and a packet of Twiglets.

Tuesday 26.9.89

IT'S ALL COME OUT TODAY. I go down the phone box to ring Mort, and Mum is already in there. I ask her what she is doing, and she tells me she is making enquiries. Turns out Mum IS going to try to get Adnan into the country permanently. Thanks a bunch. In my A-level year, she is moving in a Moroccan bodybuilder who she has known for all of five minutes. She just leaps from one husband to the next, like . . . like . . . WHY CAN'T SHE JUST BE SINGLE FOR FIVE MINUTES??!!

What was I meant to do when she told me? Be delighted?! She says stuff like, 'It's my time now – you are nearly 18.' BUT IT'S ME WHO SHOULD BE DOING STUFF LIKE THIS! I should be having exotic affairs!

The good news is that this process will take ages, even if they do get married. The immigration service is apparently really strict. I hope they are. I'm just a bit worried because that South African runner Zola Budd got a British passport just like that! If I remember rightly, technically Adnan is an athlete. I hope they don't fast-track him or something.

Wednesday 27.9.89

Late (too fucked off to even read the clock)

MUM HAS SPENT MOST OF the late afternoon and evening going down the phone box or filling in forms trying to get Adnan in the country. All day at school everybody was talking about relationship troubles. I am so sick of being alone.

Everywhere I am a gooseberry.

BIG, FAT, DIRTY GOOSEBERRY

Big, fat, dirty gooseberry
Juicy, good for a laugh, makes the set
While the strawberries go out and play
It spends the night alone
Don't pity the gooseberry
Understand it
Hold it, nurse it, hurt it not

Don't leave it alone on the plate
Even though it's a big, fat, dirty gooseberry
Like the strawberries
It needs the cream of your love too.

Thursday 28.9.89

6.05 p.m.
JUST WHEN YOU THOUGHT THINGS couldn't get any worse in my life, there is a rumour going round that the school nurse is coming next week. And you know what that means: nit check, teeth check, how are your periods? and then those bloody clinical scales will be out. The ones where she moves the little thingy up and down to try to balance it. I am telling you now – I am finding out when she is coming in and then I am faking illness big time.

I can't face being given that pie chart again. The one that has 'eat lots of these' and 'eat less of these'. The 'eat less of these' section is full of the only things I have got to look forward to at the moment.

10.15 p.m.
Just watched *Black Adder Goes Forth*. Can I just say Ben Elton is my bloody hero for ever. If it wasn't for him I would still think voting Tory was OK. And he is piss funny.

Friday 29.9.89

11.10 p.m.

FOR SOME REASON I HAVE developed the most humongous crush on Rowan Atkinson (but only when he is wearing a WWI uniform). I don't know where the hell that has come from!

You know – sometimes with Battered Sausage when he looks at me I feel weird. Like tonight in the pub he was sitting on my knee and just . . . all the eye contact. I could read everything – and yet nothing all at the same time. I wonder if blokes go home and go over and over and over conversations in their head? Do they wonder what really goes on underneath everything? I wonder if there are pages and pages written about me? I mean – blokes must wonder, surely?

Big party tomorrow night. Excited but also bricking it as I am wearing a dress and will be looking very feminine for me.

Saturday 30.9.89

2 p.m.

I HAVE JUST TRIED ON MY outfit. Oh God, there is all this overhang of flab over the bodice – it looks like I have side tits. I will have to put a jacket over the top. Just tried some make-up too. I always look ridiculous – I am too pale. Blue eye shadow makes me look like I have been beaten up. Brown eye shadow makes me look like I am a member of the living dead and haven't slept for three centuries.

Oh, you know what, Diary? Forget it! I am going to put the Beatmasters and Betty Boo on full blast, and I am just going to enjoy tonight. I am going to bop till it hurts and have a laugh. I can't lose six stone before tonight, so I might as well just bloody enjoy it. With a little help from the bottle of Baileys Mum has hidden in the larder behind the Weetabix! HA! I have spotted it!!

Sunday 1.10.89

11.33 a.m.

JUST WOKE UP! THE PARTY at RAF Wittering in the Officers' Club was completely and utterly brilliant. Vodka and lime was only 40p! I have never felt so rich in my life. I know there's a chance you could die in a war if you are in the RAF but the subsidised bar is excellent. At the end of the night, though, our taxi was an hour and a half late. Still, everyone was having a laugh outside, near the model of the Harrier jump-jet. Ryan Bates groped me! It was only in a jokey way, though. He's a bit of a weirdo. His dad wants him to be a vicar – but after seeing him strip nearly naked last night for seemingly no reason at all, I don't think he is cut out for it.

New torture, though. Big thanks to the Bangles who created 'Eternal Flame' – the new choice for the Leo Mobile Disco end song. Thank God for toilets. Thank God for a cubicle to hide in when the smooch pile of songs come on. Thank God for graffiti – I am happy to read stuff like 'Vanessa is a slag' and 'Bros are toss' when I am avoiding being left on the edge of the dance floor like the world's biggest walrus.

Going down pub tonight. Principally on the hope of seeing Haddock. I have withdrawal symptoms.

Monday 2.10.89

7.50 p.m.

FEEL VERY BAD AT THE moment. Home is very mixed up. Mum is obsessed with immigration forms and legal issues and love . . . and I just feel empty. When I write here, though, I feel better.

So, last night was brilliant – had the best time with Haddock ever. AND HE WALKED ME HOME. We were having a laugh, and he said a few significant things:

1) 'I don't like people getting to know me.'
2) 'I would be really lonely without my girlfriend.'
3) Something along the lines of 'I'm not Haddock without her.'
4) 'I really like you.' (Felt sick when he said that.)
5) His fit rugby mate said to him, 'Rae is a good laugh and a good dancer' – but Haddock didn't want to tell me that because he thought it might offend me.

So he drops me off at my front door, and then I can't sleep. I just was lying there last night listening to the Janis Ian album and wishing. I'm doing it now.

Tuesday 3.10.89

8.10 p.m.

THE SCHOOL NURSE IS AT school tomorrow with her bloody scales – Daisy overheard two teachers organising lessons around it. So today I have been building up the story with Mum. I haven't eaten anything – yes, it's a sacrifice, but it makes it more real. I've also said hardly anything. If you are loud, everyone knows that there is something wrong when you do this. Mum has just been up to ask, 'Are you OK?' I croaked, 'I am fine.' If I had said, 'I am feeling poorly,' she would have sussed it. I have also got a hot-water bottle to put on my forehead so I can fake a temperature! You have to build it up layer by layer. Tomorrow morning I will put a bit of talcum powder on my face. HA!!! I am going to bed now. Yes, it is early – but it adds to the lie. I have even turned the music off. She will think that there is a major problem.

Wednesday 4.10.89

3.10 p.m.

MUM FELL FOR IT THIS morning. I rubbed my head like crazy, she felt it and said, 'You better stay off today. I think you might have the flu coming.' She then said, 'You haven't got a test or anything, have you?' I could answer honestly 'No!' – BRILLIANT!!

She went out at about 8.30 a.m. and ever since then I have just been sitting on the sofa watching schools' programmes. You can learn shit-loads off telly! This morning I have learnt about escarpments in *The Geography Programme*; how a small town like Thetford in Norfolk can market itself as a tourist resort in *Near and Far*; how milk is bottled in *Stop, Look and Listen*; and how heat makes metal expand in *Experiment*. I turned *Good Health* off as I have seen the episode about bad footwear 'blockaboots' about 20 times since the early '80s. In *Rainbow*, Zippy was still a twat – so I turned that off too.

I have also just made a new compilation tape. I have called it 'Fish I

Love' – AKA HADDOCK!!! At the moment here's what is on it:

'THE BELLE OF ST MARK' – SHEILA E. It is so Haddock's song! It's about a bloke who is brilliantly good-looking but actually doesn't think that much of himself. Everything fits.

'ACE OF SPADES' – MOTÖRHEAD. Haddock loves this song.

'CONVOY' – C. W. McCALL. He always put this on the Vaults jukebox.

'HOLD YOUR HEAD UP' – ARGENT. Always on the Vaults jukebox too. It goes on for ever, and is '70s rock shit, but it brings back good memories.

That's it at the moment.

I'll have to have another day off tomorrow to make it look less suspicious.

Thursday 5.10.89

4.40 p.m.

MUM FELL FOR IT AGAIN this morning. She is
currently making me a stew downstairs. I feel a
bit guilty as she is being dead nice.

Getting a bit bored now – so WEIRD!! Just doing
fortune telling with *The Guinness Book of British Hit
Singles*: ask the book a question, then turn to any page.
Whatever the song title is, that's the answer to your
question.

Like I just said to it, 'Haddock – the future?' and it
said, 'MADNESS – "It must Be Love."' Honest to God!
Total truth. I swear on my cat's life.

I also asked about:

A LEVELS – 'A Sign of the Times' by Petula Clark.
BATTERED SAUSAGE – 'Apache' by the Shadows.
    (OK, this is a bit hit and miss.)
MY LIFE SONG – 'I've Been in Love Before' by the
    Cutting Crew.

Actually it should be 'I've Been in Love Before but No
One Has Been in Love With Me' by the sodding Cutting
Crew.

273

Friday 6.10.89

6.16 p.m.

MUM THOUGHT I MIGHT AS well have the weekend to recover. I feel like mega crap now because she has just bought me a new pair of shoes from Stu's Shoes on the market, and unbelievably for her – they are really nice. Feel like such a cow.

I had a totally classic letter from Fig this morning too. The thing I love about Fig is he is sweet and he really bothers. Polytechnic sounds like a right laugh, but I still can't imagine Fig as a chartered surveyor. He is just too much of a laugh for a boring job. He'll never be able to do all his impressions if he is having to be serious. I can't imagine working either. Wonder if you can draw the dole for life? Probably not, with Thatcher in charge.

Mum just came up and said, 'I am really proud of you, Rachel – still doing your schoolwork even though you don't feel very well.' Couldn't admit that I've only been writing my diary . . . YES, YES, YES. I feel like a total shit.

I need to make a gradual recovery for tomorrow night. though. Can't miss a Saturday at the pub.

Saturday 7.10.89

5.35 p.m.

I HAVE JUST SAID TO MUM that I think I may benefit from some fresh air – I may take a walk. She said, 'Oh, you are not going down the pub, are you?' I said, 'I might

– just for one.' She said, 'If you end up with pleurisy, don't moan to me!' I said, 'I won't! I'll only have one.'

Can't wait to see everyone tonight. I feel like I have been on an island cut off from everything!!

11.45 p.m.

BLOODY HELL!!

Bethany came up to me last night just before she left the pub. Dieter was with her, and she said, 'Well, Rae – I am about to make your life a whole lot easier. Goodbye, and have a nice life.' What does that mean??!! Is she eloping to Switzerland with Dieter? I am gagging to find out but she wafted out before I could question her more.

I only said a few words to Haddock tonight. Him and his girlfriend were mooning over each other. He told me he was working so hard because he wanted to get me a good marriage dowry, and then he said I was a bargain at the price. Oh – that man! Those big bloody eyes. When I see him appear from behind the jukebox my heart leaps ten foot in the air – and it doesn't matter what song is on – he floats in. Tonight that rubbish old song 'A Pub With No Beer' by Slim Dusty came on, and the atmosphere felt charged even with that on.

But I have to pretend I don't care.

The RAF Wittering party groper Ryan Bates was out tonight. He is a laugh, but he is odd.

We keep having conversations that go nowhere. For example:

RYAN: Do you like going to the cinema?
ME: What's the punchline to that one, then?

RYAN: No – I really want to know.
ME (SARCY QUEEN): Yes, of course you do!
RYAN: Sort it out.

What a knob! He must think I'm thick. I'm not setting up his jokes for him! I am no one's straight man.

Battered Sausage and I have got a lot closer since he messed up his A levels. I wish people wouldn't say, 'Here comes the biggest lad in Stamford,' as he takes it as the world's biggest compliment and his head swells. He is, in his own inimitable vocal style, knocking off his bird. I don't care – girlfriends come and go. Friendships are around for ever.

When I sit and think about it, this is the compensation I give myself for never getting action: I am adopting the spiritual high ground. But I really would prefer to be having temporary low-down and dirty encounters with men that did only last a couple of months, but who cares!!!

Sunday 8.10.89

11.05 p.m.
I HAVE A STINKING COLD. WE did karma in RE in the fifth year, and I can now tell you it exists. I have got a nose like Rudolph, and Mum keeps saying, 'It was that pub that did it.' But I am going to school tomorrow. I need to know what is happening with Bethany. This could change everything.

I taped the charts tonight and I have to say it was full of shit. Richard Marx 'Right Here Waiting' is a bloody dirge. Milli Vanilli 'Girl, I'm Gonna Miss You' is just soppy crap. I compare it to, say, five years ago, and pop has lost its way. I know it has.

Monday 9.10.89

4.02 p.m.

BETHANY IS LEAVING STAMFORD – THIS IS POSSIBLY THE BEST NEWS EVER.

She has to, as her dad has got a new job or something . . . ANYWAY – SHE IS GOING!!!

And you know what that means – no more worry. No more being uncomfortable. NO MORE BETHANY.

THE DEPARTURE OF THE BETRAYER

Goodbye, then, the betrayer.
EVERY TIME you took and stole
And made the men I loved a prize
(Exploiting your much smaller size).
And now you are gone my field is clear
I will get those I hold dear.
To demean me was your intention
You've lost now – I am the centre of attention.

HA!!

It was brilliant at school today. The thought of no more HER being a sarcy cow is brilliant. AND the school nurse isn't due in again until next year, AND I missed a surprise history timed essay. It has just been superb today.

Just reading back . . . I am beginning to think I may
have been a bit of a prat over Haddock. I mean – he's
just a bloke, isn't he? Nobody must ever find this diary.
All the bits about him are bloody embarrassing.

Tuesday 10.10.89

11.06 p.m.
I WASN'T A PRAT OVER HADDOCK.
    He is a one-off. Different. Worth thinking about,
worth wishing about. My love for him is real and true
– I can't imagine a time when I don't think about him.
I can't imagine a time when I don't beg for the
moments when I might bump into him.
We played a brilliant game at school today: 'How much
to shag . . . ?' which quite simply means how much
would you have to get paid to do it with certain men:

- Compo from *Last of the Summer Wine* – £1
  million.
- Prince Charles – £10,000. None of us can understand what Diana is doing with him, apart from
  the money.
- Dirty Den from *EastEnders* – actually only about
  £1,000. He is old but he 'has something'.
- Dave Lee Travis – £100,000. It's the beard.
- Cliff Richard – we all decided no point specu-
  lating. He wouldn't do it until he was married
  anyway.

Wednesday 11.10.89

5.16 p.m.

FOLLOWING ON FROM YESTERDAY, a great conversation today: 'How much would you pay to do . . . ?' How much money would you give (if money was no option) certain blokes to do it with you? Not just a shag – say, a weekend in a country hotel where they were dead nice to you. It's unbelievable who people fancy!!

- Marti Pellow from Wet Wet Wet – everybody agreed at least £50,000. We all think he would be dead sweet.
- Jason Donovan – at least £40K. But he might love himself a bit too much. And we all think he would never get over being with Kylie, even though he says he never has been with her.
- Morrissey – £10K. Might get on your tits all weekend if he is on a downer.
- Phillip Schofield – £60K. Best to lose your virginity to. He would be dead sweet.
- Bruce Willis – £30K, from the people who have just seen him in *Moonlighting*. The people who have seen him in *Die Hard* reckon he is worth more than that.
- Johnathan Ross from *The Last Resort* – I said this one! Even with a lisp which would make most blokes geeky there is just something about him. I would pay £30K.

279

- Michael J. Fox – £10K. Cute but too short.
- DC Carver from *The Bill*. Daisy said she would pay £7K, but the rest of us say he needs to pay us for a weekend.

For the record: Haddock – I would rob every bank in Britain.

Thursday 12.10.89

IALWAYS HAVE TO PLAY THE joker. I always go into that role when I am in a group. I hate that in me. At school today Jasmine dared me to go into the lunch queue twice. I had four fishcakes, two scoops of creamed potatoes, peas, cheese and biscuits, and then Angel Delight. Did it for a laugh – but then felt sick all the way through double history. Scoured the room – full of pretty girls with futures that just burst with boyfriends and big dreamy wedding days, and then there's me – Humpty Dumpty perched on the chair. Humpty Rae on the wall, Humpty Rae had a big fall. And NO BUGGER HELPED HER UP, THEY JUST HAD A BLOODY GOOD LAUGH.
   Probably.

Friday 13.10.89

UNBELIEVABLE . . . MUM CAME IN TONIGHT, threw a Rosemary Conley book at me and said, 'You are fat – lose some weight.' Right, dear . . . I am going to, and I will show you – just to spite you. Then

I'll be the one with the boyfriends, and you will be bricking yourself that I may get up the duff and never go to your sodding precious university.

Saturday 14.10.89

8.02 p.m.

WELL, IT'S A SATURDAY NIGHT but I am going nowhere. Terrible day. Went to buy some jeans from Sevens. Very sweet young assistant kept getting bigger and bigger sizes. She went downstairs to the men's section – eventually got one pair that fitted. I am a 38 waist. 38. 38. 38. 38. Huge. If a 14 is a 28-inch waist, then I am a . . . SIZE 24!!

Got them. Went along the High Street in a daze. I think someone's mum said hello to me outside Tesco but I was off it. You know when you can feel you are about to sob and sob? Saw the old bookshop Staniland and headed upstairs to room 4 'Religion' because no one goes in there – sat in the leather chair and just cried and cried. Just could not believe I have got this big. Must have been there for about half an hour. Thought I better buy something so went downstairs with the Ladybird *Book of Ballet* – it was only 70p. Bloke there with the beard is so sweet. I love that bookshop.

Now back in my room and staying here. Thinking about what to do and how to do it. It will take me ages to become ONE OF THEM – the skinny ones. We would have left school by that time. So sat here, resigned to hoping that one man can see through it all, and hoping that man is Haddock.

I think Mum realised I was upset because she announced that we would have a Chinese tonight. Hence I am writing this with a battered bit of pork in my gob, feeling a little bit better.

Sunday 15.10.89

5.10 p.m.

ANOTHER BORING SUNDAY. STARTING A diet tomorrow. I have to. I can't be this fat.

It seems logical to me that like an addict I must clear temptation from my way. So today while Mum was at Nan's, I cleaned out the cupboards. All fat gone. Crisps, Lincoln biscuits, Clubs, cakes, K. P. Skips – EVERY-THING GONE.

Keep looking at my jeans. They are huge. I know I am fat but I must have the opposite of anorexia because every time I look in the mirror I know I'm fat – but not _that_ HUGE.

I must see myself smaller. God, I have to get thinner.

Monday 16.10.89

6.45 p.m.

MUM CAME HOME LAST NIGHT and went mad about binned food. God knows why, because half the stuff we get we get cheap. Mum got eight Mr Kipling French Fancies the other day for 12p, just because the packet was ripped. It's for the best.

Of course Mum decided to have chips tonight, but I

saw through it and resisted. But when she wasn't looking I sneaked in just one chip. I swear Mum could smell curry sauce on my breath this morning. She set a trap and I fell into it.

11.22 p.m.
That's probably a bit paranoid – she probably just fancied chips. I have to be less of a nutter.

Tuesday 17.10.89

HAVING TO FILL OUT THE UCCA and PCAS forms for entry to universities and polytechnics. I'm pretty set on American studies and I quite fancy Exeter University – as the prospectus makes it look very green, and there is a very good-looking man holding a test tube on about page 5. If that's the standard of man you can expect, then yummy! PLUS Devon cream teas – EXTRA YUMMY! At the end of the day – I can't lie – Battered Sausage is going there, so I'm guaranteed at least one friend.

Wednesday 18.10.89

10.02 p.m.
HAVE TO SAY, I HAVE bullshitted massively about hobbies and stuff on my university application forms, as my only hobbies are sitting in the pub talking crap with my friends. Have said 'fell walking' (there's loads of potholes in Mountbatten Avenue) and 'horse-riding' (this is what I would like to do and intend to do).

Have also said 'current affairs', as I am very aware of what goes on in the world. Too aware. Worry about everything. Worry that one day some Russian bloke might accidentally fall asleep on a button, launch 60,000 nuclear missiles and start World War III. Fuck the diet – we might all be dead tomorrow.

In the pub tonight me and Dobber were having a chat when Ryan the RAF Wittering groper came to join us. He must fancy Dobber because we couldn't get rid of him. He started possibly the dullest conversation about university application forms and where we were both going. He is so insensitive! When I said I liked the sound of Exeter, he said:

RYAN: Oh, that's a bit far away from everything, isn't it? It will be hard to get there.
ME: Thanks, mate, for that. Where are you going?
RYAN: Leeds. That's miles away from Exeter. Are you sure you want to go there?
ME: Errrr – yeah!
RYAN: Not a lot there, and it's full of the green-welly brigade. Not very you!
ME: I'll bear your comments in mind, guru.

He didn't say to Dobber that her college in Canterbury just had a big cathedral in it and nothing else. WHY PICK ON MINE???

Like I've said before . . . knob.

Thursday 19.10.89

Late

THIS COUNTRY IS JUST CRAP. The Guildford Four have been released after being in prison for 15 sodding WRONG years. All they were was Irish, in the wrong place at the wrong time, and that bloody sums this place up. If you are slightly different, if your face doesn't fit, they judge you and consign you and throw away the fucking key.

They never, ever stop to think that THEY might be wrong, that THEY are making a mistake. Don't get me wrong, I haven't been the victim of a massive miscarriage of justice – I'm not saying that – BUT I know what it's like to be stinking judged before people have even bothered to find out what you are about. They have boxed me off into the ugly group even before I have opened my gob.

SOCIETY IS SHIT.

Friday 20.10.89

JUST BEEN TO SEE *Dead Poets Society* with Dobber. Roared my bloody eyes out. Brilliant film. Really weird to see Mork from Mork and Mindy do something serious, but it was really good. It was all about feeling repressed in private schools – I know how that feels. One of the main characters kills himself because his dad

285

won't let him be an actor. Exactly the same thing with me. I want to be a radio or TV presenter, but apparently I have to get my A levels first!! WHY??!! Just because she hasn't got any, Mum thinks A levels and degrees are the be all and end all. Has Madonna got them? No. Has Simon Mayo got them? No – AND HE DOES THE BLOODY RADIO 1 BREAKFAST SHOW!

Saturday 21.10.89

10.02 p.m.

DAD CAME TO VISIT TODAY. I haven't seen him for ages. Of course he doesn't come to the house, so I have to go and meet him at Blackstone's Club. It feels like the end of the world, with old men drinking bitter, playing dominoes and darts. Fantastic crusty rolls, though, with cheese and onion, AND they do scampi-flavour fries. It's incredible the amount of women that ring up and ask if their husbands are there – and the barman lies and says they aren't. These women must have dreadful lives. No wonder Mum divorced Dad after all those years, if this is what happened. At least I am old enough now to go in the pub with him. I used to have to wait outside in the car park. There was a load of us actually, with a packet of crisps and an old-fashioned Coke bottle with straw, and Dad coming out every half-hour with a refill. Is that a good memory, or a bad one? I can't remember.

Sunday 22.10.89

10.30 p.m.

MY RELATIONSHIP WITH MY DAD is so weird. He's not like a dad – he is like a mate. I can't ever imagine him telling me off. Mind you, he did make a few comments today like 'You're getting like your mum, Rach' or 'You've put on a lot of weight – it's not good.' I'll be honest – it's hard to take his health advice too seriously. He said to me after I had had one single vodka and lime, 'Mind that stuff, Rach – it will rot your liver.' He said this without any irony, as he sank his sixth pint of the day. It was only about 2 p.m.

Monday 23.10.89

9.40 p.m.

JUST BEEN DOWN TO DOBBER'S house. She has some scales in her bathroom. I couldn't resist. After the waist size 38 I just wanted to know how bad I had got, without some doctor there shouting at me. Weighed myself. Now fair enough, I'd just had spaghetti bolognaise when I did, but I weighed nearly 14 and a half stone!!!

Yes, 14 and a half stone.

I suspected this was huge, so looked it up in my mum's height/weight chart. I am in the bright-red sector – VERY FAT. I should be a maximum of ten stone six!!!

So down. I've come home and gone to bed with a Wagon Wheel.

10.33 p.m.
Mum just came in before she went to bed. Spoke to her about my weight. How did I ever get this way – nearly 15 stone? And then she said, 'Well, just think about what you have eaten today.'

six slices of toast with Marmite and Flora
crisps (onion rings) dunked in a tub of Primula cheese
jacket potato with cheese
two make-your-own Morrison's hamburgers
spaghetti bolognaise
cheese and crisps at Dobber's
and a Wagon Wheel just then.

I said, 'But I walked for 20 minutes – I thought that was enough.' She said, 'Not even a marathon runner could eat that and burn it off.'
What's the point?

Wednesday 25.10.89

11.45 p.m.
I KNOW YOU ARE PROBABLY BORED with this, but HADDOCK, HADDOCK, HADDOCK! I had a complete attack of adoration in the pub tonight. He is SO gorgeous but seems really, really quite screwed up to hell. Apparently, according to Haddock's girlfriend, he doesn't regard himself as attractive at all. I have heard

this before but I just can't believe it. He is so bloody handsome and charming – he is the epic slice! She wanted to tell me more but she wouldn't because of loyalty to him. But I think some bad stuff has gone on.

Yes, yes, yes . . . I DO feel like the world's biggest bitch BUT there is no chance. They could split up and I would be the last woman on his list to snog, I am telling you now. So I keep all this to myself and that's where it stays and that's why it doesn't matter and why I can still be friends with her.

I told Haddock's girlfriend that I was thinking about a serious diet. She said, 'Don't bother, Rae – you are lovely the way you are.' She is sweet – but she's not right, is she? I'm not.

Thursday 26.10.89

7.35 p.m.

YOU KNOW, OTHER WOMEN LIKE fat women because we are 'safe'. If I lost loads of weight, I KNOW I would find that a lot of so-called mates would sort of fall out with me, even if I didn't do anything bad. I've seen it happen to Mum – when she lost all the weight years ago people said to her stuff like, 'You've changed,' and, 'You're not as much fun as you used to be.' I remember the woman from Anne Close stopping her on Broad Street and saying, 'You've lost enough now. Any more and you'll look gaunt.' It actually means, 'Any more and you'll be thinner than me'!

If I lost weight, everything would change. I couldn't be friends with Haddock any more. Because if he likes me, AND he wants to do me, well, that's basically marriage!

Friday 27.10.89

Late

I SUPPOSE I MUST BE happy, because I am not unhappy. Sometimes, you know, I feel so left out – and out of everything. It's the old 'end of the night' syndrome. Like tonight – I don't really think Haddock likes me now, you know? He didn't give me the neck squeeze that he normally does. I'm trying to make myself dislike him. Well . . . not dislike him, but . . . trying to dissuade my emotions. When I do speak to Haddock I just feel like I am intruding on his time with his girlfriend.

Sometimes, you know, I just want to curl up and see if anyone notices I'm not there.

But I know time is short. Moping around wastes time. I always get attacks of paranoia. Big deal. Fed up of worrying what people think of me and what they feel for me.

But I wonder what they do feel for me, though. Am I loved? Perhaps in somebody's bedroom I am secretly fancied?

Probably not.

Saturday 28.10.89

11.45 p.m.

NOTHING MUCH HAPPENED AT THE pub tonight (Haddock was working). But Mum really annoyed me when Battered Sausage came to pick me up. She started to have a real laugh with him – showing him pictures of Adnan, and making him cups of tea. She made Battered Sausage get the giggles – so I asked her how her hot flushes were. She soon got the message.

Apparently Bethany has gone for a study visit in Switzerland to Dieter's college. Sex visit more like. No doubt she will be sucking his neck off up a mountain while he yodels.

Sunday 29.10.89

4.30 p.m.

RIGHT, I AM JUST GOING to write this. I have been thinking about this all day and I have been listening to *What's Going On* by Marvin Gaye, and I just want to purge this down.

I am happy to play the big fat comic joker cow because it comes easy, and losing the weight would take too much hard work, and in the end I just can't risk not being loved by people. Pathetic, but true. I'm worried if I get thin no one will like me any more. But then I'm worried that if I stay fat no man will ever love me.

I'm such a total twat. Please believe me – I know I am.

7.10 p.m.
JIVE BUNNY ARE NUMBER ONE AGAIN WITH A DIFFERENT PILE OF MONTAGE SONG VOMIT SHIT. WHO IS BUYING THIS UTTER TOSS?

Monday 30.10.89

THERE IS A BIG HALLOWEEN party tomorrow. It was the talk of the school today. It's being held by the fittest boy in our year and seemingly only really, really gorgeous girls have been invited, and they are keeping quiet as to what is going on. This is because it is apparently going to turn into an orgy. The dress code is 'vicars, tarts or gorgeous ghouls'. There is a lot of talk about garter belts and stockings. The people who have been invited are walking around like Miss World. Everyone else is calling them slags. You can't crash it – apparently the bloke has got someone on the door rating the girls out of ten!! This is what you are dealing with – public-school wankers with small cocks who will end up running accountancy companies, shagging their secretaries, becoming Tory MPs or doing all three at once . . . And half of them are PIG ugly.

Yes, of course, part of me is slightly pissed off I wasn't invited, but it is hardly a surprise.

Tuesday 31.10.89

9.20 p.m.

DEPRESSING TO THINK IF I went trick-or-treating now people would regard me as a beggar. I don't want to grow up. We have had a few kids round. They always look pissed off when you give them sweets and not cash – especially because Mum buys cheapo versions of everything, including Tesco's version of a Club biscuit. But they might as well realise now that life is shit, Father Christmas isn't real, and adults rip you off.

Funny to think right now some of my friends are wearing stockings and doing who knows what. Might as well be from another planet.

Mum asked me today if Jive Bunny had an album out! God help us all.

Wednesday 1.11.89

7.02 p.m.

ALL THE GORGEOUS-GHOUL PARTY girls were back in school today and keeping themselves to themselves and whispering in corners looking serious. All the information we can get out of them is that the party went on quite late and everyone was 'bobbing apples'. This is obviously code for some sort of sex thing but we can't work out what. We think it might be something to do with oral sex as apparently that makes

293

you bob up and down, but no one can be sure. A few people are going to ask their boyfriends at the boys' school if they know anything about it.

Thursday 2.11.89

9.40 p.m.

MORT'S 18TH BIRTHDAY. Had no money to buy a present so made her a card and bought a with-drawn-for-sale children's picture book from the library for 15p called Millicent. It's about a woman who feeds pigeons in Sydney in Australia. I customised it with cartoons about me and people at school. I was quite proud of it actually, and Mort was creasing herself – so I think she liked it. She got a great birthday present later, though . . . We all did!

We found out what 'bobbing apples' is code for. It's code for . . . BOBBING APPLES!! Apparently Mr Gorgeous Boy's parents decided to stay at home at the last minute and organise some 'silly party games with a few drinks'! He was left with his mates – and a load of his parents' mates – sticking their heads in buckets of water. BRILLIANT!! The orgy did not take place, and he is a social outcast. No wonder the gorgeous girls were looking serious – they spent most of yesterday working out how to keep this information to themselves. TOO LATE, DEARS – we know the only thing you experi-enced at that party was soggy hair!!

Friday 3.11.89

11.49 p.m.

MUM HAS PISSED ME OFF majorly twice in less than 12 hours today. Firstly, this morning I was woken up by the theme tune to *Hawaii FIVE-0*. Mum has bought the new Jive Bunny single and was playing it loud. I couldn't hear Simon Mayo over the RACKET OF TOTAL SHIT. Shouldn't it be me playing crap music loudly?? Then, as I was going to the pub tonight, admittedly looking a bit scruffy, she shouted at the top of her voice, 'Penny for the guy.' Ha, ha. This is the '80s, dear – you are allowed to have messed-up hair. It's called 'come to bed/just done it' hair these days. That's what I would like mine to be – but the fact is, I can't be arsed to comb it.

Saturday 4.11.89

I CAN'T WORK THIS ONE OUT.
I am totally freaked out and I am shaking so much I can hardly write.

Tonight everyone was hugely pissed. It was just one of those nights. And in the Vaults pub garden somebody had some sparklers and we were all playing with them and having a laugh. Haddock was there, and just to make him laugh I was drawing the shape of a bum in the air with a sparkler, and he was drawing a cock, and we were having a right laugh. He was on great

form, but then he had a couple more beers and went
quiet and weird. He then dragged me to the window
ledge on the stairs between the front and back. He was
very pissed. He was acting so weird, and then he goes:

HAD: There is just something I want to say . . .
ME: Yeah!
HAD: I know what . . .
ME (I was laughing at this stage – I thought he
was winding me up): What?!
HAD (DEADLY serious): I know what you think
underneath it all, and I don't think it will always
be like this.
ME: Pardon??
HAD: Things will get brilliant, I think. For both of us.
And things could change like that . . . (Clicks his
fingers.)

Then he just legged it out of the pub.
    Battered Sausage came up to me and said, 'Oh, what
have you said to him now?' I said, 'Nothing – should you
go after him?' and Battered Sausage said, 'No. Come and
see this bloke out here – he reckons he can make a
rocket shoot from his backside with a fart and a match.'
    'Things will get brilliant. For both of us. And things
could change like that . . .'
    What does he mean? Does he mean the fact that we
were so pissed? Does he mean how totally crap our lives
are? Does he mean how we feel about ourselves? What????
    He looked at me – like – his eyes are like lasers
piercing into you. I feel I should know instinctively
what he is on about, but I don't.

I'm not being superficial – but he is horny as hell when he is intense.

Actually, that does sound superficial, but believe me it's true.

Sunday 5.11.89

4.23 p.m.

CAN'T STOP THINKING ABOUT LAST night. It's going to be weird when I see him again.

I am just full with regrets. Big fat doner-kebab regrets. Could write loads tonight about rejection, love and divine retribution, but more earthly issues such as GCSE maths retake loom tomorrow, so sleep is called for. Who wants to be arsed with fractions when you could be thinking about things that really matter? Like what Haddock meant last night, and Haddock's magnificent arse.

FIREWORKS

Haddock is like a rocket
Exploding in my brain,
My fat puts out his sparkle
Like a firework by the rain.

I wish for bangs and whooshes
For desire that makes me thud,
I have to settle for a sparkler
And a cheese and bean jacket spud.

8.47 p.m.

Apparently something is kicking off in Germany. I don't know the full details, but East Germans are rioting. According to one of the hippies in the front bar of the Vaults, this 'could be it'. Oh please God – my head is going mad with this. I feel I need to do all the things I need to do to stop war and I know it's mad but I know I will have to do them tonight. Touch everything. Pray 30 times until I say it perfectly. Check everything.

For the record – I love my mum, I'm sorry that we don't get on at the moment, and my biggest regret is that I didn't do it with Haddock. Pathetic but true.

Monday 6.11.89

5.50 p.m.

MATHS GCSE RETAKE WENT OK. Filled in all the gaps. But you don't need GCSE maths to be a TV presenter, so frankly I don't care.

Talked to Mort about what Haddock meant. Mort said, 'Are you sure Haddock doesn't like you?' I said, 'Well, of course he likes me – I am like a sister to him, remember? I can't help but wonder, though – if I was slim, would things be different?' Mort said, 'Well, why don't you lose a little bit of weight and see? My sister lost half a stone when she ate nothing but fruit for three days.'

I start tomorrow.

Tuesday 7.11.89

7.05 p.m.

HAD A BREAKFAST OF TWO apples. At lunchtime had a massive bunch of grapes – but felt like crap when I realised they were South African and I had inadvertently helped to keep Nelson Mandela in prison for another couple of years. Tonight I have had three more apples, and I think about 70 tangerines. You could make a scale model of Big Ben from the amount of peel that is on my bedroom floor.

10.22 p.m.

No you couldn't. Tangerine peel can't be made into anything, I have just discovered. Not even into a miniature dog. It crumbles.

STARVING.

Wednesday 8.11.89

5.26 p.m.

WOKE UP THIS MORNING RAVENOUS. Managed to avoid the smell of roast dinners at school by going for a walk in Burghley Park. Almost can't write. I feel so weak, and I can't stop going to the loo. In double politics today I had to go at least five times. The teacher was getting well narked off.

8.55 p.m.
Just rang Mort and apparently peaches in syrup are not counted. Buggering hell. I was looking forward to them.

So hungry I could cry.

Thursday 9.11.89

Lasted all through school, but on the way home went past Pacey and Canham's fruit shop and spotted an apple dipped in chocolate and covered in hundreds and thousands. I had to eat it. I don't know if I am diabetic or something, but if I didn't eat it I don't think I would have made it to the Lincolnshire Poacher 200 yards away. Their special today was fisherman's pie. I saw it through the side door. I smelt it all the way home.

I don't think I have lost much weight. My skin might look better, though.

Friday 10.11.89

THE BERLIN WALL IS COMING DOWN! THE BERLIN WALL IS DOWN! CAN YOU BELIEVE IT?! THERE ARE PEOPLE ON TOP OF THE BERLIN WALL HAMMERING IT DOWN WITH AXES – CHEERING AND SHOUTING – IT'S BRILLIANT!

ALL THOSE YEARS BRICKING MYSELF ABOUT NUCLEAR WAR – ABOUT FOUR-MINUTE WARNINGS – ABOUT MELTING – ABOUT BEING AWAY FROM MY MUM WHEN IT STARTS – HAVE GONE! God . . . all that stress for nothing.

Kids like my nephew have no idea what a better world they will be growing up in. I bet Sting is pissed off, as his song 'Russians' will seem increasingly stupid. However, Elton John can go and see *Nikita* now!

But I've just realised something depressing: even bloody Communism has collapsed and I still haven't lost my bloody virginity.

11.25 p.m.
I went on the world's crappiest history trip today. Four old boring speakers going on about bollocks. We have only just got back, so I have missed a night down the pub – a night down the pub with Haddock. Nobody mentioned that I had lost any weight. Mort said she thought I had lost some round my face, but she was the only one and she knew I was dieting.

Rather than take notes, I wrote a poem. Says it all.

MY KNIGHT

My knight hides under his armour
So nobody else will know
How his soul shines
When corroded by time
His inner light will show.
And I will say I told you about him
But it will be too late by then,
I would have missed my chance
And he will be
Spearing someone else with his noble lance.

It's getting a bit pervy. Never mind, it's saying all the things I cannot say for fear of mass turbulence.

Saturday 11.11.89

LATE (AND WILL TOMORROW EVER happen?) Haddock at the pub acted like nothing had happened last Saturday. I don't think he even remembers saying anything. When I came in he yelled, 'Funky Chick, get me a pint – I will give you the money', then for the rest of the night he mooned over his girlfriend – who I shouldn't hate but do at the moment with every bone in my body.

Ryan Bates – the RAF party groper – rubbed my hair tonight when he came in. He says I remind him of his mum's Labrador, Penny. When I asked why, he said, 'You just make me laugh when you take no shit.'

What the fuck is he on?

Monday 13.11.89

4.58 p.m.

EVERYONE TALKING ABOUT THE BERLIN Wall at school. This changes everything. Our GCSE history already means nothing – we did a whole year on the Cold War and the Warsaw Pact and NATO. It's like a completely new world. And it makes you think. Even things that have been the same for years and years can change. Maybe I can change. I can bring my own wall down, and let people in.

9.45 p.m.
Bloody hell – just read that last bit back, and I sound like a right pretentious cow. Sorry!

Tuesday 14.11.89

10.10 p.m.
PARENTS' EVENING WENT OK. GOOD reports for English, politics, theatre arts. Semi-good for Euro history and British history – same old teacher 'has run out of inspiration' crap . . . 'She is capable but she is not working.' They didn't add, 'Rachel thinks it's a total waste of time to be learning this utter shit as it bears no relevance to today at all, and she is right.'

I've got a head full of dates, when all I want is a date WITH A BLOKE. And why can't they tell me this? Why does a man grab hold of you, look like he is going to burst into tears, say something really profound, and then the next weekend conveniently forget that he ever had the conversation with you in the first place? Why isn't there an A level in men? The handling of men, talking to men, being with men. It should be bloody compulsory – and there should be a practical exam!!!

Wednesday 15.11.89

9.56 p.m.
NOW I DON'T WANT TO sound desperate, but honestly, Diary, I am. I need to at least experience love now. The boys' school is full of looks-fascists. The

person I think is my absolute soul mate, the potential love of my life, is with somebody else and can't see through the fat anyway. So I have to look elsewhere and get some practice in. Preferably with someone who doesn't know me.

That's why I am considering Dateline. It's in the middle of my mum's *TV Guide*. Basically you fill in a questionnaire and they match you up with someone like you in your area. They even seem to cater for people who are really old and not that good-looking, according to the photos in the advert. The couple 'Rose and Harold' look ancient, and Mary from 'Mary and Tony' looks like a poodle! The advert says, 'You too can find love,' and best of all it doesn't ask you about your looks – and it is FREE! It has to be worth a try. I know this is normally for middle-aged divorced people with droopy bits, but right now I have no choice.

Thursday 16.11.89

9.20 p.m.

MUM HAS JUST BEEN UP. I forgot to cut the Dateline questionnaire coupon out of her *TV Guide*. She obviously had read it. She sat on my bed (always a bad sign) and said, 'Can we have a chat about Dateline, please, Rachel?'

I was dying with embarrassment.

MUM: Why are you applying to Dateline?
ME: I'm not – just got bored and filled it in for a laugh.

MUM: You have ticked that you like classical music and pop music.

ME: Well, I thought – hypothetically – that richer men would like classical music, and that – hypothetically – they would be good to meet.

MUM: What about saying you are adventurous and shy?

ME: I wasn't really paying attention.

MUM: It costs a bit this, you know. It says just three first-class stamps, but there is a membership fee.

ME: Oh, is there? I'm not really bothered . . .

MUM: OK, then. It's funny – for a lot of these people who use this service, if they just looked around a bit harder somebody would be there for them.

ME: Yeah . . . well, like I say . . . I just did it during *The Krypton Factor* in an idle moment.

Then she went. I think she fell for it. I put her off the scent.

Well, that's that, then. I haven't got money for stamps let alone a membership fee. Back to the man drawing board.

Friday 17.11.89

SO, MUM – IF THERE IS somebody waiting for me if I look hard enough, tell me this.

Why did I go down the pub tonight and feel so totally alone? Why did I have to watch Haddock rubbing his girlfriend's back, kissing her like she was the best thing on earth? Even Fig came back from polytechnic tonight, so Dobber was in a couple too. Why did I have to watch the entire pub dance to the bloody 'Lambada' on the jukebox – with knees sticking in groins – while I stood at the bar making jokes about everyone, and acting like I am the best thing on earth, when inside I am dying? Why do I laugh when they chant 'Walrus' at me and say, 'Mind that belly'? Why do I have something smart to say?

And why at the end of the evening does Haddock look at me like he wants to say something but can't – or am I so desperate that I am reading too much into everything?

Please – I hope other girls feel this way sometimes.

Saturday 18.11.89

5.10 p.m.

RANG UP MORT THIS AFTERNOON and she told me she had to go into Grantham to buy the latest UB40 song for her dad. She was surprised because it was about a transsexual. I said, 'Pardon?' She said, 'It's about a bloke called Miguel who is now a beautiful woman.' I said, 'It's not called "Oh, Miguel" – it's called "Homely Girl"!' Mort was pissing herself. She genuinely thought it was about a Hispanic cross-dresser. It's always great to come in useful where the subject of pop is concerned!

7.40 p.m.
Mum has just announced that Adnan is coming back for Christmas. Oh great.

Battered Sausage was meant to pick me up in Clarence the Cortina ten minutes ago. He is late.

Sunday 19.11.89

11.45 a.m.

Dear Battered Sausage,
   So you have got yourself another floozy, eh?
That's why you didn't even turn up last night.
Now, I wonder what SHE means to you? Dispen-
sable like me? I wish I could believe your chants
of 'I love you, you're a classic', but sometimes I
cannot accept them – in fact most of the time.
   One day . . . one day I intend to lose five stone
and do my pretty little self up, and see just how
you treat me. Because let's be honest: the only
reason you haven't fallen into my arms is because
I am a fat, ugly cow.
   I think you do like me. But do you know what
love is? It's missing someone, wanting to see them
happy, and being happy because they are happy.
Have you EVER had that?! I doubt it, you selfish,
stupid git.
   I'm used to being the centre of attention and
you even take that from me! Perhaps this new
woman can give you everything you need but I
bloody, bloody doubt it. You will flit from one bird
to another and still be crap to all of your mates. I
don't want you, though.
   And you will never see this letter – I just need
to write it all down. One day either I will realise

307

how daft I've been or you will realise how daft
you have been.

Either way – it will be too bloody late.

Monday 20.11.89

7.36 p.m.

GOT BOLLOCKED AT SCHOOL TODAY for not
doing enough work and not 'fulfilling my potential'.
History teacher dragged me outside the class to ask me
why I hadn't done my essay on the Duke of Norfolk. I
told him that I had had a very heavy period. This is the
only excuse guaranteed to shut up every teacher – male
or female – but particularly male.

He said it must be done by Wednesday. Then the
theatre arts teacher and the politics teacher said exactly
the same thing. So you'll excuse me if I just give the
headlines this week, Diary, as I am in the shit big time.

Just watching *Coronation Street*. Ken Barlow is still
having an affair with Wendy Crozier. Deirdre is being
shafted – like we all are, in the end.

Tuesday 21.11.89

8.45 p.m.

I'M TRYING TO DO A bloody essay on the Senate
and the House of Representatives, and all I can hear
is Mum wetting herself at *Birds of a Feather*. I wouldn't
mind, but it's not even that funny.

Selfishness. Total, total selfishness.

Listening to 'Pacific' by 808 State, which is like this mad bit of house dance music. It is brilliant – I must try listening to it in a field at dusk as I think it would do my head in – in a brilliant way.

Wednesday 22.11.89

10.15 p.m.

ACCORDING TO DOBBER, HADDOCK AND girlfriend have broken up/are breaking up, and it is hell for them both. I have sympathy for both of them – but for her mainly. Fancy losing that. You would be gutted. No . . . this does not mean I can get right in there. Even though that's the first thing I thought of too.

Thursday 23.11.89

11.01 p.m.

HADDOCK AND GIRLFRIEND ARE BACK together. I'm still on my own. Funny that.

All essays nearly done, and all teachers nearly off my back.

By the way – New Kids on the Block all want shooting.

Friday 24.11.89

6.02 p.m.

MUM HAS JUST COME HOME in a bit of a state.
Nan has been put in hospital. Apparently she had a
funny do in her bathroom and then keeled over. Mum was
there, so she is a bit freaked out by it. I know Nan is not
her mother or anything, but she might as well be. I made
Mum a cup of tea, and asked, 'Do you think she might die?'

I just can't imagine life without Nan. It just seems
ludicrous, and almost funny. I said to Mum, 'I think she
has got a lot more years left in her yet!' Mum didn't say
anything. Oh God . . . please let her live until I have
actually done something with my life. She saw me as a
loon last year – and I need to make up for it all. And I
was a loon. At one stage I thought she was trying to
poison me because her cups of tea tasted funny. It was
because she watered down milk to make it last longer –
it's what they used to do in the war apparently.

How could I have thought she was trying to hurt
me? See – I was off it.

I've rung Dobber to tell her I won't be down the pub
later. She was really sweet.

Saturday 25.11.89

7.30 p.m.
JUST BEEN TO SEE NAN. Bloody Stamford Hospital – hateful place. I went in to see her. She is a bit confused. She said as I left, 'Put the catch down, Rach,' like she always does when I leave her flat. I said, 'Nan, you are in hospital,' and she goes, 'Oh yes, I know.' Left her feeling really upset – so sad. Walked home. Got rid of that horrid antiseptic smell. Hope she won't have to go into a home – she will hate that. Sitting around smelling of wee, singing 'We'll Meet Again'. Oh, just awful places. In fact any institution that has a room called 'the sluice' is always bloody awful.

Not going out. Flat, shit, and done in by it all.

Sunday 26.11.89

8.35 p.m.
JUST BEEN TO SEE DOBBER at her house. We were listening to the charts. (Shockingly she thinks New Kids on the Block are 'OK . . . just a bit of fun.' Can I still be friends with this girl?!) According to her, last night Haddock was asking where I was. When Dobber told him about my nan she says he looked really worried and said, 'Shit – is she OK?' She thinks Haddock sees me as a really close friend, and 'You know – he hasn't got that many.' I know he hasn't. I should be grateful, but inside

311

I think a hug from him would make everything better.

But do you know what I said when she told me that? 'He's a big gay girl twat, isn't he?'

WHY do I say that? Inside I am melting, but my gob spouts shit.

Listening to *Viva Hate*. Wish someone would sing 'Angel, Angel, Down We Go Together' to me, and mean it.

Monday 27.11.89

11.40 p.m.

CAUGHT MYSELF SINGING 'THE RIGHT Stuff' by New Kids today. Yes, I feel disgusted with myself.

Hormones are really playing up. All I want is SOMEONE – ANYONE – to give me a hug and tell me everything will be OK. I want to stop feeling this way by the end of the DECADE!! The '80s are gone – hello, '90s. I'll be 28 by the year 2000, if we get that far. Apparently Nostradamus says not – we are all dying in 1999. Not now the Berlin Wall is down, mate. Now even I think I could make it to 28 – even though that is bloody ancient.

Dobber came round tonight. She was wearing quite a short skirt. Mum gave her a lecture on how in the '60s no one had worn shorter skirts than her, and now due to 'excessive drafts and winds' her legs were a 'varicose-vein paradise'. Then she looked at me and said, 'Thread veins are hereditary, Rachel.' Dobber had only come round to borrow my notes on *Twelfth Night* – she didn't need a lecture. And why did I need to know that one of my few OK features – my legs – will eventually look like a map of the Underground??

312

Tuesday 28.11.89

7.45 p.m.

GOT HOME TONIGHT FROM A shit day at school (I got two Cs and a D for all the essays I did last week) to Mum – who decided to give me a talk on what medical ailments I should expect in later life:

- terrible diabetes – from her Canadian dad she only met a few times. Not helped by his tendency to lose his temper and brood in his cellar drinking Japanese rice wine for two days. ('You are like him,' she said. How would you know, Mum? You have only met him three times.)
- bad legs – from my great-granddad. 'Ohh . . . your great-granddad's legs were a mess!' (Yes, but bless him – he was gassed by the Germans in World War I. That couldn't have helped.)
- hiatus hernia – from her. Makes you burp a lot. I don't need to be told this. After some meals it's like being with a sea lion.
- rheumatism, arthritis, diverticulitis, stomach ulcers and a menopause with hot flushes, which is apparently like wearing a fur coat in the Sahara.

The good news is that you don't really die from these things, but they can hurt. Of course none of them are helped by 'being podgy'. Great. FAT IS EVIL. I AM EVIL.

I have had to put on *Now That's What I Call Music*

313

2. It's old, but '99 Red Balloons' by Nena and 'Get Out of Your Lazy Bed' by Matt Bianco are cheering me up no end. Mainly because it reminds me of the time Matt Bianco got called 'wankers' on *Saturday Superstore* by a kid.

Wednesday 29.11.89

9.16 p.m.

TONIGHT I HAVE HEARD THE FUTURE.

For ages everyone has been going on about the Stone Roses down the pub, but I thought it was just hyped-up, pretentious crap. I like the new single, though – 'Fools Gold' – so I taped the album off Dobber and listened to it tonight. It is honestly even better than – and I feel bad saying this – *The Queen Is Dead*. Sorry, Morrissey, but every track on this is fucking brilliant. It's like four blokes who just got pissed one day and said, 'Let's make the best record in history.' 'I Am the Resurrection' – just genius. The words . . . you could sing them to Mum, to Bethany, to anyone who tries to do your head in.

Mum heard it and said, 'Are they druggies? Why is there a lemon on the front cover?' No, Mum, they don't need drugs, they have an imagination – and unlike Jive fuckwit Bunny they are not shitting out records on our heads.

Thursday 30.11.89

7.34 p.m.
I'VE JUST UPSET MUM AND I DIDN'T MEAN TO.
Mum said to me, 'I shouldn't go and see Nan for
the moment.' I said, 'Why?' Mum said, 'She is a bit . . .
not herself.' I said, 'You think I can't cope with Nan
being a bit confused and not knowing what is going
on? Well, I can. How many people have I been dragged
to see in old people's homes over the years who have
lost the plot? What about that time when I went with
Nan to see someone in St George's Nursing Home and a
bloody mad nun started shouting at me because she
thought I was a pregnant schoolgirl or something?'
Mum said, 'Rachel, today she didn't know who I was.'
Then she went quiet. I didn't know what to say, so I
said, 'I'm getting a yoghurt. Would you like one?'
Why did I say that?
Oh, this is awful.
And then the bloody 'Boxer' by Simon and Garfunkel
comes on the radio.
Can't stop crying.

Friday 1.12.89

7.12 a.m.
JUST WOKE UP AND THEN remembered why I feel
like shit. But I have to get over it. I love Nan but I
can't do anything to help her right now. Just have to

315

get on and hope she gets better. Or doesn't suffer. Now I'm crying again. Have to go to pissing school now.

5.20 p.m.
This is unbelievable. My nan is dying. Mum is going out with a Moroccan bodybuilder. I am in the hardest year academically, and we are all going through one of the most difficult stages of our lives. But at school they call us in for a special meeting because someone has been picking the foam out of one of the common-room chairs! The fact is, we all do it absentmindedly, but Daisy Connor owned up and took the flack. I don't know why – it's not like Duke of Edinburgh – you can't put 'foam picker' on your CV.

Can't school get some perspective?? HELLO?????

Saturday 2.12.89

12.33 p.m.
MUM HAS BOUGHT MY FOUR-year-old nephew an advent calendar this year, but not one for me. He's four – he can't even work out how to open the bloody doors – why does he get one? You are never too old for Christmas and chocolate – everybody knows that.

I can't believe December is here. Which means Christmas and my birthday are on the horizon. I don't want to get too overexcited, as that inevitably means that things go badly. Don't know what the hell I am going to do for Christmas presents this year. I used to make stuff – but I don't think that would go down too well now.

Sunday 3.12.89

3.45 p.m.

LAST NIGHT AT THE PUB we (Battered Sausage,
Haddock and girlfriend, Dobber, Fig and me) all had
a game of confessions. I dread this game because I
have nothing to share, as I have snogged one bloke and
slept with a total of no blokes.

I don't know why, but it got on to the most embarrassing thing you did as a kid. I had had a bit to drink,
so I told the truth. I once got an empty bog roll and
peed down it standing up – to see what it would be
like having a knob. I bet loads of girls have done it – it
must be one of the most common things in the world.
Everybody pissed themselves – which is fine – but then
ALL NIGHT Battered Sausage called me 'Cardboard
Cock' – like he was Jim bloody Davidson. Twat.

And conveniently, after I had told my story everyone
decided they were bored of the game and that mine
could not be topped.

Everyone has done that, surely? I am just the only
one who has the balls to admit it.

Haddock winked at me, though, on the way out. I
love it when I make him laugh. He is so grumpy I see
it as an achievement. Last night I said, 'I've got a
present for you – guard it with your life.' It was just a
bunch of old receipts. He said, 'Thanks – I will treasure
them for ever,' and he shoved them down the back of
his trousers. His humour is as dry as a bone. As he left,

he ripped the backside of his jeans on the side of the table. I couldn't look – Haddock's pants! It's right, but it's wrong – if you know what I mean.

Monday 4.12.89

EVERYBODY AT SCHOOL IS TALKING about two things:

1) Cardboard Cock. It's got round. BIG DEAL. They are all laughing a bit too hard at me. They have done it too. I can tell.
2) This film that is out called *When Harry Met Sally*. Basically two things happen in it: a woman fakes an orgasm, and a bloke and a woman who are meant to be just mates sleep together. The whole point of the film seems to be that men and women can never just be good friends. Sex, according to the film, always gets in the way. How I wish this was true. Unfortunately the female lead they have got for the film is this thin blonde woman called Meg Ryan. OF COURSE BLOKES WANT TO DO HER. Change the female lead – put ME in it, for example. And I will prove to you that you can just be mates with a man. WHETHER YOU LIKE IT OR NOT. Men can see you in a totally asexual way. If you're fat, all you have is just good friends. EVERYWHERE.

Tuesday 5.12.89

10.14 p.m.

I HATE THIS HOME. I HATE this place. You do a tiny
thing and it just turns into recriminations and hatred. I
was sitting in front of the telly and I had a few of the
chocolate decorations off the tree. It was only when I had
a few that I realised that Mum had only bought a few, so
I tried to reshape the foil and hang them back – but
Mum knew the moment she walked in. Then it all started:
'You do nothing all day – you contribute nothing to this
house – all you do is eat – and they were £1.89 for six.'
Oh, big deal. Everywhere there is a trap, a reason for her
to yell. Even in decorations.

FAIRYTALE REWRITTEN

Chocolate is a trap
You have caught me
Like the witch in Hansel and Gretel you lured me
    into your
Evil cottage
But remember – the witch died in the end.

Wednesday 6.12.89

8.19 p.m.

MUM HAS JUST GOT BACK from the hospital.
She looks awful.

I don't want to ask.

Everything is falling apart. Today I lost my Swatch. I
know it sounds pathetic but that Swatch has been like
a faithful companion to me since Christmas 1985.
Where I went, the Swatch went. It was like a dog. I
tried to retrace my steps – no joy.

Perhaps I should see it as a chance for a new image.
The clear strap had gone green and manky with sweat.
The loss of my Swatch could be a beginning. Just like
the snake sheds it skin so I have shed my Swatch.

Thursday 7.12.89

BAND AID II SHOWS THAT everything in life truly
is on the slide. Yes, I know it's for charity, but they
could have made more of an effort. The first Band Aid
had George Michael, Duran Duran and Culture Club.
Band Aid II has CLIFF RICHARD, SONIA and BROS.
Mind you, secretly I love Kylie and Jason.

Mum says no news is good news from the hospital.

Friday 8.12.89

4.03 p.m.

NAN HAS DIED. MUM WENT down to the hospital early this morning. I knew it was bad news because she came from the hospital with a Rupert the Bear cuddly toy for me – this is because she cannot give me a cuddle. She is just not the hugging type.

Didn't go to school.

I have cried for most of the day. Now I think Nan can see everything, and she must see what a big nutcase I am, and all the dodgy things I think. And last year when I was ill she saw all that too and I was off my head. All so sad. I am meant to be doing the music for *Antigone*, the school play, at the Arts Centre, but what with Nan dying I've asked for someone else to do it. Can't believe I will never see Nan again. Could almost laugh because it seems so stupid, but it's not. It's real.

Saturday 9.12.89

6.35 p.m.

OBVIOUSLY NOT GOING OUT TONIGHT. I know everyone will be lovely – but if they are too nice I will cry and then people will try to hug me, and I can't cope. And I am so ugly when I cry, my face almost collapses.

Rang Mort – she was lovely.

Mum and me were just talking and Mum reminded me

of the time when Nan said, 'Don't eat unpasteurised ice cream it's full of orgasms.' She meant to say organisms. We both pissed ourselves and I said it seems wrong to laugh now. Mum reckons dead people have an 'advanced sense of humour, and Nan would be laughing too'.

Hope she is because it was funny and she was lovely. Bloody crying again. Can't bloody stop.

Sunday 10.12.89

9.28 a.m.
I HAVE JUST GOT UP THIS morning to find a note pushed through the door. It looks like it was written on a waiter's order pad. All it says is:

> Rae
> Hope the Funky Chick is OK.
>   Love
> Haddock

He must have put it in last night. In fact – unless someone gave him a lift – he must have walked for 25 minutes to push it through.

It seems wrong to be excited at a time like this, but I honestly could be sick.

He came all this way. Is it wrong that I just want to listen to some very loud music and dance round the room? It doesn't make sense to me either.

Nan would understand. She loved her husband, and she loved music. Well – Val Doonican, and *The Black and White Minstrel* racist *Show* – but you know what I mean.

322

7.12 p.m.

JUST HAD THIS CONVERSATION WITH Mum:

> MUM: The funeral is on Tuesday. You don't have to come, Rach.
> ME: I hadn't even thought . . .
> MUM: Nan wouldn't mind . . . And they are . . . funny things.
> ME: Is it wrong not to go?
> MUM: Don't be stupid. Nan knew you loved her. It's your choice.

I think she is worried I might lose it again if I go. Once you've had a breakdown, everyone thinks you could lose it at any point – so they keep you away from nasty stuff.

Am I a bitch if I don't go? Aren't funerals just for people who can't get their head round stuff and haven't been nice to the dead person when they were living?

I can't decide what to do.

Monday 11.12.89

9.30 p.m.

NAN'S FUNERAL IS TOMORROW. I am not going. Can't bear the thought of that coffin going in the ground.

Had to stop then – can't think about it. Just remember the good times. The times she told me Cinderella without

her teeth in, the toast on the Aga, her enormous Yorkshire puddings, the smell of her Consulate menthol fags,
whenever I bumped my head that great semi-
whistle/groan noise she made as she went, 'Mind!'

Tuesday 12.12.89

3.15 p.m.

MUM SAID . . . IT WENT OK. She was OK. It was nice. What can you say? She's gone.

10.55 p.m.
I just had to write – it's my 18th birthday tomorrow. I
suppose now I can reflect on my so-called childhood.

My childhood was strange. And my teenage years . . . ?
Well, they weren't catastrophic – there were good times
and bad times. It was often . . . Well, it seemed
completely marred by certain events that I don't really
want to write about here. I think I am happy – but
what is happy? Having laughs is easy. Spiritual peace is
far more difficult . . . and I am still HUGE.

I still struggle with my head. Not as bad as a year
ago, but it is there. I think the worst things – I think I
can control things. I still hit myself to punish myself
for the thoughts I have. I have irrational, horrible
thoughts, and I shall never, ever understand why. But I
am an optimist, and in the past year the change in
what I can do is phenomenal. I mean, this time last
year approaching my 17th birthday I had never been
near a boy, never went out, was tortured ALL THE
TIME with the bad thoughts, and NOW . . .

NOW, I have been with a boy – however totally unsuccessful that was. I know loads of blokes, I go down the pub every weekend – all the time in the holidays. Only sometimes I am plagued with it all, and those times – oh, those times – I need a field and some paper and I am soon OK.

A man would make me better. One man in particular, but I can't get him over the counter at Boots.

Wednesday 13.12.89 (my 18th birthday)

11.30 p.m.
  CAN HARDLY WRITE.
  MY BIRTHDAY BRILLIANT.
  HAVE BRILLIANT MATES.
  THEY SO CLASSIC.

Thursday 14.12.89

11.40 p.m.
EXTREMELY DRUNK LAST NIGHT AS you can tell by that entry. Stupid question of the year award goes to Mum, who asked when I stumbled in, 'Have you had a drink, Rachel?' Errr . . . IT WAS MY 18TH BIRTHDAY, WOMAN!!!

Hangover from hell. Thrown up most of the day. Mum was her usual 'full of the milk of human kindness' self. I swear she did extra cooking today because the smell would make me boff more. I will never drink snakebite and black again – I'm telling you now I was gone. When they put 'Pump Up the Jam' on at Oliver's I went mad. Me and Mort were pretending to pump it with a bike pump. It was funny at the time.

It was brilliant last night, but I have to say the most amazing thing was A PRESENT FROM HADDOCK. I didn't expect it but he turned up with a compilation album called 'Lovin' Seventies' and all round and round the inner sleeve he has written a message:

Dear Rae.

Not your sort of music, you Funky Chick. Dig the Abba and all be well. Sound bit of ripped jeans the other night and thanks for the receipts (about the most interesting thing you have ever given me). Anyway I could keep on writing until I get to the middle but I won't. Hope you like the record and note that the sleeve is an early version of a Reading Rock Festival. Just think, in about 20 years when a daughter or son of yours buys an '80s record there will be me in my Dead Kennedy's T-shirt and khaki shorts knocking back a beer with Fig on the front cover. Better go now. My girl-friend needs a seeing-to. Love Haddock.

The record is shit. It has got 'Rose Garden' and 'Seasons in the Sun' on it, but it is the best present ever.

His girlfriend got a better present, though. A seeing-to.

Friday 15.12.89

4.35 p.m.
WALKED INTO TOWN. COUPLES. WALKED to get *Smash Hits* from the Green Lane shops. Couples. Even in Queen Eleanor playground bloody kids in couples. And what I don't understand is – lots of them aren't even attractive. Lots of them aren't pretty or thin or special or with a great personality, and yet they've got someone.

> I wish I was Rapunzel
> Letting down her hair
> But at the bottom of my tower
> There's nobody stood there.
>
> No prince to carry me off to the sunset . . .
> The reason why of course,
> I don't look like his princess,
> I look like his horse.

Saturday 16.12.89

23.59 p.m. (so says the video)
I FEEL LIKE A MASSIVE ENTRY.
I seem consumed with worry about everything at the moment. I hate the impression people get about me. Dobber told me last night that she hated me at first.

Now LOADS of people say that. She thought I was just a really loud twat. Now we really get on. I am such a gob – I do people's heads in. No one would be able to believe what I was like on the quiet. Oversensitive – I laugh everything off but inside I just remember it all and go over and over and over it.

Battered Sausage is being a bastard at the mo, and his new girlfriend is a tart. Actually that's a bit strong – she is actually really nice. But I hate him and I hate her. Love and hate do run an extremely fine line. What the hell do I feel for Battered Sausage? I can't get my head round it.

Fig came back and he was a bit of a jibber to be fair. Haddock and girlfriend broke up and then were back together in five minutes as predicted correctly again by Dobber. I hardly saw him all night but I can't make it obvious. I have to pretend I am just his friend. Good old 'one of the lads' Rae.

Didn't even get a wink.

Ryan the RAF party groper winked at me on the way out and stuck his tongue out. But knowing him it might just be a nervous tic.

Sunday 17.12.89

11.47 p.m. (excuse the handwriting – a bit drunk)
WHAT I HAVE DONE BEGGARS belief. I am just a two-faced cow – you will hate me.

Tonight I got a bit tipsy in the Vaults. Was sat with Haddock's girlfriend and she asked me if there was anyone I fancied and I said, 'Yes'! Then I talked about him for ages . . . but didn't mention a name or say who it was! Then she said, 'If you think this much of him, why don't you tell him?'! I felt like saying, 'How can I? He's YOUR on-off boyfriend!!!'

Haddock then came in with the 12-inch of a song he thinks is brilliant. It's called 'Getting Away With It' by Electronic. He has let me borrow it. He added that he 'doesn't like lending stuff out but I know you will look after it, Rae'. (GOD, I WILL!!!) He then said, 'Give it back to me when we go out on Thursay.' I am a sad cow but it almost sounds like a date! I know it's not but . . . you know.

Monday 18.12.89

Late

LISTENED TO ELECTRONIC ALL DAY. It is an astounding piece of music with Johnny Marr from the Smiths and the bloke from New Order. The lyrics are just... IT COULD BE MY SONG – I COULD HAVE WRITTEN IT. It talks about mirrors making you look shit and I do hate mirrors. And do you know what else I HATE about this time of year? Mistletoe. If there's one thing that forces the issue about how unattractive I am to men, it's that stuff.

When we are down the pub – one of the lads gets some – puckers up to everyone – gets to me – and decides he needs a pint. It happens EVERY TIME.

It seems wrong to me that Electronic have to share the same chart as Jive Bunny AND THEIR LATEST PILE OF FESTIVE TOSS.

Tuesday 19.12.89

11.54 a.m.

THE FIRST CHRISTMAS PRESENT – opened it
early and it's utter crap. A cute black ceramic
elephant with MAKE-UP BRUSHES!!!!!!!!!!!???????

HELLO?! DO THESE PEOPLE KNOW ME???

A) I DON'T WEAR MAKE-UP, AND B) I HATE CUTE
THINGS.

Have customised the elephant with Mum's nail
varnish, and written on it 'Vanity kills'. Mum came
upstairs and said I was an ungrateful so and so. But
why don't people get the message and buy me stuff
that I want, like records and books?

Wednesday 20.12.89

5.50 p.m.

WROTE A CHRISTMAS CARD TO Haddock to give
to him tomorrow but I never will. I ended up
putting too many kisses on it – he's bound to get
suspicious. I wish you could see Haddock. Then you'd
appreciate him for what he is visually. And down there
under all the crap is a shining soul – a gem of a man.
Yes, he is screwed up, but the best ones are as far as I
can see. He is meant to be going to South Africa for
six months next year. I'd love to be able to say in that
time I could make a caterpillar-to-butterfly-type trans-

formation, but while prawn-cocktail crisps exist, this seems unlikely.

What I feel for Haddock is so positive, but totally wasted. Depressing really.

Thursday 21.12.89

12.20 a.m.

IT DOESN'T SEEM LIKE CHRISTMAS, you know. When I think what I was doing a year ago, it isn't pleasant. I was off my head after the breakdown. I kept thinking I was dying every five minutes. On Christmas Day I got it into my head that I was slowly choking on a 5p that Mum had put in the Christmas pudding.

Last night Fig bought me a Jack Daniel's, then gave me a fireman's lift from near Beewise to outside the old cinema. A fair way – I was quite impressed. It's the lightest I've felt in years, though he looked red afterwards.

I think Haddock's girlfriend has clicked on to the fact that I have a huge crush on Haddock. I just get a vibe. Oh, so what? I've got a 38-inch waist – I am hardly a threat!!

11.37 p.m.

Oh, Haddock looked so horny tonight, I swear . . . He makes my heart nearly come out of my bloody ribcage. I don't think his girlfriend has clicked on actually – I cover it up well. He was wearing a grey wool jumper that just smelt of Lenor and aftershave, and a little tartan scarf. You could just eat him. And then we had the most brilliant conversation about the record he lent me:

331

HAD: What did you think, then?

RAE: I thought it was bloody brilliant, mate.

HAD (LOOKING ME STRAIGHT IN MY EYE – BAM!!): It's my song.

RAE: Piss off, it's my song. It says it all.

HAD: Well you and me have got a lot in common, then.

(GAP – GAP – GAP. QUICK, RAE, FILL IT BEFORE YOU BURST WIDE OPEN WITH SO MUCH LOVE FOR THIS MAN YOU MIGHT VOMIT OR DIE.)

RAE: That album you bought me for my birthday has got some prime shit on it. Hot Chocolate?? Sonny and Cher?? Where the hell did you get it from?

HAD: Bargain bin at work, mate. It was £2.99.

RAE: Thanks – I hope you won't starve because of you lavishing so much money on me.

HAD: Nah, there's a big tin of Quality Street in our front room. I'll be fine. Do you want a drink, Funky Chick?

RAE: Yes, you tight arse – get me a beer.

So he goes to the bar, none the wiser . . . that I may just die if I never go out with him.

Fucking hell, I deserve an Oscar. No one covers shit up like me. People think I am confident and happy with myself. Haddock thinks I am just a friend of his. I am the Meryl Streep of Stamford.

I was going to a review of the '80s, but I've decided it would be too depressing.

Friday 22.12.89

10.50 p.m.

WELL, ADNAN IS BACK FOR Christmas. His
English has improved. He must have been having
lessons, as when I wished him happy Christmas, he said,
'You also. Jesus prophet me too.' Mum was quick to tell
me that Islam has Jesus as a prophet. They are mooning
over each other like a couple of teenagers . . . and keep
disappearing into the kitchen muttering and kissing.

Tonight in the pub Battered Sausage said I looked like
the inflatable Father Christmas that was hanging off the
bar. So I said, 'Rudolph the Reindeer has got a bigger
cock than you, and is prettier to shag.' He laughed.
Everyone laughed. He has gone somewhere to snog. I am
sat here looking at my Father Christmas figure.

That is my life. The smart comment. Then fuck all.

I can't cope with Christmas like this. I am so lonely I
could cry.

I am depressed. No one has noticed.

Saturday 23.12.89

Bloody late (knackered and pissed off beyond gooseberry
belief)

WELL, IT'S LATE, AND FRANKLY it's not the
23rd but I refuse to have a crap Christmas Eve.
Tonight was a right snog-fest for everyone BUT ME!!

Battered Sausage and girlfriend sucking each other's faces off. Haddock was snogging his girlfriend like something I didn't want to see – but like a car crash I couldn't stop staring. At one stage he caught me looking at him. I just stuck my Vs up. He came over and said:

HAD: The Funky Chick looks pissed off. What's the matter?
ME: Just a bit pissed off, mate.
HAD: Why?
ME: Doesn't matter.
HAD: Tell me.
ME: All right, then. I'm fucked off, fat and a gooseberry everywhere I go. And if you must know, my mum's bloody foreign boyfriend is back.
HAD: Let's go out tomorrow and get ratted. On me – I've just got paid.

He then kissed my hand in a comedy way and ran off.

He is so horny it's . . . Oh, I wish you could see him. Too knackered to write now. Going to sleep on that thought.

Sunday 24.12.89

LATE
CRIMBLE EVE!!!
    Went down the Vaults. Elva the landlady gave me a Vaults diary for Christmas. Got loads of Christmas kisses off people and had such a laugh with Dobber.
    Oh, BUT . . .

HADDOCK . . .

Took me on a pub bender to cheer me up. He succeeded. If he had taken me to a building society he would have cheered me up. In the snog way Battered Sausage is repulsive – leering, uncaring, cold. Oh, he reckons (and he tells me) that he is good at 'it', but so what? But Haddock is so funny, gentle, yet strong. How I contain myself I don't know.

We had such a laugh. He is witty, he is kind. He is grumpy, but only in a comedy way. He is . . . And on a few occasions tonight I caught him looking at me, and I swear . . .

No, that is just bollocks, Rae. Don't kid yourself. Don't spoil what you have, because what you have is a lovely, wonderful thing. What you pray and hope for, and what you wish he thinks – he doesn't.

I swear he is my ideal man and I'm not joking. I don't think anyone will come close to matching him.

But his presence plagues me with the 'if only's more than anyone. If only he wasn't spoken for, etc. If only I wasn't fat.

I swear – if it means lettuce leaves for three years, and my mum's Green Goddess video – I will snog that bloke one day.

His poor girlfriend had family commitments tonight. Her loss – bloody hell – was my gain.

Monday 25.12.89 (Christmas Day)

8.34 a.m.

MUM HAS JUST WOKEN ME up with a turkey sarnie . . . at 8.31 a.m.!

Two things can be relied upon today:

1) I won't get anything I want.
2) Mum will force me to eat a ceremonial Brussels sprout 'just for her'.

3.50 p.m.

Mum is watching the Christmas edition of *Bread*. It is not funny.

The more I think about it, the more I realise that Haddock is desperate to put me off him. He probably finds me repulsive, and the little things he says are there to prove a point.

The more I think about it, the more I realise just how much I want him – I mean really, really want him. Totally impossible situation.

8.32 p.m.

Sitting here feeling really worried. Have had about 50 Just Brazils and a couple of walnuts and now I am beginning to feel like I am blowing up like a balloon. Told Mum I think I am allergic – she just laughed and said I'd eaten too much. BUT what if I DO have a fatal

336

nut allergy? I really don't want to die – I've only
snogged one bloke. And what is beyond death?
Nothing. A void. I don't want to die for nuts.

Tuesday 26.12.89

11.05 p.m.

JUST BEEN DOWN THE PUB. Loads of people got
CARS for Christmas! It's the hazard of being poor
while going to a private school. One girl even got a car
and a private numberplate. I was moaning about this
loudly, so Ryan the RAF groper made me a car from a
beermat and wrote, 'RAE 1,' on the back. I said,
'Thanks, mate – that really makes up for it.'

Dobber thought he was trying to be sweet. He is a
sarcy shit of a man.

No Haddock. Bet he looks cute in a paper hat from a
cracker. That's the mark of a true man.

I had a bit of Pimm's before I started on the vodkas.

Everyone out. Everybody got off with each other. The
year is ending just like it started – with snogging couples
everywhere and me lurking around the fruit machine.

THE CORNER OF MY EYE

The corner of my eye
If I could
I would disown you.
When I'm looking away you catch glimpses of
    torture.
Corner of my eye always sees couples kissing

It reminds me of the things I'm missing.
Corner of my eye is where agony lies – I look
   straight ahead but you see love.
Corner of my eye – be useful – FIND
Someone who doesn't mind my fat – someone
   blind.

Wednesday 27.12.89

3.35 p.m.

JUST WATCHED *GREASE*. WHAT I need in the
year 1990 is an Olivia Newton-John-style transformation. You know the bit at the end where she goes,
'Tell me about it, stud,' in all that tight black stuff like
Mrs Sex on Legs? That's what I need! I need a
complete image change so people think, 'Who the hell
is that? Is she available? And can I do her?'

Going down pub later. Haddock apparently –
according to Dobber – will not be out. He is having an
evening at his girlfriend's house.

She mentioned this in passing. Obviously to me it was
like the most important news ever, but I just grunted.

11.55 p.m.

Shit-stirrer of the year BETHANY turned up out of
nowhere tonight in the pub and said, 'What's going on?
Haven't you got off with Haddock yet?!' SILLY BITCH.
Luckily it fell on mainly deaf ears, but Dobber heard and
said, 'What??!!' And I said, 'Don't worry – just a private
joke.' Luckily Haddock and girlfriend were not there.

Bethany is a shit-stirring cow. Wish I had not told her a thing EVER. That's a lesson if ever there was one.

Thursday 28.12.89

4.28 p.m.

FORGOT TO TELL YOU – GOT a CD player for Christmas. Unfortunately I currently only have one CD and that's *The Eagles Greatest Hits* borrowed off one of my mum's friends. Still, it's brilliant – and no more record jumping when I dance.

The end of the decade is fast approaching. Here is a list of objectives and resolutions – AKA ALL THE THINGS I INTEND TO DO (first two in order – rest not in order):

1) Get spiritual peace and fight for a better world.
2) Lose weight and learn how to LOVE!
3) Fall in love with someone who can give it back – not some glorious unobtainable.
4) Try to be kind even to people who I can't stand.
5) Never sell out to materialism.
6) Get to university.
7) Fight for good.
8) And try to beat all bad.
9) Get rid of mental confusion.
10) Marry Haddock.

No. 10 just being silly.

Well, only partly silly.

Friday 29.12.89

RIGHT – NOTHING ON TV, AND no money for sales, so it's time for the:

REVIEW OF 1989

A year that I greeted in an extremely strange way. I had been ill for six months, both primarily physically and mentally. I was unhappy. The pub then came along: the Hole in the Wall primarily, then the Vaults (said 'primarily' twice – bad English – I do apologise). That's where I met everyone, including Harry. I let that one get me down for a bit – well, more than a bit. Heaven knows why I bothered. He was a crap snogger with the personality of a duster.

At first I hated the Vaults – I thought it was a really grubby, sleazy dive of a place. I have now grown to love it – it's an epic. Elva the landlady is fab, the atmosphere is brilliant. That's where I first met Battered Sausage and Fig. Fig has introduced me to a top mate in Dobber – who has replaced Bethany as the person to socialise with. The key improvement between Bethany and Dobber? Dobber is not a bitch.

Haddock
The first time I met Haddock he was pissed and trying not to chunder on the stairs by the Hole in the Wall. He still looked gorgeous then. I thought he was a rugger-bugger twat. I was wrong. He is . . .

340

. . . just something for the moment I can't tell anyone about. But he is worth changing for.

I don't know what 1990 or the '90s will bring. But I hope they bring more Haddock and less Jive Bunny.

Saturday 30.12.89

JUST GOT IN AND I AM FREEZING AS SOON AS THIS YEAR IS OUT OF THE FUCKING WAY I WILL BE HAPPY.

Tonight I realised that all these things I write here are just nonsense. What I feel belongs to dreamland, not reality. Tonight it was a lads' night out – so Haddock, Fig and Battered Sausage were all getting ratted on their own. So me, Dobber and Haddock's girlfriend all sat there. And while Dobber was at the bar, Haddock's girlfriend was telling me about an argument her and Haddock had about her being possessive. Let me quote to you what Haddock said, as a basis for an argument with his girlfriend, about jealousy:

'You don't let me have any female friends other than Rae.'

You see? I am ALWAYS the fat, ugly-cow exception. I am safe. No threat. I mean – who would? That was quoted to me in all innocence – but it cuts me up so much.

And to him I am just the sister, and that's why I am the agony aunt to her – because I will never, never be a threat.

She said, 'He thinks the world of you, Rae. You know that, don't you?'

341

Yes – and you are fine with it because the way he thinks of me will never be in competition with you.

At the end of the night Haddock said, 'How is my Funky Chick?' I said,'Your Funky Chick is fucked off.' He went to ask why but I just left.

I feel off it.

I can hear my mum giggling.

And if I hear 'Merry Xmas Everybody' by Slade one more time I will smash everything to shit and I don't care if they lock me up again.

Sunday 31.12.89

ACTUALLY IT'S 1.1.90. I AM lying on Dobber's mum's sofa with Wally, Dobber's budgie, going mad at me.

OH MY GOD.

MEN ARE ALL NUTTERS.

FREAK-OUT NIGHT. I CAN'T GET MY HEAD ROUND IT.

The pub was packed tonight. You could hardly move, but it just turned into the most surreal night in history. Dobber and I were just sat there getting pissed, when honestly out of the blue Ryan the RAF groper marched up to me and said in a really angry way, 'You missed your chance. I am seeing someone else. You know, you shouldn't be such a sarcy bitch – it gets tedious after a while.' He then grabbed this girl he was with and stuck his tongue down her throat right in front of me. HELLO??? He's obviously on something. Dobber said, 'What the fuck was that about?' I said, 'I don't know, mate. But WHAT A WEIRDO!'

Then almost immediately Battered Sausage got dumped by his girlfriend and started semi-crying by the fruit machines in full view of everyone!!! When I went to see if he was OK, he wouldn't let go of me – and started saying, 'All women are bitches, Rae. I'm just shagging the flange. I won't marry a slag. Just want special minge long term.'

So basically the mega lad Battered Sausage just wants to be loved like the rest of us!

Bloody hell.

Dobber agreed – it was getting more weird the more pissed everyone got. Some twat even put the Nolans on the jukebox – it was like the world was ending.

We stayed in the Vaults until 11.45, then we all ended up in Red Lion Square. We didn't hear the bells but the word went round it was 1990. Had a moment of 'total fat cowness' when every man went to kiss Dobber first, then seemingly everyone else next and THEN me. I got an uncomfortable peck off most . . . It was one of those 'I am Jabba the Hut' times. I thought, 'Bugger it,' though. Was trying to make the most of the rest of the night, when the following happened:

Haddock and me had been having a laugh all night but all of a sudden in the square he grabbed me and dragged me to Horseshoe Lane by the men's toilets. I was pissing myself laughing . . . but he wasn't. He told me to shut the fuck up and shouted at me to LISTEN!!

When I said, 'Calm down, mate,' he said, 'Fucking shut up. I know you were down yesterday, and I know you get down.' Then he put his fingers in my hair and said, 'Do you know . . . it's just a bit of weight you need to lose. You've got a pretty face . . . Other people

343

have said it. And you are funny . . . and if you just toned up a bit . . .' (STROKING MY HAIR – I AM TELLING YOU I WAS DUMBSTRUCK) ' . . . things would change for you. Fuck other people! You'd feel better, and I would–'

THEN SODDING BATTERED SAUSAGE APPEARED, and shouted to Haddock, 'Come and get a kebab – my knackers are frozen!'

He didn't say anything after that. He just looked at me and ran off.

That happened about four hours ago.

'I would . . .' I could fill in the gaps. What would he do?

Don't want to analyse it. Just want to keep playing it back in my head.

Hands in my hair feel . . . right.

Come on . . . what is five stone? I can do it.

'A pretty face.'

Just looked in Wally the budgie's mirror. For the first time ever, I think Haddock may have a point, you know.